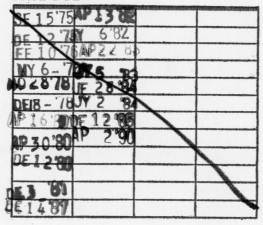

Elements of Judicial Strategy

Elements of Judicial Strategy

WALTER F. MURPHY

THE UNIVERSITY OF CHICAGO PRESS / CHICAGO & LONDON

International Standard Book Number: 0-226-55369-8
Library of Congress Catalog Card Number: 64-24973

THE UNIVERSITY OF CHICAGO PRESS, CHICAGO 60637
The University of Chicago Press, Ltd., London

For Terry

Preface

One of the occupational hazards of writing in a realistic fashion about the Supreme Court of the United States is that one runs the double risk of being accused of muckraking by those who, at a given moment, identify themselves as the friends of the Court and the sometimes even more unpleasant fate of being lauded by those who currently proclaim themselves to be its enemies. When one dares to use the private papers of deceased Justices to bolster one's analysis, the likelihood of both dangers actually occurring becomes great indeed. Let me make, then, the protestation that, while I bow to none in my respect for the Court, this book is neither an effort to debunk or belittle, nor an effort to praise or defend. It is an attempt to understand—to understand how, under the limitations which the American legal and political systems impose, a Justice can legitimately act in order to further his policy objectives.

Since the aims and approach of this book are set out in detail in the introductory chapter, I shall deal here only with certain peripheral matters. The first concerns the use of private papers of Justices. I have carefully gone over the papers of Charles Evans Hughes, Horace Lurton, James C. McReynolds, Harlan F. Stone, George Sutherland, William Howard Taft, and those parts of Frank Murphy's papers which were open by August, 1963. In addition, my good friend David F. Hughes of Centre College generously allowed me full use of his copious notes on the Salmon P. Chase Papers at Philadelphia and Washington. My empirical data are largely drawn from these collections. I went through parts of the Franklin D. Roosevelt and Harry S. Truman papers, and the Oral History Files at Columbia University, but I used very little material from them.

There is a feeling in some quarters that the private papers of Justices—papers which the Justices themselves sometimes compiled and arranged for public use—should not be looked into lest the image of the Court be somehow tarnished. Taking an opposite stand, Charles Evans Hughes claimed that if the inner workings of the Court were widely known and understood, popular respect for the judiciary would be vindicated.[1] Certainly Hughes's faith was well founded.* The private papers of the Justices which have been relied upon in this book do reveal some human frailties. To a much greater extent they reveal also a truly remarkable degree of personal integrity, intellectual vigor, and selfless dedication to duty—qualities which these judges directed toward the attainment of what they earnestly believed to be sound law, wise public policy, and, not least of all, justice.

A more intelligent objection to the use of private papers of Justices is that such use might discourage the free exchange of ideas within the Court. There may be some validity in this objection. Candid discussion among Justices is an important value,† but so is responsibility, and responsibility usually does inhibit free choice. Because they are not restrained directly by the check of the ballot box there is all the

---

* In his case this was no accident. With the aid of a research assistant Hughes carefully edited his private papers by destroying many documents. See Alpheus T. Mason, "Charles Evans Hughes: An Appeal to the Bar of History," 6 *Vand. L. Rev.* 1 (1952). Lurton, McReynolds, and Sutherland also destroyed a large part of their papers. Apparently Chase, Taft, Stone, and Murphy did not tamper with their papers—which may indicate there is a certain value to historians in a Justice's dying in harness.

† The conflict between candor and responsibility is not by any stretch of the imagination peculiar to the judiciary. Compare the problems caused the Kennedy administration by the publication in the December 8, 1962, issue of the *Saturday Evening Post* of an article by Stewart Alsop and Charles Bartlett purporting to be an inside story of the advice the President got from his staff during the Cuban Crisis of 1962. See the *New York Times* editorial of December 5, 1962, castigating this as a "breach of security." A somewhat similar controversy has arisen over the publication of Emmet John Hughes's book, *The Ordeal of Power*, in which he used material gathered while working as a speech writer for Dwight D. Eisenhower to bolster criticisms of the General's concept and use of the presidency. See Hughes's reply: "Is It Confidential or Is It History?" *The New York Times Magazine*, May 12, 1963, p. 24.

more reason why Justices should be checked by the informed judgment of history.

I have not quoted from the private correspondence of any living Justice, sitting or retired, without his permission.* On the other hand, I have used and used heavily the private papers (repeating, I hope, neither gossip nor scandal) of deceased Justices in the belief that judges, like all public officials, have to bear the criticism of good and bad scholars and run the risk of being misunderstood—a risk that every author shares—in the hope that truth will ultimately triumph. With his typical pungent wit, Karl Llewellyn stated my position far better than I ever could:[2]

> It is well to remember that neither secrecy of the court's deliberation or later secrecy about what went on during that deliberation rests in the nature of things or in any ordinance of God. The roots of each are either practical or accidental, and it is only either ignorance or tradition which makes us feel that we have here something untouchable, a semiholy arcanum. . . . Thus the storied sanctity of the conference room represents to me as pragmatic and nonmystic a phase of appellate judicial work as the handling of the docket. Our modern fetish of secrecy reminds me of the shock German lawyers displayed at the notion of such dangerous things as published dissenting opinions.

I find that the use of private papers entails a more serious hazard than that of lifting secret veils. Collections of letters and memoranda are always incomplete records; this is especially true of papers of men who are in daily face-to-face contact with each other or who frequently use the telephone. There is as great a danger in trying to fill the inevitable gaps as in not understanding that a writer's point of view may destroy the validity of a letter or memorandum as a factual account of contemporary events. These are well-known problems of historical research, and I hope I have avoided at least the more common errors in using personal documents.[3]

In this context it should be noted that I have drawn most heavily on material from the Taft Papers for illustrations of judicial efforts to exert personal influence in the political processes. Because of his

---

* I have, however, in several places utilized without direct reference to their source quotations from a Justice's private correspondence which I felt the Justice would prefer not to be attributed to him at this time.

long political career and especially his term of office as President, it may be objected that Taft's position was unique. It is true that Taft had unique advantages; but he also had unique disadvantages. The advice of a former President, as no one had better reason to know than Taft himself, is often far less welcome in the White House than suggestions from a former senator, governor, or Attorney General. And, over the years, Taft had made enemies as well as friends on Capitol Hill. It should also be kept in mind that most members of the Court have extensive political careers before they come to the bench,[4] and that not many of them have showed less understanding of the realities of politics than did Taft before 1921. I believe that, insofar as they relate to previous experience, Taft's net advantages over the "typical" Justice were of degree rather than of kind, though it is entirely possible he made more of these net advantages in his dealings with other government officials than any other Justice either before or since.*

Almost as jarring to some readers as quotations from private papers will be my use of terms which are familiar to economic reasoning and the theory of games but which are alien to public law literature. Words like "bargaining" may seem badly out of place—and out of taste—when applied to the judicial process. But if one strips such concepts of their emotive connotation and tries to utilize them as descriptive rather than evaluative expressions, I think any nefarious overtones will be quickly dissipated. We all bargain—unless we are willing and able to employ superior brute force to settle disagreements, or we are in the enviable position of being so obviously and perpetu-

---

* Taft may have engaged in more political activity than any other Justice, with the possible exception of Salmon P. Chase. Comparisons are difficult to draw because of the relative scarcity of materials on other Justices and the relative clarity and completeness of the record Taft left. Every Sunday morning when he was in Washington, the Chief Justice would dictate long, chatty letters to members of his family, explaining in intricate detail many of the political maneuverings in which he was currently engaged. Furthermore, he much preferred to communicate with other government officials by personal notes rather than by telephone, undoubtedly as great a burden to his secretary, Wendell W. Mischler, as it is a boon to historians.

For an account of the activities of a state judge who operated politically much like Taft, see: Gilson G. Glasier (ed.), *Autobiography of Roujet D. Marshall, Justice of the Supreme Court of Wisconsin, 1895–1918* (2 vols.; Madison, Wis.: A. McCleod, 1931).

ally infallible in our judgment that all affected men agree with us, or we are so supine as never to disagree with our peers. At first reading, other terms may be equally disagreeable as "bargaining," but I hope they will become equally neutral if it is understood that they are meant to imply neither diabolic nor angelic qualities.

This book is not intended, however, as an essay in the formal theory of games. Most of what we call game theory is a mathematical development of zero-sum games, or games of pure conflict. The judicial process, I think, is one of the areas in which a zero-sum model is inappropriate. Now a model need not be, if in fact it ever can be, a replica of reality; certainly the model of judicial decision-making I offer in chapter ii is not. But models should be simplifications not distortions of reality, and I hope to demonstrate that judicial decision-making, at least from the point of view of the judges, is not in most of its aspects zero-sum.[5] Following Thomas Schelling, I believe that games of pure conflict form one limiting point of the real world, with games of pure co-operation at the other extreme.[6] As I will often state in the text of the book, I have used game-theory concepts and vocabulary, but of a kind of game theory which Schelling calls "mixed-motive"; that is, where elements of both conflict and co-operation are present. I think these concepts are appropriate and fruitful in the study of judicial behavior.

This book, as with everything else I have ever done, has been built on a foundation of enormous debts. I am obliged to the Social Science Research Council for financing several summers of research and one of writing, as well as to Princeton University for various funds and time off to pursue this work at a pace which for a more industrious person would have been leisurely. The directors and staffs of the Manuscript Division of the Library of Congress, the Alderman Library of the University of Virginia, the Michigan Historical Collections of the University of Michigan, the Franklin D. Roosevelt Library at Hyde Park, New York, and the Harry S. Truman Library at Independence, Missouri, supplied cheerful and valuable assistance to me in my work with document collections. Miss Helen Fairbanks of the Firestone Library of Princeton University helped run down many esoteric bibliographical references, and my research assistant, Stephen Beckwith, of the Princeton class of 1964, aided in checking citations. Mrs. Helen Wright typed the manuscript with her usual skill and acted as a welcome general editor both on matters of style and substance.

A number of people have read all or parts of the manuscript. Stanley Kelley, Jr., of Princeton University read in full an early draft with a care that must have been as tedious to him as it was painful—and valuable—to me. David Danelski of Yale University, Robert K. Faulkner, Alpheus Thomas Mason, Louis Werner of Princeton, Joseph Tanenhaus of New York University, and C. Herman Pritchett of the University of Chicago read the final draft and made many useful suggestions. Others whose comments on particular aspects were especially helpful are Robert H. Birkby of Vanderbilt University, Duane Lockard of Princeton, John Nolan of the Washington law firm of Steptoe and Johnson, Harold Spaeth of Michigan State University, Sidney Verba of Stanford University, and Gerald E. Wheeler of San José State College. I am also indebted to my two daughters, Kelly and Holly, for remembering to turn down the television so that I might write in peace. Last, this book would not have been possible without my wife's willingness to have our collective lives regulated by my irascible Muse.

Contents

xiii

1 *Introduction*

As long as law remains one of the most common means of formalizing public policy, the judicial office in the United States will involve political, i.e., policy-making, power. Judges are asked daily to decide disputes between individual litigants by interpreting statutes, executive orders, and constitutional clauses. Because the meaning of these legal documents often vitally affects the basic economic, social, and political order of the country, such decisions can be of fundamental importance to the nation as a whole as well as to the particular parties to a case. Thus, in settling disputes judges inevitably play a part in shaping public policy; and they do so, as J. W. Peltason has said, "not as a matter of choice, but of function."[1] Judges are rulers, rulers in different and perhaps more limited ways than legislators or executive officials, but rulers nevertheless.

Moreover, because the legal documents which judges are asked to interpret are frequently phrased in broad language, there is room—and sometimes need—for the exercise of considerable discretion in performing the judicial function. There may be more certainty in law, even constitutional law, than the Legal Realists were once willing to admit; but the preferences and predilections of judges can be significant factors in construing the vague language which sometimes decides the allocation of goods, benefits, and advantages in society. The effect of judges' own notions of proper societal arrangements is especially evident in the decision-making process at the Supreme Court level, since, generally speaking, the Justices get the most difficult and far-reaching cases in the least settled areas of federal law.

A generation or two ago, despite the solid scholarship of men like

1

Introduction

Edward S. Corwin, discussions of the policy aspects of judicial decisions or of the impact of value judgments on judicial decision-making usually occurred in the context of attacks against particular rulings. Judges were condemned for exercising discretion and molding public policy. Surely no one familiar with the literature of vitriolic protest against the School Segregation cases believes that the day is past when men of intelligence and learning cruelly upbraid judges for such "sins." Nevertheless, the role of the scholar who accepts the existing political system is not to criticize judges for acting as judges must within that system. The role of that scholar, insofar as it is critical, is to hold decisions and opinions of judges up to the highest criteria of craftsmanship and statesmanship—to determine not whether judges have exercised discretion but whether they have done so to an extent and in a manner permitted by relevant standards; to determine not whether judges have influenced policy but whether that influence is to the benefit, both in the long and the short run, of society.

The scholar has other duties than criticism, of course. Among these is the duty of providing lucid explanations of the genesis and application of the formal rules which courts apply to individual and official conduct. This job is basically that of the lawyer, though certainly historians, economists, sociologists, and political scientists may throw some light on the problems involved. Another duty of the scholar is to increase knowledge about the way in which the judicial process operates, and here lawyers and political scientists share responsibility. A third task, given the inevitable policy effects of judicial decisions, is to explore the capabilities of the judicial branch of government to influence public policy formulation. Responsibility for this function falls primarily on the political scientist, though he needs help from lawyers and other social scientists.

This book tries to fulfil the third task. This, then, is a study of judicial power—not of judicial power in the lawyer's sense of jurisdiction but in the sense of the capability of an individual Justice of the Supreme Court of the United States to shape, through the peculiar kinds of authority and discretion inherent in his office, the development of a particular public policy or set of public policies.

Because of its focus this book is concerned with efficacious means rather than with desirable ends. For the same reason, the orientation of this book is both toward the traditional approach to the study of public law as well as toward more recent research which, for lack of a

2

more descriptive term, has been called behavioral. The research techniques used here are largely those of traditional legal-historical scholarship; but the overriding purpose is to offer an approach to analysis of judicial behavior which will contribute to theorizing about judicial decision-making and, in a larger context, about the role of the judiciary in the American system of government.

To formulate useful theories of judicial behavior, we need to know more than how judges act. We must also answer at least two additional questions: (1) What range of choice is actually open to a judge? (2) How can possible choices be expressed? Despite the basic nature of these queries, one looks almost in vain through the literature of political science for conscious, systematic attempts to answer either. While no writer of the traditional or behavioral persuasion has argued that a Justice's range of choice and method of expression are limited to voting and writing opinions for or against a specific policy, neither—to my knowledge—has any scholar made a systematic effort to outline what other modes of expression are practically possible and what is the range of real choice open to a Justice.* Ironically, one of the studies which comes closest to a direct attempt to cope with these two questions was written by a lawyer rather than a political scientist.[2]

I do not believe that at this stage of the development of political science one can offer—or should even yet seek—precise or all-inclusive answers to these two questions. But I do believe that a start should be made. Like most early efforts, the one represented by this book may be crude and groping, and, as will be discussed later in this chapter, has its full share of difficulties. The approach to the problems of range and expression of choice which is used here is that which has loosely been called capability analysis.[3] This kind of analysis is concerned not so much with the exact behavior patterns of a given set of public officials or private citizens, but rather with how a person or group of persons can act in a fashion which society considers legitimate, in order to attain certain goals. Thus, the focus of this book is the question: How can a Justice of the Supreme Court most efficiently utilize his resources, official and personal, to achieve a particular set of policy

* To some extent Glendon Schubert has done so in his application of zero-sum game theory to judicial behavior. See especially, *Quantitative Analysis of Judicial Behavior* (Glencoe, Ill.: Free Press, 1959), chap. iv; and "Policy without Law," 14 *Stan. L. Rev.* 284 (1962).

objectives? To allow the broadest scope for investigation particular policy objectives will not be specifically identified.

In order to supply a rough notion of the framework within which judicial decision-making takes place, the next chapter will examine the sources of and limitations on judicial power. Its purpose is to refresh memories and to put well-known facts in an orderly arrangement rather than to supply new information. The four chapters which follow are organized around a discussion of how a Justice can minimize, though he probably may never overcome, the major institutional checks on his power. The last two chapters attempt to draw some more general conclusions about the ethics of limited choice as well as about judicial behavior.

In much of subsequent chapters I shall be talking about a policy-oriented judge or Justice. By this term I mean a Justice who is aware of the impact which judicial decisions can have on public policy, realizes the leeway for discretion which his office permits, and is willing to take advantage of this power and leeway to further particular policy aims. I do not mean to predict or forecast how any ideal type of judge will act. I only mean to show as fully as I can within certain space limitations the kinds of factors which a policy-oriented Justice would weigh and the courses of action which would be open to him.

It should be noted that a Justice who would take fullest advantage of the strategies and tactics analyzed in the following chapters would have to possess or acquire a rare combination of characteristics. He would have to have a consciously and systematically arranged hierarchy of policy values, or, in more traditional phraseology, an ordered and articulated jurisprudence. Since every Justice has only a finite supply of time, energy, research assistance, and personal influence, he would not be able even under optimum conditions to accomplish all that he wanted. A Justice would thus have to choose between goals and probably between parts of any particular goal. Often he would not be able to choose intelligently without such a hierarchy or ordered jurisprudence.

A Justice would also have to be intensely committed to his objectives, willing to devote almost all of his limited resources to attainment of those ends. To allow himself the greatest chance of reaching his aims, a Justice would have to galvanize his resources and utilize them as rationally as he could. Under these conditions, rationality would mean simply "geared as efficiently as possible to maximize goal

4

achievement."*⁴ It may well include taking advantage of the propensity of others to respond to extra-rational appeals.

It may be true that no Justice who has ever sat on the Court could have taken complete advantage of the strategies and tactics outlined here. Probably relatively few Justices have had a systematic jurisprudence; more but probably still relatively few have been so intensely committed to particular policy goals as to establish rigid priorities of action that dominated their entire lives; probably few have been able to act only rationally in seeking to achieve their aims. Even fewer—if indeed any single Justice—have possessed all of these qualities. Yet the facts remain that these strategic and tactical courses are open, that many if not most Justices could increase their policy influence by conscious efforts along these lines, and that until we know better how a Justice can extend his policy influence it is impossible with any degree of precision to evaluate or criticize the influence he did exert, does exert, or will exert.

To keep analysis within manageable limits, I have eliminated from consideration several possible courses of action. First, I have decided not to discuss illegal behavior. I shall not take up such tactics as fraud, bribery, or threats of or use of unlawful violence. Since no evidence has yet come to light that any Supreme Court Justice has ever engaged in such activity, this exclusion is, I believe, most reasonable. On the other hand, some readers may conclude that several of the strategic and tactical maneuvers outlined in later chapters are unethical if not illegal. It is certainly true, as one novelist has pointed

---

* Herbert Simon, in grappling with the problems of utilizing the term "rational," has concluded that the only way to avoid difficulties is to use the word with appropriate adverbs. "Then a decision may be called 'objectively' rational if *in fact* it is the correct behavior for maximizing given values in a given situation. It is 'subjectively' rational if it maximizes attainment relative to the actual knowledge of the subject. It is 'consciously' rational to the degree that the adjustment of means to ends is a conscious process. It is 'deliberately' rational to the degree that the adjustment of means to ends has been deliberately brought about (by the individual or by the organization). A decision is 'organizationally' rational if it is oriented to the organization's goals; it is 'personally' rational if it is oriented to the individual's goals." *Administrative Behavior* (2d ed.; New York: Macmillan Co., 1959), pp. 76–77. Here I am referring to behavior which is "subjectively," "consciously," "deliberately," and "personally" rational. For a more complete discussion of the problems involved here, see Sidney Verba, "Assumptions of Rationality and Non-Rationality in Models of the International System," 14 *World Politics* 93 (1961).

out, that the greatest danger in Washington politics is not that the decision-maker loses his ideals but rather his ethics.[5] I do not, therefore, request the reader to forgo moral judgment, only that he suspend such judgment until chapter vii. This is not an easy thing to ask since the moral element in judging is usually much closer to the surface than in other fields of public-policy formulation. I would prefer, however, to establish how the judicial process can and at times has worked before attempting to seek standards for passing moral judgment.

Second, I will not discuss the possibility that a Justice might seek to harm the Court as an institution in order to accomplish his policy goals.* That is, for purposes of analysis, I assume that a policy-oriented Justice would not deliberately attempt to injure or destroy judicial power, though he might try various means of overturning particular decisions. While this distinction may seem clear, the line between injury to judicial power and reversal of a specific decision may be difficult to draw in many circumstances; and this problem of differentiation will be discussed at several places in later chapters.

Despite its operational difficulties, this distinction is realistic in terms of logic as well as of historical practice. Pleas for self-restraint are far more common among Justices when they feel their policies may fare better in another governmental forum than are efforts from within the Court to maim judicial power. In fact I am aware of only two instances—and neither of these is free from doubt—in which a Justice seemingly acted to curb the Court's power for the sake of short-term policy goals; and both instances involved Salmon P. Chase, a judge whose extrajudicial ambitions were as notorious as they were frustrated.[6]

Moreover, unlike members of Congress, lesser executive officials, and state officers, Supreme Court Justices are unlikely to influence public policy except insofar as they do so as judges. In this century only two Justices, Charles Evans Hughes and James F. Byrnes, have been able to secure important government posts after leaving the bench, and Byrnes served only a single term on the Court before resigning. The record of the last century, with its string of disappointed presidential ambitions, would scarcely be more encouraging

* I do not exclude the possibility that a Justice might feel some goals so important as to risk the future existence of the Court or even to accept what he feels sure will mean institutional martyrdom.

6

to a Justice who was ambitious for himself or for his policy goals. Thus the loyalty to the Court as an institution which one expects from a lawyer reared and educated in the American legal tradition would also be a prudent emotion.

Last, I will exclude from discussion the possibility that a policy-oriented Justice would try to expand his own power or that of the Court beyond limits which would be legitimate under traditional theories of the judicial function in American government. Since these theories have ranged all the way from supremacy in domestic policy to severe restraint in all fields, this exclusion may seem meaningless. Yet it does serve a double purpose. It eliminates the necessity of considering the implausible possibility that a Justice would want to set himself up as a dictator and destroy constitutional democracy or free government—though he might disagree with his colleagues and with other political officials on exactly what these terms mean in a complex situation. In addition, this last exclusion allows the book to maintain its attention on how judicial power *can* operate, leaving to another work the equally if not more important question of how judges should behave.*

Several disclaimers are also in order before beginning a book like this one. First, I do not say that Justices always or frequently do act or must act in the fashion I shall describe. I say only that a Justice must weigh all of the alternatives I discuss (and probably many more which I do not) if he truly wants to maximize the chances of achieving his policy objectives. By "must" I mean that a policy-oriented Justice would have to consider these factors if he is to act most efficiently to realize his policy goals—which is to admit that judges often do not consider such factors. But, as Theodore Sorensen said of presidential decision-making, a Justice "may ignore these forces or factors—he may even be unaware of them—but he cannot escape them. He may choose to decide in solitude, but he does not decide in a vacuum."[7]

Second, I neither state nor mean to imply, when I cite examples of prior judicial action, that the judge or judges involved acted from any but the highest motives or that the actors recognized, much less intended, the power implications in the situation. Sometimes it is

---

* On reading a similar statement in an earlier version of chap. iii, published in the *University of Chicago Law Review*, my former colleague Robert Birkby chided me for deliberate question-begging. I would prefer to think of this exclusion as question-avoiding.

manifest that a Justice was quite aware of the power factors inherent in the situation he faced and was carefully and deliberately manipulating those factors to the best of his ability. On many other occasions, the question of motivation is unclear. I use these examples only to illustrate the possible effects of the action described, not to impute motives to the actors. I simply want to show by these incidents that strategies and tactics which are theoretically applicable are also practically possible.

The third disclaimer has to do with two problems raised by any discussion of influence—a concept which has not yet lost all of its original mystic connotation. The initial difficulty in any such discussion is the matter of definition. That offered by Lasswell and Kaplan has the double advantage of simplicity and utility; they state that the exercise of influence "consists in affecting policies of others than the self."[8]

The next and related problem is that of the degree of influence. "Affecting" covers a wide spectrum of possible impacts on the behavior of others, a spectrum ranging from the inconsequential to the decisive. Influence then by no means implies domination; indeed, it implies something far less than absolute control. And herein lies the disclaimer. It is always difficult—and usually impossible—to know that A does x *because of* B's activity. This statement may or may not be true. To prove or disprove it, we would have to know whether A would have done x even if B had not acted. A may also have been under pressure from C and D and have yielded to them rather than to B; he may have made up his mind before anyone attempted to reach him. Furthermore, there is often the possibility that A may have made up his mind because of the requests or reactions he had anticipated coming from B or from other actors.

The sort and quantity of evidence needed to show cause and effect in a complicated public-policy decision are, to say the very least, hard to come by. Although we frequently have indications of how A planned to act before B intervened—if B has close knowledge of A's plans, B's intervention is of itself evidence that A was seriously considering an alternative to x—we rarely have incontrovertible proof one way or the other. We lack such proof mainly because we seldom, if ever, know either all of the actors who were involved in a particular decision or all of the factors which were making an impact, consciously and subconsciously, on the decision-maker's perception and judgment.

Thus no claim is made here that where, for instance, a Justice asked a President to make a certain nomination and the President made that nomination, the President's action proves that the Justice caused the nomination. Rather, the empirical evidence offered here performs two functions, each very different from trying to prove cause and effect. Primarily the evidence attempts to show that certain kinds of activity which one would expect to further a Justice's goals have in the past been carried on in the real world. Secondarily, and only secondarily, this evidence is usually meant to imply that such activity has had some influence on the development of public policy.* The degree of influence is indicated, albeit roughly, by the particular circumstances of each illustration. Further and more exhaustive research into any specific illustration may well show that the Justice's influence was somewhat different from that implied here.

The final disclaimer is a personal one. My immediate mission in this book is to explore how a Justice can act to influence public policy. I do not intend what follows to be construed as advice to judges, present or future. My own preference in behavioral styles, were I giving advice, is for that of the blunt, straightforward soldier over that of the suave, shrewd, carefully controlled professional diplomat. A personal preference, however, does not constitute an intelligent basis for limiting analysis.

As I mentioned earlier capability analysis of this sort is not without its serious difficulties. First, there is the problem of a distinction between strategy and tactics. Neither writers on military affairs nor compilers of dictionaries have yet been able to lay down very exact demarcations between these two concepts, and the fact of a hazy distinction simply has to be lived with. To minimize semantic distractions, I have used here a set of definitions somewhat like those of Clausewitz.[9] *Tactics* will refer to maneuverings designed to obtain advantages in dealing with colleagues, lower court judges, other government officials, interest groups, or the public at large. *Strategies* will refer to the over-all plans under which such maneuverings against specific obstacles are co-ordinated and for which scarce resources are

---

* I say "usually" because the analysis accompanying some illustrations points out that the particular activity of the Justice had no visible impact on policy development, though again without knowing all of the factors one cannot say that the Justice's intervention had no impact at all.

allocated in order to further the accomplishment of the broad policy objective.

Second, the kind of reasoning used here is far more difficult to apply to Supreme Court Justices than to most other highly placed government or party officials or to businessmen. If a firm does not act rationally and does not allocate its resources in the most efficient way, it is usually "punished" by a loss of profits if not by financial ruin. Similarly, elected officials who wish to stay in office must organize their behavior according to rational standards;* if not they are likely to be defeated at the polls or at least will face expensive and harrowing campaigns for re-election. With an assured salary and life tenure, a Justice, assuming he does not have to worry about impeachment, need not fear loss of money or position if he does not act rationally in terms of his policy aims.

Furthermore, although neither money nor votes are without their own peculiar difficulties as terms of analysis, each lends itself far more readily to use as a reference point than does the concept of achieving a policy objective. As tangible items both money and votes can be measured, and the efficiency of the way in which resources have been expended to attain them can be judged, at least ex post, with some degree of accuracy. Advance toward achievement of a policy objective, however, is a highly subjective concept, not a collection of empirical data that can be counted and weighed. One must therefore speak in very general and unfortunately sometimes vague terms when discussing the efficiency of judicial behavior oriented toward a policy goal.

Closely related is the price that must be paid for not identifying any particular policy which a Justice may wish to see triumph. Without knowing either the specific policy or circumstances, it is always difficult and often impossible to rank various strategies and tactics according to their probable efficacy. The best that can be accomplished is to identify the conditions under which various strategies and tactics would be most apt to yield success. On the other hand, to label a specific policy and to set a specific moment in time as the mode of analysis would raise even more serious problems of generalizing from

* Due to a number of factors, including public indifference, apathy, and lack of information, as well as the forensic skill of the particular official involved, an elected politician usually has considerable leeway on most issues, and it would be rational for him to take advantage of this leeway.

an individual situation—though, of course, such examples may frequently illustrate broad principles.

Finally there is a difficulty relating to the copiousness of the evidence and the demands of literary style. Since this kind of analysis, in spite of its reliance upon traditional methods of research, has rarely been used in public law and much of the data is little known or unknown even among close students of the Court, I have felt it necessary to present my evidence in some detail. To a certain extent this abundance of factual material may distract attention from the fundamental purpose of the analysis. But were this evidence not offered, the analysis would be open to a charge of being both divorced from and a distortion of the real world of the judicial process. Furthermore, since much of what I offer as illustrations has not been previously published, its printing now may help other students of the Court to improve this sort of approach, and it may also serve as useful raw material for very different kinds of studies.

2 *The Framework of Judicial Power*

The American system of government bestows a "stupendous magnitude"[1] of power on Supreme Court Justices. That same system imposes significant limitations as well. The Justices are subject to political, legal, institutional, social, ideological, and ethical restraints. Any Justice who wishes to do good—or evil, for that matter—will have to take into account not only the scope and sources of his power and the instruments available to him, but also the restrictions on his power and the points at which those restraints could be most damagingly applied.

I SOURCES OF JUDICIAL POWER

Max Weber has distinguished three "pure" types of legitimate authority: (1) *legal,* those whose claims rest on the rationality and utility of a pattern of normative rules and the right of persons in authority under those rules to issue commands; (2) *traditional,* those "resting on an established belief in the sanctity of immemorial traditions and the legitimacy of the status of those exercising authority under them"; (3) *charismatic,* those whose claims rest on the peculiar personal magnetism of a ruler "touched with grace."[2]

Like that of many other agencies of government, the authority of the Supreme Court partakes of all three claims to legitimacy. As a court of law established by order of the Constitution, the Supreme Court grounds its right to rule on the specific wording—and what to many judges are the logical implications—of the fundamental legal charter of the nation. In addition, the Justices have historical claims, not only as inheritors of the traditional authority of British common law courts but also as successors to the prescriptive rights built up through American judicial practice since the early days of the republic. The "cult of the robe," the concept of the judge as a high priest of justice with special talents for elucidation of "the law," that sacred and mysterious text which is inscrutable even to the educated layman, forms a sort of institutional charisma which is bestowed on judges with their oath of office.

A political system which combines separation of powers and federalism needs an umpire if it is to function. The Justices of the Supreme Court quickly utilized both traditional and legal arguments to place themselves in the role of arbiter between the other two branches of the national government and, with the help of those other two branches, between the states and the nation. Whether or not intended by the founding fathers, judicial review has become a fact of American political life, one now long sanctified by time. Although decisions frequently provoke vitriolic criticism that the Court has wrongly said what the law is or suggestions that the Justices should be divested of their interpretive authority, only an occasional maverick politician or scholar[3] thinks it worth the effort to challenge the historicity of Marshall's dictum that "It is emphatically, the province and duty of the judiciary to say what the law [the Constitution] is."[4]

Since the Constitution is written in broad terms of such convenient vagueness as "due process," "equal protection," "unreasonable searches and seizures," "commerce among the several states," saying what this law is allows, perhaps even requires, the Justices to apply their own value preferences. The words of the Constitution, Professor Frankfurter once claimed, "are so unrestricted by their intrinsic meaning or by their history or by tradition or by prior decisions that they leave the individual Justice free, if indeed they do not compel him, to gather meaning, not from reading the Constitution, but from reading life."[5]

STATUTORY INTERPRETATION

Under the Constitution and accepted legal traditions, the Court also has authority to interpret federal statutes and executive orders. Statutory interpretation is usually less dramatic than constitutional interpretation, but it is nonetheless a fecund source of power. As Theodore Roosevelt commented with no more than his usual exaggeration, "The

President and Congress are all very well in their way. They can say what they think they think, but it rests with the Supreme Court to decide what they have really thought."[6]

No less than in the broad wording of the Constitution, judges may find their own policy preferences in the vagaries of legislative language. As in constitutional interpretation, the task of applying the words of a statute to specific situations often demands rather than merely permits policy-making as well as policy application. Few important or controversial bills can run the legislative gauntlet without considerable compromise; and vague, indefinite phrasing is a common means of obtaining general consensus. Certain points are agreed upon, and both sides tacitly consent to transfer to judges or administrators the authority to settle some of the issues on which agreement is impossible.

Perhaps the most striking example of judicial legislation under the guise of statutory interpretation has been the Court's handling of antitrust cases. The Justices at times have insisted on sterile definitions of monopolization practices; they first denied that the Sherman Act embodied the common law's "rule of reason,"[7] then, without even admitting a change of policy, read this rule into the statute.[8] Meanwhile, they exempted many activities of gigantic trusts from the law's coverage while including many of the activities of small labor unions.[9] The Court soon became, as one standard text has said, "the ultimate maker of antitrust policy."[10]

Without a doubt, the Justices were writing their own policy preferences into the law; but they were doing so at the invitation, implicit if not explicit, of Congress. In the legislative debates of 1890 Senator Sherman had been candid about his solution to the complex problems caused by growing threats of monopoly. "I admit that it is difficult to define in legal language the precise line between lawful and unlawful combinations. This must be left for the courts to determine in each particular case. All that we, as lawmakers, can do is to declare general principles, and we can be assured that the courts will apply them so as to carry out the meaning of the law. . . ."[11]

In the final statute Congress provided neither a definition nor criteria to determine what was meant by monopolization. Legislative history was equally devoid of guidelines, even had it been general judicial practice at the time to use such history. According to two close students of antitrust policy, "The bill which was arduously debated was never passed, and . . . the bill which was passed was never really discussed."[12]

Other factors may force the Court into a policy-making role. Over a period of years Congress may enact several pieces of legislation which embody contradictory public policies without repealing earlier statutes. Again the antitrust field provides an excellent example. In the Sherman, Clayton, Federal Trade Commission, and Celler acts, Congress has taken what appears to be a position, however unsure, against restraints of trade and in favor of vigorous competition. On the other hand, in the Robinson-Patman, Miller-Tydings, and McGuire acts, in patent and tariff legislation, and in niggardly appropriations for the antitrust operations of the Department of Justice and the Federal Trade Commission, Congress has apparently chosen to oppose "too vigorous" competition.

Adoption of these conflicting policies has left it largely to the courts to draw the line between vigorous and not too vigorous competition. Under the circumstances, the Justices have frequently been open to valid criticism for making unwise policy, but they can hardly be censured for playing a policy-making role.[13]

Even if it were possible that a complex and controversial bill could survive the political pressures of the legislative process without compromises effected through deliberately vague phraseology or without being subjected to later modification by inconsistent statutes, limitations inherent in the use of words would still leave a wide field for judicial interpretation. "Such is the character of human language," John Marshall once wrote, "that no word conveys to the mind in all situations, one single definite idea; and nothing is more common than to use words in a figurative sense."[14]

Executive orders, while immune neither to Washington "officialese" nor to compromises caused by the agitation of affected interests, are usually more direct in language than statutes. But, when the application or meaning of those administrative directives is challenged in a law suit, they must be interpreted by judges acting with notable discretion.

PRESTIGE

At frequent intervals the Supreme Court is asked to settle some of the most volatile issues of domestic policies. These range from the validity of state bankruptcy laws, paper money, income taxes, state or federal regulations of wages and hours, antitrust policy, and transportation and public utility rates to the legality of slavery in the territories, suspensions of habeas corpus, compulsory racial segregation, restrictive real estate covenants, congressional investigations, prosecutions of Jeffersonians, Copperheads, pacifists, socialists, Wobblies, Trotskyites, or Stalinists, test oaths for southern sympathizers or left-wingers, public school prayers, and legislative apportionment. Decisions on such problems are bound to excite heated controversy. The remarkable fact is not that such decisions have stirred opposition, but that this opposition has not been more frequent, more strenuous, and more successful.

In large part the explanation for this phenomenon lies in the charismatic source of judicial power. "Among holy things," Hamilton and Till have observed, "likeness passes by contagion,"[15] and much of the sacred, mysterious character of the Constitution has been caught by the Justices in the performance of their priestly duty of expounding the meaning of that holy writ. "Since the Constitution is America's covenant," Max Lerner has said, "its guardians are . . . touched with its divinity."[16]

As protection against more mundane forms of infection, the Justices early appropriated to themselves the myth that their function was solely expository. They claimed to decide pressing public-policy questions not by reference to any personal or partisan value system but solely by reference to the terms of the Constitution itself. The judicial function, John Marshall asserted, echoing Alexander Hamilton in the *Federalist*, No. 78, involves an exercise of judgment not of will.[17] The fact, as one iconoclastic Justice remarked in 1952, that the materials of constitutional interpretation are often "as enigmatic as the dreams Joseph was asked to interpret for Pharaoh,"[18] has been utilized to make the secret process of judicial decision-making more occult and therefore more appealing. As Charles de Gaulle, a stranger neither to the mystique of power nor the maneuverings of politics, has stated, "There can be no prestige without mystery. . . . In the designs, the demeanor and the mental operations of the leader, there must always be a 'something' which others cannot altogether fathom, which puzzles them, stirs them, and rivets their attention."[19]

Magic and mythology cannot long survive, of course, if they do not seem to contain some truth and do not in fact perform a useful function. The intellectual acumen and strength of character of Justices like

16

Marshall, Miller, Harlan, Holmes, Brandeis, Hughes, and Stone, and the unmarred record of integrity of the other Justices indicate that the judicial claim to primacy in guarding the chastity of the Constitution has considerable merit. Moreover, the Justices themselves have generally been captives of this myth rather than its cynical exploiters. Brought up in a tradition which sets the proper role of the judge as that of a strictly impartial arbiter, Supreme Court Justices have typically done their utmost to act in the expected fashion. Their failures to be truly objective can usually be attributed to an inability to distinguish between their personal values and those values essential to the working of a free political system. The Justices have frequently succumbed to the human tendency to self-deception, rarely to the temptation to deceive others.

On another level, the judicial myth has not only protected the Court against assault because of controversial decisions, but at the same time has also smoothed the path of acceptance for such decisions. People, it would seem, are more ready to accept unpleasant decisions which appear to be the ineluctable result of rigorously logical deductions from "the law," than they are rulings which are frankly a medley of legal principle, personal preferences, and educated guesses as to what is best for society.

LEGITIMATION

The charisma of the Court's prestige has combined with its traditional and legal authority to create a subsidiary but nonetheless important source of judicial power. In a pluralistic society many important public policies adversely affect the aims and interests of a number of powerful individuals and groups. This antagonism not only creates opposition to the wisdom of the policies involved but also stirs up controversy as to the very authority of government to pursue such policies. To meet this situation there must be some way of legitimizing political decisions, and the American political system provides for many means, such as the campaign process, the ballot box, and the constitutional amendment. Acting through the ritual of the lawsuit, the Supreme Court plays a significant part in this process by declaring *constitutional* contested policies.[20] Sharing the legitimizing role means that the Court has a more positive function to perform than might appear from the superficially negative character of judicial review. This legitimizing authority also means that elective officials who real-

17

ize that they will often have need of the Court's imprimatur will be less likely to use their checks against judicial power lest they kill the proverbial goose which lays the golden eggs.

The Court may similarly be of use to elected officials in serving as a welcome scapegoat. In 1961 and 1962, the problem of federal aid to parochial schools was one which cut deeply into the ranks of both parties. It was the sort of explosive issue on which a vote either way could cost an official his re-election. In this situation Supreme Court pronouncements about "a wall of separation" between Church and State were godsends to a cross-pressured Chief Executive and to harassed congressmen from districts with heterogeneous religious populations. Constitutional decisions of the Court, it was widely said, had settled the issue, and the Court had to be respected, no matter what the feelings of the individual official or citizen. Few legislators took time to enlighten their constituents with the knowledge that the Court had never directly passed on the issue under consideration, and that if the Justices adhered to their past decisions on "standing to sue,"[21] it was extremely improbable that any person could challenge in a federal court the constitutionality of such aid.

II INSTRUMENTS OF JUDICIAL POWER

From the varied sources of their power, Justices have at their disposal several different kinds of instruments.[22] Among the legal instruments the most obvious, but also the most important, is the authority to decide cases between parties, one or both of whom may be a state or federal official acting in the name of his government.

Reinforcing this power to grant or deny legitimacy to private or governmental action is the judicial practice of writing opinions. Great Justices like Marshall can utilize their eloquent rhetoric to educate public and official opinion and so shape public policy. More specifically, to carry out their decisions, judges may, for example, issue injunctions and declaratory judgments to private persons or public officials, or writs of habeas corpus to jailors, fashion decrees breaking up mammoth corporations or apportioning a state's electoral districts. Judges can also punish, often summarily, as contempt of court any disobedience to their orders. While as an appellate tribunal the Supreme Court does not normally issue such writs[23] or hold trials for

18

contempt,[24] it can direct lower courts to proceed in a given manner in a case which has been brought before the High Bench.

Prestige is an important source of judicial power. When combined with professional reputation it can also become an important instrument of judicial power. Prestige refers to the Court's hold on popular esteem. Reputation refers to the judgment of other government officials about the skill and determination with which the Justices use their power to their own advantage or that of the policies they are supporting.[25] Since public officials are likely to have been brought up to respect the judiciary as an institution, they are also likely to share to some extent the widespread belief that they *ought* to obey Supreme Court decisions. When the Justices can reinforce this feeling of obligations with professional respect for their abilities and determination, they have fashioned a very potent weapon to secure obedience and co-operation from the very people who have the physical power to ignore or even to defy them.

The Court also has certain passive instruments. First, it has control over its own jurisdiction. In the overwhelming majority of cases which come before them, the Justices are able, without giving any reason whatever, to decide which disputes they will hear and which they will not. Offering only the delphic explanation "want of a substantial federal question," the Court is able to reject almost any of the remaining requests for review. Second, the Justices have at their disposal a number of legal technicalities, such as an order for reargument or a remand to a lower court to clear up a record. These procedures can be used to delay a decision on a case until a time which the Justices feel would be more appropriate. Third, and this is an extension of the last technique, the Justices may avoid indefinitely a decision on the merits not only of a specific case but also of a larger policy issue by restricting their decision to peripheral procedural matters. In short, one can bring a case before the Court, but no litigant, not even a government official, can force the Court to take the case or, once the Court has taken the case, to decide the substantive issues.

III LIMITATIONS ON JUDICIAL POWER

The Restraint of Public Opinion

If prestige is one of the major sources of judicial power, it must follow that public opinion is one of the major limitations on the authority of the courts. To speak of public opinion, V. O. Key has quipped, is not unlike wrestling with the Holy Ghost;[26] but public opinion, however elusive a concept, is as real to government officials as is the Holy Ghost to orthodox Christians. The relationship between the Court and public opinion is complex. To some extent the Justices reflect the prevalent views of the day. According to Cardozo, "the great tides and currents which engulf the rest of men do not turn aside in their course and pass the judges by."*[27] Yet the Supreme Court usually has been staffed by older men, many of whose values and outlooks were formed in an earlier social milieu. The advent of new political or economic theories may, despite Cardozo's assurance, leave a majority of the Justices stranded on a sparsely populated ideological island.

The Justices thus have the unenviable task of differentiating between political fads and deeply felt—and more or less permanent— changes in social outlook. A series of wrong or imprudent judgments about such matters can undermine public faith in the Justices and strengthen interest-group leaders and government officials who support policies contrary to those of the Court. Looking back, in 1951, with a great deal more perception than he showed at the time, Owen J. Roberts remarked of the Justices' war with the New Deal: "it is difficult to see how the Court could have resisted the popular urge for uniform standards throughout the country—for what in effect was a unified economy."[28]

A Justice must also realize that because judicial prestige is high does not mean that its supply is inexhaustible. As Robert H. Jackson once noted, overuse can cheapen the currency of judicial power. The Justices cannot, therefore, hurl constitutional thunderbolts every Decision Monday, lest such pronouncements become too commonplace to be effective.

In addition to limitations on its store of prestige, the power of the Court is checked by technical law-court restrictions, by institutional factors, by the political power of Congress, the President, and the state governments, and the access which offended interest-group leaders

---

* In a similar vein, Professor Frankfurter commented: "To a large extent the Supreme Court, under the guise of constitutional interpretation of words whose contents are derived from the disposition of the Justices, is the reflector of that impalpable but controlling thing, the general drift of public opinion." *Law and Politics,* eds. A. MacLeish and E. F. Prichard, Jr. (New York: Harcourt, Brace & Co., 1939), p. 197.

have to other government officials, and by the concept which each Justice has of the proper role of the Court and of ethical standards of judicial conduct.

TECHNICAL CHECKS ON THE COURT[29]

The first of the more important technical checks is that the Supreme Court lacks a self-starter. The Justices cannot initiate action. They can make policy only by deciding individual cases, cases which litigants must bring to the Court. Furthermore, Justices are supposed to decide only the issues which the litigants themselves raise; it is not considered good form for the Court to give litigants more than they ask for, at least not without allowing opposing counsel to argue the matter. Then, too, judicial decisions legally bind only the parties to the particular case, persons who co-operate with those parties, or, where government officials are involved, their successors in office. It is true that under certain circumstances a small number of plaintiffs may use a "class action" to sue for themselves and "all others similarly situated" to protect a specific legal right which is common to an easily identifiable group. The right vindicated by a class action, however, is still protected by the court's order only against the specific defendants in the case or against those who co-operate with them or who succeed to their office or station. A Supreme Court decision, for example, that segregation is unconstitutional in Louisiana does not legally compel officials of any other state to desegregate. Indeed, the decision is likely to be restricted in binding effect to one school district within a given state. Such a decision does, of course, serve as an invitation to potential litigants to initiate legal action and as a guide to lower court judges in their decisions on future cases.

A second set of technical checks is that which limits the conditions under which persons may bring suit. Congress and the Constitution have set the general jurisdiction of federal courts. These regulations are complex enough, but following common law tradition the Court has established over the years a series of additional rules determining "standing to sue," i.e., to help decide under what circumstances federal jurisdiction can be lawfully invoked. First, there must be a "case or controversy." To have a case or a controversy litigants must have a real dispute in which injury has been done or is immediately threatened against a right protected by federal statutory or constitutional law. The injury and the dispute must be real, not feigned. To have "standing" a litigant must also show that the right involved is a personal one. As a general rule, one may not invoke the rights of other private citizens or of the public at large.[30]

If governmental action is challenged, that action must be sufficiently "final" to be "ripe" for review. The Court has usually ruled that a person has no standing to contest government action as long as administrative remedies have not been exhausted; i.e., until the litigant has availed himself of all the valid procedures which an administrative body has set up to correct its own errors. In keeping with the historic practice of common law tribunals, the Supreme Court has also refused to allow federal courts to take cases in which the judicial decision in the particular controversy would not be final between the two parties to the dispute. Thus the Justices have declined to decide cases in which their rulings would be subject to some kind of administrative review by non-judicial officers.

Last, to have "standing" a plaintiff must raise a "justiciable" question, one which is suitable for determination by the judiciary, rather than a "political" question, for which the Constitution delegates responsibility to one of the other branches of government. Since the Court has tended to give circular definitions of what questions are "justiciable" and what are "political," this distinction is exceedingly imprecise. The doctrine of political questions, as John P. Frank has pointed out, is "more amenable to description by infinite itemization than by generalization."[31] There are, however, some issues which the Court has clearly ruled to be beyond its competence: conduct of foreign policy generally, and, in domestic politics, guaranties to the states of a republican form of government, qualifications of members of the House or Senate, and ratification of constitutional amendments.

Another of the more important technical restraints on judicial power is *stare decisis,* the great touchstone of judicial regularity. "We do not write on a clean slate," is a lament which appears frequently in court opinions. Precedent, the wisdom of the past, not the free choice of the present, is the typical rationale of judicial decision-making. Judges are expected to follow their own decisions as well as the decisions of their predecessors, not only when similar situations arise but when confronted with new problems. "To reason by analogy" and carry over established principles into fresh fields is the widely accepted standard of judicial craftsmanship.[32] *Stare decisis* gives the law stability and predictability; it also provides harried judges who face difficult choices with a welcome decision-making crutch. In so doing, it limits judicial discretion,* making the traditional way the "proper" way.

A further technical check is the limited kinds of remedies which are available to the Court to settle disputes. Although the Justices have much discretion, by the nature of judicial decisions they can make policy only on a restricted basis. The Justices can hold constitutional or unconstitutional a minimum wage statute passed by Congress or by a state legislature; they cannot write such a law on their own motion. They can rule that certain kinds of conduct by public officials are illegal; but they cannot uphold convictions against guilty officials unless other officials prosecute. Thus the law-court status of their institution puts far greater limitations on the Justices' power to influence policy positively† than it does on their power to influence policy negatively.

INSTITUTIONAL RESTRAINTS

The power of the Court and more particularly of the individual Justice is restricted by institutional factors. The Court is a collegial body of nine men. Any decision must have the approval of at least five of them, as must any opinion which purports to speak for the Court rather than for individual members. Getting five Justices to agree on a common result in a case is often more complicated than it might seem since the Court usually has more than two alternatives open to it. It can reverse or affirm or it can merely modify the lower court's decision by reversing in part and affirming in part.‡

Obtaining a majority for a decision, however, is relatively easy when compared with the problem of getting five or more intelligent, strong-willed and individualistic Justices to agree in whole with an opinion written by one of their number. The degree of difficulty is likely to increase with the importance and complexity of the issues which the case presents. A Justice who is determined to write without giving in to his colleagues' wishes is apt to find he is writing for himself alone.

---

* It should be kept in mind, however, that one may *increase* his power by decreasing his range of discretion. See Thomas Schelling, *The Strategy of Conflict* (Cambridge, Mass.: Harvard University Press, 1960), esp. chap. i.

† They may, of course, sometimes "find" more policy in a statute than congressmen put there; see below, chap. v.

‡ Read *Screws* v. *United States* (1945) and *International Ass'n* v. *Street* (1961), in terms of the "theory of cyclical majorities." See below, chap. iii.

On the other hand, a Justice who is willing to make all the modifications suggested by his colleagues is liable to find he has fathered an amorphous mass of doughy sentences rather than a strong statement of law. Holmes once complained to Sir Frederick Pollock about his fellow Justices, that "the boys generally cut one of the genitals" out of opinions he circulated.*[33]

Lower court judges constitute a second institutional check on the power of a Supreme Court Justice.[34] Bureaucracy in the executive branch of government, Dahl and Lindblom have noted, "more nearly resembles the arena of international politics than a group of disciplined subordinates responsible to the control of common superiors."[35] While state and federal judges may resist more often than administrators the temptation to drag their heels or otherwise hamper execution of high-level policy decisions, opportunities for such action are an everyday occurrence in the judicial process.

Even where there is no desire to sabotage high policy, the frequent necessity to exercise discretion may have a thwarting effect similar to that of deliberate misunderstanding. Just as mixed problems of language and political compromise permit and sometimes force judges to make their own policy choices in interpreting statutes, semantic difficulties and opinion compromises within the Supreme Court often allow or require the exercise of lower court discretion. In addition, even where the Court has spoken precisely on general principles of law, the work of applying these principles to new and complex situations of muddled evidence and tangled pleadings may demand ingenuity, imagination, and the insertion of value preferences which may not conform to those of the Justices. Moreover, a lower court judge may think he perceives a change in Supreme Court doctrine and thus feel confronted with the choice of following the Court of yesterday or tomorrow.

A number of factors operate to increase the range of lower court discretion. One is that the Justices rarely make either the first or last decision in a case. When a piece of litigation gets to the Court, the facts and legal issues have usually been shaped by several sets of lower court judges, and most cases will be returned to those judges for final

---

* In the 1958 term, Justice Brennan solved this dilemma by writing two opinions in one case, one for the Court and a somewhat different one as a separate concurring opinion for himself. *Abbate and Falcone* v. *United States* (1959).

disposition. A second factor is the vague remand formula which the Court uses when it reverses a decision of lower tribunal. Typically the Justices send a case back to state courts with instructions that the litigation be handled by further "proceedings not inconsistent with this opinion." Instructions to federal judges are often equally imprecise.

A third factor is that if and when lower court judges choose not to follow Supreme Court decisions they are far more insulated against retaliation than are administrators. Federal judges hold their office during good behavior, and although appointed through the same legal process as Supreme Court Justices they are generally chosen through a different political process. State courts are staffed through a variety of ways; but the judges in these courts do not owe their original appointment or tenure to the pleasure of the Supreme Court. Since they are chosen according to different considerations, it is inevitable that, although Supreme Court and lower court judges share many basic values of American society, they have many different specific values, outlooks, and ambitions which produce conflicting interpretations of law and policy.

The enormous number of cases which courts in this country decide forms an additional protection against even the mildest of sanctions: reversal. Lower federal courts handle about a hundred thousand cases a year and the state courts literally millions. Appeal is a lengthy and expensive business, so much so that probably only about 3 per cent of all cases go beyond the trial court level. Since the Supreme Court consents to a full-scale review of less than two hundred cases a year, the chances of any particular decision, even one involving a question of federal constitutional law, getting up to the Court are statistically small.

Last, there is the matter of conscience. A judge who felt that policy endorsed by the Supreme Court in a given field was unwise, unconstitutional, or unjust and did not use the latitude available to him would face ethical problems no less serious than would a judge who chose to exploit his opportunities for exercise of discretion. As Justice Frankfurter once said, "the ultimate touchstone of constitutionality is the Constitution itself, and not what we have said about it."[36]

The common law tradition—as well as the counterpower of the Supreme Court—restricts the courses of resistance which a judge may pursue, but these lower court judges have at times: (a) interpreted

25

Supreme Court decisions, distinguishing or explaining the case before them so that if their own policy preferences did not prevail at least they were not snuffed out;[37] (b) carried Supreme Court decisions to an extreme which made them absurd;[38] (c) simply ignored—whether deliberately or through lack of time or information or through Freudian slips—contrary Supreme Court decisions:[39] (d) invited a change by the Court itself or by other branches of government by sharply criticizing Supreme Court decisions in official opinions, at bar association meetings or judicial conferences, or before congressional committees.*[40]

POLITICAL CHECKS

Congressmen have an impressive array of weapons which can be used against judicial power. They can impeach and remove the Justices, increase the number of the Justices to any level whatever, regulate court procedure, abolish any tier of courts, confer or withdraw federal jurisdiction almost at will, cut off the money that is necessary to run the courts† or to carry out a specific decision or set of decisions, pass laws to reverse statutory interpretation, and propose constitutional amendments either to reverse particular decisions or to curtail directly judicial power. Furthermore, senators share to some extent the President's power to appoint judges to all federal courts.

As Chief Executive, the President may order executive officials from marshals on up to the Attorney General or the Secretary of Defense to refuse to enforce Supreme Court decisions. He can pardon persons convicted of criminal contempt of court for defying judicial decisions. In his choice of nominees for vacancies on the Supreme Court and the lower federal bench, the President can influence the future course of judicial power. As chief legislator and as head of his party, he can try to persuade congressmen to impeach offensive Justices, to increase the size of the Court, or to utilize any of the other legislative checks against judicial power. In opposing the Court, a President, a senator, or a representative could also throw his own prestige onto the scales.

* The Supreme Court has almost no formal sanctions to apply against criticism by judges. By the Court's own decisions judges cannot punish as contempt out-of-court criticism unless the comments are so strong and the judges so weak that the administration of justice is impaired. *Nye* v. *United States* (1941); *Bridges* v. *California* (1941).

† The Constitution explicitly forbids cutting judicial salaries, but it would be impossible for the Court to force Congress to appropriate the money.

Local constituencies may well support a member of Congress who attacks the Court, especially if a recent judicial decision has adversely affected them. And it is no mean thing for the Justices to be opposed by a President to whom a majority of the nation looks for leadership or by a legislator whom local majorities revere.

It would be comforting for judges to be able to say that these are only possible limitations. But as every schoolboy knows, Court opponents through the years have attempted to use each of these checks against the Justices, and, at one time or another in American history, Court foes have been successful in employing most of these means to curb the judiciary. The Eleventh Amendment withdrew the Court's jurisdiction to hear suits against states. The Judiciary Act of 1802 summarily abolished the office of circuit judge without making any provision to pay the salaries of the incumbent judges. This act also postponed the next session of the Supreme Court for ten months in order to delay a decision in *Marbury* v. *Madison*. The Jeffersonians impeached Justice Chase in 1804 and failed by a narrow margin to convict him. Presidents from Washington to Johnson have tried to put on the bench men who were "ideologically sound," and senators have made similar efforts to assure themselves of the correctness of the nominees' political views.

Removal of jurisdiction has been a perennial suggestion from those who oppose Court policies, though the Judiciary Act of 1868 was the only successful use of this weapon against the Supreme Court.[41] The size of the Court has also been changed over the years. During the Civil War and Reconstruction periods, the political efforts to interfere with the Court were especially blatant, as they were in Roosevelt's attempt to enlarge the Court in 1937. Presidents Jackson and Lincoln ignored judicial decisions, and Jackson in so doing acted on the advice of Attorney General Roger Brooke Taney. On another occasion, Lincoln subjected to house arrest a federal judge who seemed likely to hold executive action unconstitutional.[42] Jefferson and Franklin D. Roosevelt were also prepared to defy the Court. Even former Circuit Judge William Howard Taft, when Secretary of War, advised Attorney General Philander Knox to ignore claims for money made on the basis of what Taft described as a "fool decision" of the Supreme Court.[43]

State officials other than judges have no direct, legal checks on Supreme Court power. Nullification has been tried on a number of occasions and has sometimes been successful, but the development of American constitutional law has branded this as an heretical doctrine. State politicians, however, do have important means of restricting federal judicial power. Like federal officials, state officers may drag their heels and refuse to co-operate in carrying out the Court's decisions. More dramatically, state officers may throw their prestige against the Court and on an issue of local significance, such as school segregation, may so stir public opinion as to make the Court's policy practically unworkable. Furthermore, since federalism is as strong an aspect of the American political party system as it is of the formal governmental structure, state politicians can bring heavy pressure to bear at the national level both on legislators and administrators to use their weapons against the Court or at least to withhold their support from the Court or from those groups likely to benefit from Court decisions.

Political officials may fight particular decisions or even judicial power itself for a wide combination of reasons. They may disagree sincerely with the wisdom of the public policies which the Court seems to be following. They may feel their own policy-making prerogatives threatened by judicial action. Then, too, political officials, lacking the job security of Supreme Court Justices, may be reacting to the pressures of organized interest groups or broader constituent sentiment. Interest-group leaders are quick to utilize such instruments of the judicial process as the injunction and the class action when they believe the judiciary will serve their goals against other groups who may be benefiting from legislative or administrative policies. These same leaders are equally quick to complain to congressmen and executive officials when they feel their own interests are impaired by court decisions. Spokesmen for respected groups like the American Bar Association, the National Association of Manufacturers, or the Chamber of Commerce, can also effectively attack the Court's prestige.

JUDICIAL SELF-RESTRAINT

The restraints of constitutional, political, and legal philosophy which individual Justices impose on themselves are always important in judicial decision-making. As men of integrity, Justices automatically foreclose to themselves certain morally tainted courses of action. For most Justices, their anomalous position as powerful officials appointed for life in a supposedly democratic political system also imposes significant restrictions on their freedom. It would be difficult to deny that much of judicial self-restraint can be traced to a prudent regard for the existence of political checks. As Chancellor Waties of South Carolina once remarked, "The interference of the judiciary with legislative Acts, if frequent or on dubious ground, might occasion so great a jealousy of this power and so generally a prejudice against it as to lead to measures ending in the total overthrow of the independence of the judges, and so of the best preservative of the constitution."[44]

It would also be difficult to deny that a policy-oriented Justice may believe more strongly in self-restraint when his views are in the minority on the Court or when he believes that his views are more likely to triumph ultimately if the Court allows other government officials responsibility for choice. It would be equally difficult to deny that much of the force of self-restraint can be traced to individual Justices' concepts of their proper role in American government, to a realization that they are equipped by training, availability of information, and choice of legal remedies to offer only partial solutions to many problems and no solution at all to many others.

IV AVOIDANCE OF TECHNICAL CHECKS

The limitations discussed in this chapter are, in fact, limitations not absolute bars to the exercise of Supreme Court power. In the nineteenth and early twentieth centuries the mechanical theory of the judicial function saw the limits of judicial power largely in terms of legal technicalities. In the 1920's and 1930's, some Legal Realists derided technical checks as a device which judges used to mask their freedom of action. The Realists produced weighty evidence in favor of their argument.[45] The Court has no self-starter, yet many interest-group leaders and private citizens have long been fully aware that judges govern as much as legislators and administrators, and these knowledgeable citizens have been quick to bring cases—when they thought the decision would be to their advantage—up to the Supreme Court.[46]

Contrary to the official doctrine that a case means a real dispute, the Justices have sometimes accepted and decided litigation where there were strong signs of collusion between the supposed opponents.[47] On other occasions, the Justices have been engaged in what has been called "judicial homework."[48] They have found issues in the case which opposing counsel did not see and have decided those issues

29

without allowing argument. The "standing" rules have been applied with such "flexibility" and subject to such drastic exceptions that expert students of the Court have confessed as much confusion as the minority Justices.[49] Furthermore, despite frequent disclaimers, the Justices, individually and collectively, have at times offered advisory opinions.[50]

Stare decisis has also been employed in many ways. The doctrine of precedent, Llewellyn has noted, has a "Janus-face." There is one set of rules for utilizing precedents that appear helpful, and another set for avoiding those precedents which seem troublesome.[51] A skilful legal craftsman can usually reach the result he wants without directly overruling established cases or obviously making new law. Nor is the British practice as different from the American as is often claimed. "On the whole," a distinguished English jurist has written, "it is a sign of an incompetent lawyer or Judge that he is over-impressed by citation of particular authority. Authority is but a guide to juridical understanding—a servant, not a dictator."[52]

Previous decisions can be stretched to cover new situations and to provide a justification for creation of law and policy. Alternately, precedents can be contracted and their vitality sapped in a number of ways. Cases can be easily distinguished—no two factual situations can be exactly the same. The Justices can also "explain" prior decisions into oblivion or they can simply ignore precedents that stand in the way. As a final technique, a Court may misuse a precedent—weaken or even kill it by citing dicta in the opinion which runs contrary to the actual holding of the case.[53]

The Realists have properly shown that technical rules partake as much of diplomacy as of fixed law. The Justices by applying most of these rules with discretion and considerable flexibility can take the cases they wish to decide, reject problems they prefer not to hear, and often decide litigation in the way they want. As the first Justice Harlan once commented from the bench: "The courts have rarely, if ever, felt themselves so restrained by technical rules, that they could not find some remedy, consistent with the law, for acts, whether done by government or by individual persons, that violated natural justice or were hostile to the fundamental principles devised for the protection of the essential rights of property."[54] Off the bench, Harlan was even more candid. He once told a class of law students, "I want to say to you young gentlemen that if we don't like an act of Congress, we don't have much trouble to find grounds for declaring it unconstitutional."[55]

On the other hand, it would be false to think of judicial use of technical rules as a game of legal charades. These rules are not infinitely malleable.[56] They provide flexibility but not total freedom of choice. First of all, the Justices are lawyers, trained to respect and work within these technical rules. Judges are, in Llewellyn's phrase, "law conditioned."[57] They believe that these rules serve many useful purposes in protecting the legal system from the caprice of individual jurists. Second, the Court's prestige—and therefore a large measure of its power—is based on its status as a court of law in the common law tradition. No branch of government can govern a growing industrial society strictly by *stare decisis*. The Justices must frequently extend or contract and even occasionally overrule precedents. Nor can a Court in deciding cases whose outcome will affect the nation as a whole always permit counsel's choice of argument to channel decisional alternatives. Judicial homework may be the only answer under some circumstances. So, too, in varying degrees the other technical rules may have to be bent on occasion. But were such bendings to become commonplace or flagrant, the effect on the Court's prestige could well be disastrous. Technical rules do set limitations on the Supreme Court's power —vague limitations, perhaps, limits which can usually be stretched to some extent, and occasionally to a great extent, but limitations nevertheless. Thus, even a judge who had little respect for technical lawcourt rules would find it prudent to assume such respect before some of the popular, bureaucratic, or political checks were applied against his tribunal.

V THE FRAMEWORK OF POWER

This chapter has tried to sketch the framework within which a Justice must operate. A policy-oriented Justice would have to make frequent and careful appraisals of this power framework, since it is dynamic, not static. The Court's prestige, like that of Congress or the President or individual state governments or pressure groups, may be high one year and low the next. The Court's reputation at the same moment may be high with Congress, low with the President, and vary with different groups of judges and administrators. So, too, the skill and energy of the leadership of interest groups and the other branches of government may differ and affect the probability of the use of political checks, just as the policy preferences, intellectual caliber, and emotional state of individual members of the judicial bureaucracy may affect lower court reactions to Supreme Court decisions.

Any time a Justice forms an estimate of a situation, he must, of course, consider the situation in terms of his own objective. Some policies may meet with such universal approval that he need only wait for a case to come up for the Court and the rest of the nation to acclaim a favorable decision. Other issues will be more controversial, ranging from those which will create a resistance so overwhelming as to make their attainment manifestly impossible for the foreseeable future to

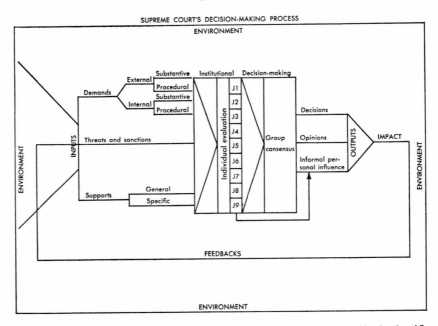

SUPREME COURT'S DECISION-MAKING PROCESS

those issues which will provoke mild criticism but practically insignificant opposition.

From this general framework within which every Justice must operate, one can abstract a conceptual scheme of the process of Supreme Court decision-making. The model used here is an adaptation of a scheme suggested by David Easton as typical of all political systems.[58] It is clearly very simple and open-ended. Like all models this one is an abstraction from, not a replication of, the real world. Its "validity" depends entirely upon its utility in furthering fruitful research or in increasing our understanding of reality.

The *environment* is the general political and social system, of which decision-making at the Supreme Court level is only one part. *Environment* thus includes not only widely shared societal values (which may or may not be fully articulated or carefully understood and may be to some extent even mutually incompatible in terms of strict logic), but also the specific political context, much like that just outlined. Certain kinds of social conflict are generated in the *environment* and presented to the Court as competing *demands* for judicial action. The particular pleas of individual litigants represent the more formal *external demands;* other actors in the *environment* may also be simultaneously making related though unexpressed *demands.* Public officials, affected interests, and the legal profession, for instance, may all want the problem resolved to produce certain, though very different, results. These kinds of *demands* are substantive in nature. At the same time, there are also *demands,* though seldom overtly expressed, that the Court handle any dispute according to particular institutional procedures, normally the technical rules already sketched.

Internal demands are those claims which a Justice puts on himself —his concept of his office, his notions of his proper function, and his standards of professional ethics. Again some of these *demands* have to do with substance and others with procedure.

General supports would include most of the integrative forces in society, in broadest terms the state of mind which desires—and therefore respects courts and judges insofar as it considers them to be fulfilling those desires—what we like to think of as the rule of law. The traditional myth of the judicial function would be an example of a cultural orientation toward *general support. Specific supports* would include the actions of persons, both in and out of public office, who back the judiciary as an institution or a particular decision as viable policy because of past benefits derived, present benefits being enjoyed, or future benefits anticipated.

For the sake of clarity, *threats* and *sanctions* are considered here as separate *inputs,* but they can also be seen as concomitants of *demands.* A *demand* may carry with it a *threat,* usually implicit, to withdraw a *specific support,* to discourage *general support,* or, more positively, to attack the Court or a particular decision if a set of *demands* is not satisfactorily met. The term *sanctions* is used here in the very narrow

33

sense of those formal political and institutional controls which may be applied from the outside against the Court.

In the *individual evaluation* stage of decision-making, each Justice weighs the *inputs* in terms of:

    a) The legitimacy—according to his standards of law or justice or some combination thereof—of the *demands* of the litigants.

    b) The relative desirability of the implications of these competing *demands* for public policy.

    c) The kinds, extent, and intensity of the *demands,* latent and active, of other public officials (including his colleagues), interests, and the public at large for each of the policy alternatives.

    d) The nature and seriousness of the *threats* implicit in the *demands* on the Court, and the likelihood that effective *sanctions* will be applied.

    e) The kinds, extent, and intensity of the changes in *supports* likely to be forthcoming from the *environment* for each of the policy alternatives.

The *group consensus* stage represents:

    f) The presentation to the Court as a whole of the individual evaluations of *a, b,* and perhaps of *c,* and/or *d* and *e.*

    g) The process of reaching an agreement on a decision of the Court.

    h) The process of reaching an agreement on a justification for that decision.

In every part of the *individual* and *group* decisional processes, each judge's choices would be heavily affected not only by his understanding of existing legal rules and his intellectual acumen but also by such factors as his emotional biases, policy predilections, personal values, and even his strength of character. Particularly in the *group consensus* phase, his choice probably would also be affected by similar characteristics of his colleagues. It could happen, of course, that a judge's *internal demands* would preclude him from consciously weighing or openly discussing *c, d,* and *e,* but a Justice who fits the description offered in chapter i of a policy-oriented judge would certainly consider such factors, though he might not publicize the fact that he did so.

Outputs are the resulting decisions and opinions—institutional and individual—as well as informally expressed personal influence. The Justice's decisions legitimize what Easton calls "authoritative allocation of values"[59] in society by other public officials or substitute therefor the Justices' own allocations, or in the case of the minority, desired allocations. Opinions justify these decisions in terms of tradition, existing legal rules, and previous societal values.

The *impact* is the actual effect of these *outputs* on the larger *environment*. These effects range from those which may be trivial except to the litigants themselves to those which may precipitate far-reaching and momentous changes in the political or social structure of the *environment*.

Outputs and their *impacts* may in turn generate *feedbacks* into the judicial process, creating fresh *demands* or altering old ones, encouraging some kinds of *supports, threats,* and *sanctions* while discouraging others. Some of the effects of the *impact* will not feed back directly into the judicial process but will be channelized into the executive or legislative process and from there possibly return to try to affect future decisions.

Under the conditions of this model, a policy-oriented Justice must be prepared to weigh the relative costs and benefits which will result from his formal decisions and informal efforts at influence. He must realize that because some litigants, and therefore some interests in society, will lose from any decision, he will have to pay supportive costs. Similarly, he will have to assess the danger posed by *threats*. Because his time, energy, and staff are severely limited, he will have to pay opportunity costs. Since on important issues some or most or all of his colleagues are apt to have strong feelings of their own, he must be ready to pay decision-making costs—costs computed again in time and energy but also in good will, prestige, and bargaining capital. A Justice would certainly have to pay the latter two costs, and possibly the first, for uses of personal influence. On the opposite side of the scale, the Justice can calculate the supportive gains which may accrue, as a result of his decision, from the winning litigants, as well as from sympathetic interests and officials. So, too, a Justice may use his personal influence to increase support from sectors of the general political system. Not least, there is always the benefit to be gained by achieving or coming nearer to achieving a desired policy goal.

Thus the policy-oriented Justice in this model acts much like the rational man of economic theory. He has only a limited supply of such resources as time, energy, staff, prestige, reputation, and good will, and he must compute in terms of costs and revenues whether a particular

35

choice is worth the price which is required to attain it. To be sure, neither in real life nor in this model can a Justice make precise mathematical calculations. He would be weighing intangibles and weighing them on a predictive basis. Moreover, a backlog of capital may make deficit financing available; and in a way analogous to investment, a Justice might rationally risk loss of support from a currently powerful interest in society in the belief that in the long run support from a currently weak interest would offer greater strength both to his institution and decisions. There is the further fact that the cultural values of society tend to keep a flow of *support* into the judiciary which enables the judges to make rational gambles on their ability to recoup short-run losses.

An additional complication is that in working toward his policy goals, a Justice may not be able to calculate in a series of stages the costs and benefits of dealing with colleagues, lower court judges, etc., but he may have to meet simultaneous and competing *demands,* *threats,* and promises of *support* from all of these people. Under such circumstances discernment of the most efficient allocation of resources is as easy to prescribe and as difficult to execute as the supposed axiom of General Nathan Bedford Forrest: "Get there fustest with the most-est."*

* In the Washington law firm of Arnold, Fortas, and Porter there is a motto known as the Paul Porter Doctrine which is of equal application: "When in doubt do the right thing."

3 Marshalling the Court

Since he shares decision-making authority with eight other judges, the first problem that a policy-oriented Justice would confront is that of obtaining at least four, and hopefully eight, additional votes for the results he wants and the kinds of opinions he thinks should be written in cases important to his objectives. Moreover, because he faces other problems as well, he must try to influence* his colleagues with as little expenditure of time and energy as possible.

His initial step would be to examine the situation on the Court. In general three sets of conditions may obtain. There may be complete coincidence of interest with the other Justices, or at least with the number of associates he feels is necessary to attain his aim. Second, the interests of the other Justices, or a majority of them, may be indifferent to his objective. Third, the interests of his colleagues may be in opposition to his own. Since there are varying degrees of coincidence, indifference, and opposition, each represents a range rather than a pin-pointed position. The coincidence may be such that the Justice need only bring the facts or implications of a specific situation to the attention of his colleagues, or it may be so imperfect that the term coincidence can be used only in the sense of an analogy. Under the latter circumstances, the Justice may have to do a great deal of persuading to convince his colleagues that their objectives are not

* In the sense influence is defined in chap. i, it can be distinguished from leadership only if one restricts leadership to the exercise of influence within a specific group. As used in this chapter, the two terms are interchangeable. I prefer to use influence because, to most persons not trained in social psychology, leadership usually connotes a formal position in a hierarchy.

incongruous and that it is important to their interests that they support his suggestions.

Indifference may be, as one might assume, the situation in which attempts to exercise influence would be most necessary and would pay the biggest dividends; but influence could also have a major effect where interests were in opposition. Where the opposition was intense a Justice might still be able to lessen its impact on his policy aims by decreasing its intensity. Where the opposition was mild, a Justice might conceivably convince his associates that they were mistaken, or he might offer a concession in another area which they valued more highly in exchange for a concession here.

Influence, of course, does not simply come into existence.[1] It is the result of interaction among human beings, of their individual interests, values, and concepts of what moral rules, if any, ought to be controlling, and of their different perceptions of the situations in which they are operating. A policy-oriented Justice must therefore want to know what factors predispose one actor to respond positively to the suggestions, wishes, requests, or commands of another. Where actors are behaving rationally in terms of their particular goals, the question, "What shall I gain if I do x because actor A suggests, wishes, requests, or commands it?" is crucial. Personal esteem can also be important in gauging reactions, and it is often tied to self-interest. We tend to like those whose actions have benefited us in the past, to interpret as beneficial the actions of those whom we like, and, in turn, to help those whom we like. In addition, we frequently find ourselves liking another person for no apparent reason at all. In the process of reacting favorably to the suggestions of those we like, we may be unconsciously reckoning on intangible as well as tangible gains, such as an increase in affection. The desire to be loved seems as important as it is widespread in our society. Furthermore, once our affections have become attached to another person, whether or not because of rational considerations, what Pepitone has called "facilitative distortion" may set in.[2] That is, we tend to attribute to persons to whom we are emotionally drawn the virtues and talents we would like them to have.

Thus, in disposing an actor to respond positively to the attempts at influence by another actor, personal esteem may merge with professional esteem—respect for judgment, knowledge, or skills—in that we might see those whom we like as having somewhat more of these qualities than they perhaps possess. Self-interest, as has already been indicated, may also be involved in professional evaluations. It is easier to esteem the abilities of those whose previous actions have been beneficial to one's own interests than to esteem the abilities of those whose actions have been harmful or indifferent. This is not to deny that such respect may be based on purely professional standards, largely apart from interest or affection, and still influence our decisions. In addition, such respect, no matter how generated, can lead to influence insofar as it operates as an economizing device. An actor might conclude that "A is an expert in this field, and I am not. The cost of becoming an expert is so high that I find it more efficient to follow A than to become an expert myself."

The concept of "oughtness" also plays a role in disposing an actor to respond to the suggestions of another. One might react positively or negatively to a suggestion because one feels that because of broad moral precepts or because of one's particular role in society, one should or should not perform such an act. In a more specific fashion, when he is a member of an institutional hierarchy, an actor might feel that he ought to carry out the wishes of those further up the hierarchy than he, at least in those matters relating to the superiors' areas of authority. Fear, too, can be a significant factor in determining influence. The question, "What reprisals shall I be risking if I do not do x at actor A's suggestion?" is central to any rational process of decision-making. And, in politics, sanctions can take forms ranging all the way from a decrease in affection to physical violence.

Since the Justices are largely equal in authority, an appeal by one Justice to his position on the Court is not likely to be an effective means of increasing influence with his associates, except perhaps in those few fields in which tradition has given the Chief Justice certain prerogatives.* The Justices, however, are not equal in intellectual ability, in perspicacity, learning, legal craftsmanship, persuasive talents, energy, determination, ambition, or social skills; nor do they hold each other in equal personal and professional esteem. Thus a Justice has considerable opportunity to try to exercise influence over his colleagues. He could attempt: to appeal to their interests—to convince them that their interests would gain from furthering his interests or that their interests would suffer injury if they opposed his; to increase or create and then appeal to their personal and professional

* The Chief Justice will be considered as a special case in sec. III of this chapter.

esteem for him; and to appeal to their concepts of duty and moral obligation.

The peculiar formal rules and informal norms of the Court would allow a Justice to operate under one or more of several simple strategies to exploit each of these possible appeals. First, he might try by force of his intellect and will to convince his colleagues not only that what he wanted was in the best interests of themselves, the Court, the country, humanity, or whatever other goals they might wish to foster, but also that it was morally incumbent upon them to act in the fashion he was proposing.

Second, a Justice might plan so to endear himself to the other Justices that they would be reluctant to vote against him in matters he considered to be vital. Conversely, he might try to capitalize on fear rather than affection and try to bludgeon his colleagues into agreement by threatening them with use of the sanctions available to him. Fourth, he might conclude that the only viable way to come near achieving his goal would be to negotiate: to compromise with those who were less intensively opposed to his policies. Last, he might decide that the best way of securing approval of his policies would be to secure new men for the Court, men whose interests would coincide closely with his own.

Taken alone, none of these simple strategies seems very promising. Occasionally a giant like Marshall can dominate the Court, but the great Chief Justice was blessed with several co-operative colleagues as well as with a magnificent sense of statecraft. As Justice Johnson explained to Jefferson:[3]

> While I was on our state-bench I was accustomed to delivering seriatim opinions . . . and was not a little surprised to find our Chief Justice in the Supreme Court delivering all the opinions in cases in which he sat, even in some instances when contrary to his own judgment and vote. But I remonstrated in vain; the answer was he is willing to take the trouble and it is a mark of respect to him. I soon found out however the real cause. Cushing was incompetent. Chase could not be got to think or write—Patterson [*sic*] was a slow man and willingly declined the trouble, and the other two judges [Marshall and Bushrod Washington] you know are commonly estimated as one judge. . . .

On the other hand, it is difficult to imagine any judge, even a Marshall, dominating men like Johnson, Taney, Field, Miller, Bradley, Brewer,

Harlan, Holmes, Hughes, Brandeis, Sutherland, Van Devanter, Cardozo, or Stone. It is equally difficult to imagine any Justice getting passive acquiescence, for any length of time, on important and controversial issues from a Court composed of Justices as brilliant, individualistic, and strong-willed as Black, Douglas, Frankfurter, and Jackson.

Similarly, Supreme Court Justices are as unlikely to be swayed by personal esteem alone as solely by the threat of sanctions being applied against them. Bargaining, too, hardly seems to be the golden key to success, unless accompanied by high personal or professional esteem, some measure of coincidence or indifference of interests, and, perhaps, by some fear of the application of sanctions.

Last, staffing the Court with men whose interests coincided with the policy-oriented Justice's would undoubtedly be very effective. It would depend, however, on (1) the Justice's being gifted with better vision than most Presidents have had in foreseeing how future judges would behave once securely on the bench, (2) enough vacancies occurring to permit a favorable majority to be formed, (3) the President and the general political environment allowing the Justice to play the chief role in the appointing process. The necessity of all three conditions happening simultaneously is a severe limitation on the practicality of sole reliance on this strategy.

It is obvious that in most circumstances a Justice would be far more prudent to pursue a mixed strategy employing some elements of each of these simple approaches—so obvious in fact that the only real question is what blend should be adopted. Without knowing the specific policy involved and the exact moment of time in the Court's history, one can only formulate some general considerations.

First would be the personality of the Justice himself. Realization of the major sources of influence potential might, for instance, induce a Justice who inclines to rely on hard intellectual argument on the merits of an issue to the neglect of considerations of the feelings, interests, and moral concepts of those with whom he is debating to pay more attention to the social amenities, so that his ideas will find a more receptive audience. Conversely, a recognition of influence potential should move every Justice toward diligent attention to the craftsmanship of his profession. By the time he comes to the Court, however, a Justice's personality is so formed that even a strong-willed man probably cannot completely remold himself. It would have been impossible, for example, for Taft to have become a scholar and to

41

have awed the conference with his legal erudition. At another extreme is the kind of man whom Justice Jackson once described: "You must go to war with him if you disagree."[4] While Jackson was hardly a disinterested critic of the particular Justice to whom he was referring, his characterization does fit a common personality type. It is improbable that any amount of effort could turn such a man into the warm, sensitive, forgiving sort of person who refuses to press an intellectual advantage or who smilingly overlooks personal affronts.

An effective, policy-oriented Justice must be able to assess with a considerable degree of objectivity his own strengths and his weaknesses and, while trying to make adjustments to minimize the latter, concentrate on exploiting his major abilities. Choosing an ally with complementary talents is one way of maximizing potentials. Taft, for instance, knew that he had a rare social skill, but he was also keenly aware of his intellectual limitations. He complained to his family on several occasions that his colleagues would "humiliate" him in conference discussion,[5] and he was struck by the contrast between his own and Van Devanter's grasp of the intricacies of the Court's business. As the Chief Justice told his son, "The familiarity with the practice and the thoroughness of examination in certain cases that Van Devanter is able to give makes him a most valuable member of the Court and makes me feel quite small, and as if it would be better to have the matter run by him alone. . . ." Taft, however, had no intention of letting another man even appear to run the office which had been his life-long ambition. Instead he shrewdly utilized Van Devanter's immense learning to improve his own opinions, to supply technical knowledge at conference, and to advise on the numerous political affairs in which the Chief Justice was constantly getting involved. Meanwhile Taft continued to make full use of his own sensitivity to the feelings of others and the personal esteem in which other Justices held him. As he told his son, he would be "content to aid in the deliberation when there is a difference of opinion."[6]

What mixture of appeals, threats, and offers to compromise would be effective would also depend in large part on the character of the Justice's colleagues. Indeed, a somewhat different combination might have to be devised in dealing with each member of the Court. It would be far easier, though not necessarily very profitable, to bargain with a born negotiator like Brandeis than with a lone wolf like Douglas; easier to reason with an open-minded judge like Holmes than

with a man like Peckham, whose major premise, so one Justice remarked, was "God damn it";[7] easier to play on charm with a genial
character like Taft or Sherman Minton than with a waspish, suspicious
McReynolds; easier to dominate a Justice who has ceased to care about
his work than a man who, like most Justices, is fully committed to the
Court's operations.

The ideal strategic formula would also be affected by the nature of
the policy itself and the kinds of cases relating to that policy which the
Court was receiving, what the policy meant in terms of existing legal
doctrine and the commitments thereto not only of the Justices but
also of the demands and supports from other government officials and
powerful interest groups. One or more such factors would certainly be
significant in determining the kinds of stimuli to which each of the
Justices would respond in a positive manner. Moreover, the general
political situation would be a key element in a Justice's capacity to
influence the appointment of new members of the Court.

I TACTICS

Once he has decided on a strategic plan to secure a majority within
the Court—and integrated that plan into his larger scheme to meet the
other obstacles in his path—a Justice would have to consider the tactics
open to him to carry out his efforts to persuade on the merits of his
policy choice, to capitalize on personal regard, to bargain, to threaten,
and if possible to have a voice in the selection of new personnel.

Persuasion on the Merits

To date all the Justices have been lawyers, and whatever the status of
their technical knowledge when appointed, their work, their friends,
their critics, their pride, and their clerks have forced most of them to
become competent and usually highly competent lawyers. Traditional
overemphasis on the logical element in judicial decision-making has
been ridiculed by Legal Realists. Yet, while it is true that the work
of courts revolves around basically subjective value judgments, judgments conditioned by all sorts of subconscious drives shaped in part
by childhood experiences, no evidence has yet been adduced to show
that judges decide cases through some automatic operation of emotional prejudices. To a significant extent judges can and do weigh

such factors as legal principles and precedents and well thought-out ideas of proper public policy.

Furthermore, judges can be persuaded to change their minds about specific cases as well as about broad public policies, and intellectual persuasion can play an important role in such shifts. As Robert Jackson once commented from the bench: "I myself have changed my opinion after reading the opinions of the other members of this Court. And I am as stubborn as most. But I sometimes wind up not voting the way I voted in conference because the reasons of the majority didn't satisfy me."*8 An examination of the notes of conference discussions which Justice Murphy filed with his papers and the memoranda in this and in other collections of judicial papers show that time and again positions first taken at conference are changed as other Justices bring up new arguments. Perhaps most convincing in demonstrating the impact of intellectual factors are the numerous instances on record in which the Justice assigned the opinion of the Court has reported back to the conference that additional study had convinced him that he and the rest of the majority had been in error. A few examples will have to suffice:

When, in May, 1922, Taft circulated his opinion in *Hill* v. *Wallace*, he attached a statement summarizing the history of the Court's handling of the dispute:[9]

> . . . we voted first that there was equitable jurisdiction by a vote of 7 to 1, Justice Brandeis voting "No" and Justice Holmes being doubtful. On the question of whether [the congressional statute regulating trading in grain futures] could be sustained as a taxing act, the vote stood 7 to 1, Justice McKenna casting the negative vote, and Justice Brandeis not voting. Later we took a vote as to whether the act could be sustained as a regulation of interstate commerce. At first, by a vote of 5–4, it was held that it could not be so sustained. Later there was a change, and by a vote of 5 to 3, Justice Brandeis not voting, its validity as a regulation of interstate commerce was sustained.

* It is interesting to observe that not only in their memoranda to one another but also in conference, the Justices argue in terms of such categories as "intent of the framers," the meaning of legislative history or previous Court decisions as well as in terms of the policy implications of possible decisions. This evidence indicates, of course, that the real process of judicial policy-making is a very subtle business, that judges often think largely in traditional legal categories, though their behavior may actually be more accurately described under different concepts.

Taft then pointed out that he had changed his mind and asked the Court to go along with him. "On a close examination of the case, the law and the record, I have reached the conclusion that the law is invalid as a taxing law and that it can not be sustained as a valid regulation of interstate commerce." When the opinion came down three days later, the statute was declared unconstitutional as a taxing act, under the authority of the Child Labor Tax Case. The vote was 8–1, with Brandeis agreeing in a separate opinion that the statute was unconstitutional but doubting that the plaintiffs had standing to sue.

In March, 1945, a majority of the Court voted in conference to affirm the conviction under the Sherman Act of several employers and union officials who had conspired to raise wages and prices by trying to monopolize the lumber business in the San Francisco Bay area.[10] The opinion of the Court was assigned to Justice Black. On May 2, 1945, however, Black circulated an opinion reversing the convictions. He explained that further study had convinced him that the trial judge had improperly interpreted the Norris–La Guardia Act.[11]

Black may have been persuaded, but his colleagues were not, at least not immediately. The case was twice set down for reargument on the construction of the Norris–La Guardia Act, and the decision did not finally come down until March 10, 1947. The vote to reverse was 5–3, Justice Jackson not participating. As the senior majority Justice, Black, possibly as a means of conciliation, assigned the opinion to Reed rather than to himself; and Reed held that the trial judge's charge to the jury had been erroneous under the Norris–La Guardia Act and ordered a new trial.

As every serious scholar has recognized, the openness of many Justices to logical persuasion on the merits points up the importance of professional skills to a policy-oriented Justice. It is almost trite to note that if a Justice is able to mass legal precedents and history to bolster an intellectually and morally defensible policy and can present his arguments in a convincing manner, he stands an excellent chance of picking up votes. Indeed, without this kind of approach it is extremely unlikely that a Justice will significantly influence any of his colleagues, although, because they have found the necessary evidence themselves or because of their own policy predilections, they may vote in the way he wishes.

As in all phases of human activity, eloquence and charm would be valuable additions to professional competence. One might suspect that

Hughes's opening remarks to the conference when the troublesome issue of a compulsory flag salute was first discussed increased the predisposition of the other Justices to accept his reasoning. "I come up to this case," Justice Murphy recorded the Chief Justice as saying, "like a skittish horse to a brass band."[12]

It does not follow, to be sure, that all or even four Justices would be open to persuasion on the policy which the Justice wanted adopted. Certainly a Justice coming to the bench after 1941 would have received reactions no more favorable than bored yawns had he urged the Court to resume its role as defender of laissez faire. Thus a Justice would also have to consider exploiting the vulnerability of any of his colleagues to non- or extra-rational arguments. He would probably feel it unethical to appeal to the strong personal dislike of one Justice for another, though there may have been occasions when such an appeal would have been effective.

Less distasteful would be an appeal to loyalty to the Court as an institution, though it would normally be possible for a Justice to utilize this argument fully only when he was in the majority and was trying to pick up additional votes or was trying to get a majority to agree to an institutional opinion in preference to a seriatim expression of views. Similarly, in situations where the Justice feels that the general political environment requires unanimity, he might play on the isolation of a would-be dissenter.

Hirabayashi v. *United States* provides one example of a combination of such tactics. After reading a draft of Stone's opinion for the Court sustaining the conviction of a Nisei for violating the curfew imposed by the military on all West Coast Japanese Americans—an opinion which ducked the more serious question of the constitutionality of the evacuation and internment aspects of the program—Justice Murphy began writing a dissent. Hearing of this, Frankfurter sent him a plea to close ranks with his colleagues:[13]

> Please, Frank, with your eagerness for the austere functions of the Court and your desire to do all that is humanly possible to maintain and enhance the *corporate* reputation of the Court, why don't you take the initiative with the Chief Justice in getting him to take out everything that either offends you or that you would want to express more irenically.

Even after an exchange of several other notes, Murphy remained adamant, and he circulated a blistering opinion branding the whole

Nisei program as "utterly inconsistent with our ideals and traditions" and "at variance with the principles for which we are fighting."[14] Frankfurter read Murphy's protest in horror, and he immediately wrote another impassioned plea:[15]

> Of course I shan't try to dissuade you from filing a dissent in that case—not because I do not think it highly unwise but because I think you are immovable. But I would like to say two things to you about the dissent: (1) it has internal contradictions which you ought not to allow to stand, and (2) do you really think it is conducive to the things you care about, including the great reputation of this Court, to suggest that everybody is out of step except Johnny, and more particularly that the Chief Justice and seven other Justices of this Court are behaving like the enemy and thereby playing into the hands of the enemy?

Murphy was apparently moved at least to second thoughts about the possible implications of what he was doing. Within a few days he had switched his vote and had modified his dissent into a concurrence, though one which still expressed concern over the "melancholy resemblance" between United States treatment of the Nisei and Nazi treatment of the Jews.

Shortly after Stone came to the bench, Taft tried to use this sort of approach with him. When Stone was considering a dissent in an important labor case,[16] the Chief Justice wrote him: "My dear Brother Stone: I am quite anxious, as I am sure we all are, that the continuity and weight of our opinions on important questions of law should not be broken any more than we can help by dissents. . . ." Holmes and Brandeis, Taft went on, had originally dissented from the line of cases on which the instant decision was based and would doubtless grasp at any minute distinction to persist in their opposition to established law. "With respect to those judges who have come to the Court since these decisions were rendered, I am sure it is not their purpose to depart from what has been declared to be accepted law."[17] Stone gave in to the extent of writing only a concurring opinion.

A few years later McReynolds used the same kind of argument in an unsuccessful effort to dissuade Stone from what was becoming a pronounced tendency to dissent. McReynolds wrote:[18]

> Please don't think me presumptuous. Certainly I do not mean to be. All of us get into a fog now and then, as I know so well from my own experience. Won't you "Stop, Look, and Listen"? In my view,

47

we have one member [Brandeis?] who is consciously boring from within. Of course, you have no such purpose, but you may unconsciously aid his purpose. At least do think twice on a subject—three times indeed. If the Court is broken down, then there will be rejoicing in certain quarters. I cannot think that the last three dissents which you have sent me will aid you, the law or the Court. Give the matter another thought.

A Justice might appeal to other emotions, for example, patriotism in cases involving issues of national security. In *Ex parte Quirin,* the Justices were unanimous in their conclusion that the government could try captured Nazi saboteurs in military tribunals rather than in regularly constituted civil courts, but they could not agree on an opinion explaining why such trials were constitutional. After the Chief Justice had circulated three different drafts of an opinion without securing full assent, one of the other members of the Court sent a long memorandum to all of his colleagues. He began by pointing out that most of the discussion was now approaching mere quibbling about words, since the Justices were agreed that the only real point of difference, the extent to which Congress could bind the President as Commander-in-Chief, should not be decided. As the clearest way of explaining his own views, the Justice offered a dialogue between himself and the saboteurs, a dialogue in which he rejected their claims out of hand, describing them as "damned scoundrels" who were attempting to create a conflict between the President and Congress which would continue long "after your bodies will be rotting in lime." At the conclusion of the dialogue, the Justice again spoke directly to his brethren:[19]

> Some of the very best lawyers I know are now in the Solomon Island battle, some are seeing service in Australia, some are sub-chasers in the Atlantic, and some are on the various air fronts. It requires no poet's imagination to think of their reflections if the unanimous result reached by us in these cases should be expressed in opinions which would black out agreement in result and reveal internecine conflict about the manner of stating that result. I know some of these men very, very intimately. I think I know what they would deem to be the governing canons of constitutional adjudication in a case like this. And I almost hear their voices were they to read more than a single opinion in this case. They would say something like this but in language hardly becoming a judge's tongue: "What in hell do you fellows think you are doing? Haven't we got enough of a job

trying to lick the Japs and Nazis without having you fellows on the Court dissipate thoughts and feelings and energies of the folks at home by stirring up a nice row as to who has what power . . . ? Haven't you got any more sense than to get people by the ear on one of their favorite American pastimes—abstract constitutional discussions? . . . Just relax and don't be too engrossed in your own interests in verbalistic conflicts because the inroads on energy and national unity that such conflict inevitably produces, is a pastime we had better postpone until peacetime."

Stone, too, was hard at work trying to woo the doubtful Justices by means of what he described as "patient negotiations."[20] Eventually the opinion which came down was unanimous.

INCREASING PERSONAL REGARD

Some people are blessed with a warmth and a sincerity that immediately attract other human beings. It is improbable that even a sophisticated version of a Dale Carnegie course, whether or not self-taught, could build up anything approaching the personal magnetism that such people have by nature. Observance of the simple rules of human courtesy and thoughtfulness, however, can do much to keep interpersonal relations on a plane where a meaningful exchange of ideas is possible.

When a new Justice comes to the Court, an older colleague might try to charm his junior brother. A gracious letter of welcome may make the new Justice more disposed to trust another's judgment or at least more disposed to compromise without rancor. When Wiley Rutledge was appointed, Felix Frankfurter, who along with Stone had been reported as working for Learned Hand's promotion,[21] wrote the new Justice:[22]

> You are, I am sure, much too wise a man to pay any attention to gossip even when it is printed. And so I depart from a fixed rule of mine—which Lincoln's life has taught me—not to contradict paragraphs. I do so not because I think for a moment that the silly statement that I am "opposed to" you for a place on this Court has found any lodgment in your mind but to emphasize it as a striking illustration of sheer invention parading as information. The fact of the matter is that the opposite of that baseless statement could much more plausibly be asserted.

Three years earlier, when Frankfurter's nomination was confirmed by the Senate, Hughes, despite the fact that his work on the Court had been sharply criticized by Frankfurter, immediately wrote a welcoming note:[23]

> Let me extend to you a warm welcome to collaboration in our work—for which you are so exceptionally qualified. We need you and I trust you will be able to take your seat at the opening of our next session on January 30th. If there is anything that I can do to aid in making your arrangements here, command me.
>
> With kindest regards, and looking forward with the greatest of pleasure to the renewal, in this relation, of the association with you that I had when you were with the Department of Justice many years ago. . . .

Once on the Court, the freshman Justice, even if he has been a state or lower federal court judge, moves into a strange and shadowy world. An occasional helping hand—a word of advice about procedure and protocol, a warning about personal idiosyncrasies of colleagues, or the trustworthiness of counsel—can be helpful and appreciated.* Particularly if a new Justice comes to Washington in mid-term, aid in securing clerical assistance and law clerks can be a means of establishing good will—with the new Justice as well as with his staff.

The new Justice may also feel it necessary to establish warm social relations with his brethren. When he first came to the Court, Justice Stone asked several of his associates for pictures of themselves. At the end of his first few months on the Court, one Justice sent Hughes this note: "I don't want to leave without telling you how forbearing and generous you have been to this fledgling judge and what an inspiration it has been to work under your chieftainship."[24] After his first year on the bench, that Justice again told Hughes of his great esteem:[25]

> Perhaps this day [Hughes's birthday] I may say to your face what I have several times—to my wife and to a few of my intimate friends— said behind your back: that no one could have welcomed me more generously to the Court than you did, nor have sustained a spirit of generosity and considerateness toward a very junior Brother in those

---

* Mode of address may seem a minor matter, but it can be important to some Justices. Taft, for instance, usually addressed his colleagues, even the new Court members, as "Judge"—except Pierce Butler, whom he almost always called by his first name. Stone was apt to speak to his senior colleagues by title, but to address others by last name—a habit which struck several of the younger Justices, accustomed to the first name informality of the New Deal, as just a bit cold, even impolite.

day-to-day joint labors which, because of the inevitable difference of opinion, test and give the quality to, the relations between men.

No outside student of the work of the Court could be unaware of the intrinsic authority with which you have exercised your Chief Justiceship. But only one who has been privileged to sit under your chief[tainship] can possibly appreciate the sweep and impact of resources and fruitful traditions and creative energy with which you lead the Court. Of your complete dedication to its function in our national life it would be almost humorously impertinent to speak.

Notations on slip opinions provide another avenue of social access. A large ego seems to be a prerequisite of political success, and large egos bruise easily—though the exigencies of American politics probably sift out most of those people with slow recuperative powers. In any event, a judicial opinion represents considerable labor, and it would be a rare man who did not enjoy appreciation of his intellectual offspring. Remarks on slip opinions are frequently glowing in their praise. Holmes could be as charmingly eloquent in his editorial comments as in his other writing. He told Taft in 1921, "I cling to my preceptor's hand and follow him through the dark passages to the light."[26] Stone received his full share of such encomia. On the back of the draft of the opinion in *United States* v. *Darby*, Douglas wrote: "I heartily agree. This has the master's real touch!" Frankfurter added: "This is a grand plum pudding. There are so many luscious plums in it that it's invidious to select. But I especially rejoice over (1) the way you buried *Hammer* v. *Dagenhart* and (2) your definitive exposure of the empty hobgoblin of the 10th Amendt. It's a superb job." On the back of Stone's dissent in *Cloverleaf Butter Co.* v. *Patterson*, Frank Murphy said: "This seems to me the finest kind of writing and it is sound too."

After Hughes had finished his opinion in the Minnesota Rate Cases (1913), Justice Lamar sent him a note: ". . . It is a great opinion and will stand as one of the greatest in our records. Your success ought to be compensation for your days and weeks and months of unceasing labor. . . . I congratulate you most sincerely and heartily on having written an opinion which not only sustains the particular rights of the states and of the United States but, will be a landmark in the history of the Court."[27] A week later Justices Day and Lurton wrote Mrs. Hughes: "Your husband has done a great work this day, the effects of which will be beneficially felt for generations to come. Con-

51

gratulations."[28] Certainly such comments make for an easier exchange of views than remarks like McReynolds' about an opinion of which he did not approve: "This statement makes me sick."[29]

Similarly, suggestions for changes in opinion should be made with tender regard for the feelings of the writer. Stone, for example, wrote Douglas about the latter's opinion[30] in a 1942 term case:[31]

> I have gone over your opinion in this case with some care, and I congratulate you on your lucid and penetrating analysis and the great thoroughness with which you have done a difficult job. If Justice Brandeis could read it he would be proud of his successor.

Stone then quietly added to these gallantries a single-spaced typewritten page of suggestions for revision.

When a Justice has won a fight over a decision, he may be well advised to offer the olive branch to the loser, knowing that today's opponent will often be tomorrow's ally. After their failure to agree in the first Flag Salute case, Frankfurter wrote Stone a gentle note: "Though we read the scales differently in weighing these 'imponderables,' I cannot but feel confident that our scales are the same. In any event our ways do not part and we care no differently for the only things that give dignity to man—the things of the spirit."[32]

A somewhat different way for a Justice to build up a reservoir of good will for later use would be to accede frequently to the majority, and to let the majority know that although acquiescence goes against his better judgment, he is stifling his doubts for the sake of harmony. As Pierce Butler once wrote on the back of one of Stone's slip opinions:[33]

> I voted to reverse. While this sustains your conclusion to affirm, I still think reversal would be better. But I shall in silence acquiesce. Dissents seldom aid in the right development or statement of the law. They often do harm. For myself I say: "Lead us not into temptation."

Sutherland, too, let Stone know his real feelings. In 1930 he commented: "I was inclined the other way, but I think no one agreed with me. I, therefore, yield my not very positive views to those of the majority."[34] In 1932 he told Stone: "I voted the other way, but I have acquiesced in other outrages and probably shall in this. Shall let you know Saturday, though I should like more time to forget."[35] Three years later, he noted on the back of the *Alaska Packers* opinion:

"Probably bad—but only a small baby. Let it go."[36] As handed down, all three decisions were unanimous. Hughes, too, on occasion abstained from dissenting. As he commented on a 1939 slip opinion: "I choke a little at swallowing your analysis, still I do not think it would serve any useful purpose to expose my views."[37]

If such concessions as these are made on issues which a Justice does not think important—or on which he would have been in a small minority anyway—he has lost very little and may have put himself in an excellent position to win reluctant votes from colleagues on other issues. Certiorari voting supplies an opportunity for such tactics.[38] The Court's rules require a vote of four Justices to bring up a case, but where one or two members feel strongly about granting certiorari in a case, another Justice—providing the final decision in the litigation is not likely to affect detrimentally his cause—can capitalize on the situation by graciously saying something to the effect that he is willing to defer to the judgment of the minority.

Members of the Court should be sufficiently sophisticated to take praise and apparent deference from colleagues no more seriously than do most senators. Judges are usually mature, educated, and experienced men, long accustomed to recognizing and thwarting efforts to smooth-talk them into favors.[39] It would be rare for a Justice to succumb to flattery to the extent of changing his vote on a case he thought important. Yet, as has already been pointed out, friendship and the social amenities, especially when coupled with genuine intellectual respect, can play an important auxiliary role in the judicial process insofar as they help determine with whom a Justice is more apt to interact and with whom he will probably continue to negotiate even after an impasse has seemingly been reached.

When Stone first came to the Court, he was, as Taft thought, fundamentally a conservative. Within a very few years, however, Stone had joined Holmes and Brandeis in what the Chief Justice considered "radical" constitutional opinions. In part this change reflected Stone's capacity for intellectual growth, but the warm and stimulating companionship of Holmes and to a lesser extent Brandeis may also have been a decisive factor. As Thomas Reed Powell, a long-time confidant of Stone, commented, it was "respect and liking for Holmes and Brandeis that turned him from his earlier attitudes."[40] On the other hand, Stone probably had slight intellectual respect for Taft. This fact, coupled with McReynolds' bigoted attitude toward Brandeis as well as his continual carping at Stone's opinions,[41] did little to keep the new Justice in the conservative camp.

Stone's change of viewpoint may be an unusual case. Probably more typical is that of the Justice who finds it easier to compromise with a colleague who has shown him respect and consideration than with an associate who has been coldly formal or even impolite. Holmes and Sutherland had very different views of the judicial function,[42] but they were able to work together in making mutual accommodations much more easily than, for example, Brandeis and McReynolds. Conversely, lack of rapport can severely limit opportunities for influencing the Court's work. The relations between McReynolds and Clarke were even more strained than between McReynolds and Brandeis, and as Clarke once told Taft, "I never deign—or dare—to make suggestions to McReynolds, J., as to his opinions."[43]

USE OF SANCTIONS

The two major sanctions which a Justice can use against his colleagues are his vote and his willingness to write opinions which will attack a doctrine the minority or majority wishes to see adopted. The effectiveness of the first sanction usually depends on the closeness of the vote, though there may be special situations, as with Brandeis in the Child Labor Tax Case, where a particular Justice's vote will greatly increase the impact of the arguments of one side or the other, or where, as in the school segregation cases, the general political environment in which the Court functions makes unanimity or near unanimity extraordinarily desirable.

The effectiveness of the second sanction depends largely on the literary and forensic skill of the particular judge. A threat of a separate opinion from one Justice may be a matter hardly worth considering where the vote is not close, while a similar threat from a Johnson, a Field, a Bradley, a Harlan, a Brandeis, or a Black may menace both one's intellectual pride and policy objectives.

A Justice may employ sanctions which are even stronger—and more dangerous—than these. In 1893, Justice Field took what might be termed extreme measures against Justice Gray. After reading Field's dissent in *Fong Yue Ting* v. *United States*, Gray changed a sentence in his opinion for the majority. Feeling this modification took some of the sting out of his dissent, Field wrote Chief Justice Fuller that if Gray did not restore the sentence as originally written, he—Field—

would add a footnote to his opinion explaining that Gray had corrected his error under fire. Gray consulted with the Chief Justice and backed down, leaving the sentence as originally written.[44]

McReynolds expressed his displeasure over Justice Clarke's votes and opinions in a more systematically unpleasant fashion. When he was Attorney General, McReynolds had been instrumental in getting Clarke appointed to the district bench; and when Clarke was promoted to the Supreme Court, McReynolds thought the new Justice should follow his benefactor's ultra-conservative constitutional philosophy. Clarke, however, went his own individual and sometimes erratic way; but, in his first few years on the Court, he tended to side more with Holmes and Brandeis than with McReynolds on constitutional cases. As a result, McReynolds cut off all pleasant social relations with Clarke, meting out only curt sarcasm to him.

Similarly, but in one swift blow, Justice Jackson lashed out at Justice Black in 1946. Roosevelt had promised Jackson—or led Jackson to think that he had promised—to promote him to the chief justiceship when Stone stepped down, but Stone outlived Roosevelt by eleven months. When Stone died, Jackson was at Nürnberg finishing his work as chief American prosecutor of the Nazi war criminals, and he heard rumors that Black and his friends were feverishly lobbying against his promotion. Infuriated, Jackson cabled a long letter to the chairmen of the House and Senate judiciary committees, charging that Black had made "public threats to the President" to resign if Jackson were appointed Chief Justice. Jackson then offered a detailed explanation of the feud between himself and Black, accusing Black of "bullying" tactics and of dealings of questionable propriety in sitting in a case argued by a former law partner.[45]

Like massive retaliation, the threat of airing disputes in public is effective to the extent that it is never actually applied. Its use may embarrass one's adversary, but even a threat to use it may enrage him to the point of total alienation as far as future consultation or compromise is concerned. More important—since, if the Justice employing such a sanction were acting rationally, he would not make the threat unless relations with the target Justice had already reached a hopeless point—public use or threats of sanctions may damage the Court's prestige and so weaken its institutional power and thereby the Justice's ability to use that power for his own ends. McReynolds' tactics were only slightly less dangerous. In fact his shabby treatment of his brethren

55

did become known outside the Court, though not with a dramatic effect comparable to that achieved by Jackson in his Nürnberg cable. On the other hand, McReynolds' tactics may have been the most successful of the three for Clarke resigned in 1922.[46] He claimed that he was bored with "the trifling character of judicial work,"[47] but Taft, who had been an appalled witness to the feud between Clarke and McReynolds, felt sure that the real reason was McReynolds.*[48]

Ridicule can be a lethal weapon in undermining the professional esteem in which an opposing Justice is held, although it is also a most dangerous device in that it will undoubtedly provoke the man against whom it is directed, and its clumsy use can engender sympathy for the target Justice even among those who disagree with him on the merits of a case. Occasionally, however, a Justice may accept these risks, as did the author of the following memorandum.[49]

> Mr. Justice ————————, concurring.
>
> I greatly sympathize with the essential purpose of my Brother . . .'s dissent. His roundabout and turgid legal phraseology is a *cri de cœur*. "Would I were back in the Senate," he means to say, "so that I could put on the statute books what really ought to be there. But here I am, cast by Fate into a den of judges devoid of the habits of legislators, simple fellows who have a crippling feeling that they must enforce the laws as Congress wrote them and not as they ought to have been written. . . ."

BARGAINING

Bargaining is most likely to occur when men agree on some matters, disagree on others, and still feel that further agreement would be profitable.[50] Where the disputants are of approximately equal authority, they must, if persuasion has failed and force is not a feasible alternative, either turn to bargaining or reconcile themselves to loss of the advantages which they would accrue from compromising over the remaining points of difference. Disputants in posts of political authority

---

* Alpheus T. Mason has found in the Woodrow Wilson Papers some interesting correspondence from Justice Clarke. In several letters to the former President, Clarke explained his growing disillusionment with Brandeis after Taft became Chief Justice. Clarke felt that by 1922 Taft had indeed massed the Court against liberalism. To continue on the bench under such circumstances, Clarke feared, would be futile. Brandeis was apparently swimming with the current during the first few years of Taft's chief justiceship, but this approach was too devious for Clarke to understand or probably to approve had he understood.

who fail to achieve some sort of *modus vivendi* will frequently find that the problem at hand will be solved by other actors—with perhaps no profit and some loss to the original disputants or to their policy goals.

For Justices, bargaining is a simple fact of life. Despite conflicting views on literary style, relevant precedents, procedural rules, and substantive policy, cases have to be settled and opinions written; and no opinion may carry the institutional label of the Court unless five Justices agree to sign it. In the process of judicial decision-making, much bargaining may be tacit,[51] but the pattern is still one of negotiation and accommodation to secure consensus. Thus how to bargain wisely —not necessarily sharply—is a prime consideration for a Justice who is anxious to see his policy adopted by the Court. A Justice must learn not only how to put pressure on his colleagues but how to gauge what amounts of pressure are sufficient to be "effective" and what amounts will overshoot the mark and alienate another judge. In many situations a Justice has to be willing to settle for less than he wants if he is to get anything at all. As Brandeis once remarked, the "great difficulty of all group action, of course, is when and what concession to make."[52]

To bargain effectively, one must have something to trade and also a sanction to apply if the offer is rejected or if there is a renege on a promise. The personal honor of the Justices minimizes the possibility of a renege in the usual sense of the term, but under existing Supreme Court practice a Justice is free to change his vote—and perhaps the disposition of a case—up to the minute the decision is announced in the courtroom. Beyond this, he may even change his position and vote for a rehearing and a reversal if such a petition is filed after a case has been decided. Equally important, he may shift his doctrinal position the next time the basic issue is before the Court.

The most significant items a Justice has to offer in trade are his vote and his concurrence in an opinion. Conversely, as the last section pointed out, threats to change a vote or to write a separate opinion, dissenting or concurring, are the sanctions most generally available to a Justice. When the Court is sharply divided any Justice can wield great influence. In 1889 Justice Gray deftly pressured Miller:[53]

> After a careful reading of your opinion in *Shotwell* v. *Moore,* I am very sorry to be compelled to say that the first part of it (especially in the passage which I have marked in the margin) is so con-

trary to my convictions, that I fear, unless it can be a good deal tempered, I shall have to deliver a separate opinion on the lines of the enclosed memorandum.

I am particularly troubled about this, because, if my scruples are not removed, and Justices Field, Bradley and Lamar adhere to their dissent, your opinion will represent only four judges, half of those who took part in the case.

Faced with the defection of one of his narrow majority, Miller had little choice but to adopt Gray's views.

It is also clear that where the Court is closely divided an uncommitted Justice has great bargaining advantages, advantages which a deeply committed Justice might assume by appearing unsure. During the Court's deliberations over the Meadowmoor Dairies case in 1941,[54] a review of a state court injunction against picketing in a labor dispute which had been fraught with violence, Justice Murphy was toying with the idea of writing a separate opinion. His law clerk, however, sent him a lucid argument against such a course. Noting that Frankfurter had already circulated a draft of an opinion for the majority and Black and Reed had prepared separate dissents, the clerk advised that "the better and more effective approach is now to take advantage of your eminently strategic position. All three will try to woo you. Wouldn't it be better to work out your own views? Then pick the opinion that comes the closest. Then start work (à la Stone) on that." In closing, the clerk reminded his Justice of the importance of his vote to the various factions: "The name of Murphy in this case means much. It adds great weight to the opinion bearing it since you wrote Thornhill.* I'd act accordingly."[55]

Murphy consented to this game of watchful waiting. While disapproving of the emotional overtones of both Black's and Frankfurter's opinions, he considered Frankfurter's the better approach† and decided

---

* *Thornhill* v. *Alabama* (1940), and its companion case, *Carlson* v. *California* (1940), held for the first time that picketing was a form of free speech protected by the First and Fourteenth Amendments—a doctrine which the Court was later to qualify, but which typified at the time the spirit of the "new" Court.

† Murphy may have been influenced in this by the comments of Edward Kemp, his old friend and former law partner with whom he was sharing an apartment, to the effect that Black had misread the state injunction so as to give an erroneous impression of its scope and effect. In his early years on the Court, Murphy apparently frequently consulted with Kemp on judicial business.

to "improve" that opinion. In a few days he received the following memorandum from Frankfurter:[56]

> 1. You know how eager I have been—and am—to have our Milk opinion reflect your specifically qualified expert views. You also know how anxious I am to add not one extra word, and especially not to say anything that is absolutely avoidable by way of creating a heated atmosphere. So here is my effort to translate the various suggestions into terms that would fit into, and truly strengthen, our opinion.
> 2. *Of course* I am open for any further suggestion. . . .
> 3. I am sending this to you, and not circulating it to others.

The final decision, which provoked one of Black's most eloquent protests, sustained the injunction against picketing. The opinion of the Court, however, stressed that the justification for this decision lay in the context of violence—the burnings, beatings, bombings, and shootings—in which the picketing had taken place. Frankfurter's opinion specifically stated: "We do not qualify the Thornhill and Carlson decisions. We reaffirm them." Then he quoted Murphy's opinion in the Thornhill case to show the basic consistency between the two decisions.

All intra-Court bargaining takes place with the understanding that if the opinion writer ignores the suggestions which his colleagues scribble on slip opinions, he risks the disintegration of his majority. The threat to pull out normally need not be expressed, though some Justices have preferred to be very explicit about their intentions. Stone, for example, once wrote Frankfurter:[57]

> If you wish to write, placing the case on the ground which I think tenable and desirable, I shall cheerfully join you. If not, I will add a few observations for myself.

Only slightly less direct was the note, attached to a draft of a concurring opinion, which Stone sent Roberts:

> I doubt if we are very far apart in the Cantwell case, but in order that you might get exactly my views, I have written them out and enclosed them herewith.
>
> If you feel that you could agree with me, I think you would find no difficulty in making some changes in your opinion which would make it unnecessary for me to say anything.

While it is probably true that accommodation within the Court more often prevents a majority from splintering into concurring factions, compromise can also serve to mute dissent. In either case the threat of a separate opinion may create a bargaining situation in which both minority and majority may gain something. Fearing that publication of a dissent or concurrence might cause the author of the prevailing opinion to make his pronouncements more rigid or perhaps draw attention to and emphasize an "erroneous" ruling, a minority Justice might reason that it would be more prudent to suppress his disagreement if he can win concessions from the majority.

Justice Johnson had the opportunity to explain one such occasion, *Sturges* v. *Crowninshield,* and to live to see a new majority erode the disputed policy. As he later wrote: "The Court was, in that case, greatly divided in their views of the doctrine, and the judgment partakes as much of a compromise as of a legal adjudication. The minority thought it better to yield something than risk the whole."[58] Other judges may not be so fortunate. "Silence under such circumstances," Alexander Bickel has pointed out, "is a gamble. . . . The risk is that if the birth is successful, silence will handicap one's future opposition. For one is then chargeable with parenthood. . . . Brandeis was to face the dilemma more than once. Instinct, a craftsman's inarticulable feel, which must largely govern action in such a matter, dictated now one choice, now the other."[59]

Publication of a dissent and *circulation within the Court* of a separate opinion serve two different functions. The latter is essentially an effort to resolve conflict within the Court by persuading, in one fashion or another, other Justices. The former is basically an attempt to shift the arena of combat. Having lost in the Court, a dissenting opinion is, as Cardozo said, an appeal to history, particularly to future judges.[60] But a dissent can be more. Whether the author intends it or not, a dissent can become an appeal to contemporaries—to members of Congress, to the President and executive officials, to lower court judges, to the bar or other interest groups, or to the public at large—to change the decision of the majority. As Frankfurter explained to Murphy in discussing a dissent in *Harris* v. *United States:*[61]

> This is a protest opinion—a protest at the Bar of the future—but also an effort to make the brethren realize what is at stake. Moreover, a powerful dissent in a case like that is bound to have an effect on the lower courts as well as on the officers of the law, just as a failure to speak out vigorously against what the Court is doing will only lead to further abuse. And so in order to impress our own brethren, the

lower courts, and enforcement officers, it seems to me vital to make the dissent an impressive document.

Although dissent is a cherished part of the common law tradition, a Justice who persistently refuses to accommodate his views to those of his colleagues may come to be regarded as an obstructionist. A Justice whose dissents become levers for legislative or administrative action reversing judicial policies may come to be regarded as disloyal to the bench. It is possible that either appraisal would curtail his influence with his associates. Even in his despair over the course of constitutional adjudication after Marshall's death, Justice Story thought this consideration limited the frequency with which he could dissent. He told Chancellor Kent that he would stay on the bench and continue to express his—and Marshall's—opinions, "But I shall naturally be silent on many occasions from an anxious desire not to appear contentious, or dissatisfied, or desirous of weakening the [word unclear] influence of the court."[62] Some years earlier, when Story's constitutional philosophy had been ascendant, Justice Johnson explained to Jefferson that he had found that one had to be wary of writing separate opinions "or become such a cypher in our consultations as to effect no good at all."*[63]

* Taft never really approved of dissenting opinions except as a very last resort, and frequently complained of the tendency of Justices like McReynolds, Holmes, and Brandeis to put what the Chief thought was personal vanity above institutional loyalty by publishing separate opinions. Taft explained to Justice Clarke: "I don't approve of dissents generally, for I think in many cases where I differ from the majority, it is more important to stand by the Court and give its judgment weight than merely to record my individual dissent where it is better to have the law certain than to have it settled either way." Quoted in David Danelski, "The Chief Justice and the Supreme Court" (Ph.D. diss., University of Chicago, 1961), p. 184.

The Chief once went so far as to lecture the brethren on unseemly oratory in the courtroom. As he recounted the story to his son: "There are going to be several sharp dissents [tomorrow], and I ventured in Conference to say that I hoped that our opinion day would not degenerate into a place to attract people as the Senate attracts people with Heflin speaking—that I thought we ought to phrase our dissents so as to be dignified at least. The Court took it in very great part and I don't know how much effect it will have in the future." Taft to Robert Taft, April 8, 1928, William Howard Taft Papers, Library of Congress.

Stone, on the other hand, at least when an Associate Justice, was an ardent believer in the right of any Justice to write for himself. After he became Chief Justice, however, he felt that several of his colleagues abused the right. See his

61

At this time we lack sufficient empirical knowledge about the norms of intra-Court behavior to know how far a Justice would have to go in writing separate opinions before alienating his associates. It is possible that a reputation for writing dissents which result in favorable legislative and/or executive action might actually increase the Justice's bargaining power. A Justice who tried to build up such a reputation would have to be aware that, damage to personal relations within the Court aside, frequent appeals, especially if they were successful, to other branches of government or to public opinion to change what the Court was doing could severely injure the prestige of the Court and thus the Justice's chances of utilizing judicial power to achieve his own goals.

A Justice has to be concerned also about the attention outside the Court which his dissents will gain. As in all aspects of life, overexposure can lead to boredom. Stone explained this to Karl Llewellyn: "You know, if I should write in every case where I do not agree with some of the views expressed in the opinions, you and all my other friends would stop reading them."*[64]

Another factor which might prod a minority Justice into accepting compromise is psychological. Most people experience anxiety when they find themselves in sharp disagreement with a group with whom they are intimately associated. Supreme Court Justices tend to be highly independent and individualistic men, but they may not be completely immune to this distaste for isolation. Their professional socialization—especially their legal training and the accepted norms of judicial behavior—to some extent encourages judges to express their own views, but only to some extent. This socialization to some extent encourages a judge to strive for harmony and teamwork with his colleagues.†[65]

---

memorandum to the Court reprinted in Alpheus T. Mason, *Harlan Fiske Stone: Pillar of the Law* (New York: Viking Press, 1956), pp. 608–9.

* Stone also wrote Cardozo: ". . . I have felt called upon to dissent so much in cases involving constitutional questions that I usually let private law decisions with which I do not agree pass without noting an objection." Jan. 19, 1932, Harlan Fiske Stone Papers, Library of Congress.

† For instance, canon 19 of the Canons of Judicial Ethics provides: "It is of high importance that judges constituting a court of last resort should use effort and self-restraint to promote solidarity of conclusion and the consequent influence of judicial decision. A judge should not yield to pride of opinion or

The strength of this tug toward agreement will vary according to the Justice's reliance on the Court as a reference group, and this reliance in turn will largely be a function of the personal and professional esteem in which he holds his colleagues. Where another reference group, either outside the Court or in the minority on the Court, is equally or more important to the Justice than the Court majority and where his views are applauded by that other group, he is very likely to be more persistent in asserting his views. Stone's reference group* of law school professors such as John Bassett Moore, Edwin Borchard, Thomas Reed Powell, Herman Oliphant, Karl Llewellyn, and Felix Frankfurter made it easier for him to maintain his position in the old Court, as did his friendship with Holmes and Brandeis and later Cardozo.

By recognizing the existence of this tug toward agreement and the factors which affect it, a Justice might be better able to control it in himself and able to use it to his advantage. Where a Justice is one of a minority group on the Court, his friends in academic life—and many Justices have had close ties with major universities, either through their previous careers or their law clerks—might build themselves into a reference group for the minority by writing encouraging letters and publishing laudatory articles about the minority's work. When the Justice is in the majority he might further isolate the minority by having his friends write critical articles, or he might try to cut the minority off from access to their academic connections.[66] More simply, where he thought the Court was the other Justices' reference group, he might stress loyalty to the Court as an institution and the implications of isolation from the majority, as Frankfurter did with Murphy in *Hirabayashi*.

On the other hand, there are factors which push the majority Justices, especially the opinion writer, to accept accommodation. An eloquent, tightly-reasoned dissent can be an upsetting force. Stone's separate opinions during the thirties pointed up more sharply the folly of the conservative Justices than did any of the attacks on the Court

---

value more highly his individual reputation than that of the court to which he should be loyal. Except in case of conscientious difference of opinion on fundamental principle, dissenting opinions should be discouraged in courts of last resort." For a fuller discussion of this problem, see chap. vii.

* The term "reference persons" might be equally appropriate here.

by elected politicians. The majority may thus find it profitable to mute criticism from within the Court by giving in on some issues. The Justice who has been assigned the task of writing the opinion of the Court may see himself as a broker adjusting the interests of his associates as well as of himself. His problems, of course, are dynamic rather than static. By making a change in an opinion to pick up one vote he may lose another. Moreover, by compromising and incorporating several different lines of reasoning in his opinion he may expose himself to even more damaging dissent, as Hughes did in the Minnesota Moratorium case.[67]

Most important, a Justice would want to avoid having to water down his policy to the point where it ceased to be an operational doctrine—though it is possible that emasculation may be the only alternative to an outright rejection of his policy by the majority. As Stone wrote a colleague about the draft opinion in *Hirabayashi:* "I am anxious as far as I reasonably can to meet the views of my associates, but it seems to me that if I accepted your suggestions very little of the structure of my opinion would be left, and that I should lose most of my adherents. It seems to me, therefore, that it would be wiser for me to stand by the substance of my opinion and for you to express your views in your concurrence as you have already done."*[68]

The opinion writer can apply some sort of marginal analysis to the

---

* Compare Pierce Butler's rejection of overtures from Stone that he tone down his opinion in *Hamilton* v. *Regents* (1934), a case which sustained against a challenge by religious pacifists the constitutionality of a California requirement that students at the state university take some military training. Stone wrote Butler on November 28, 1934: "I wish very much that I could persuade you to drop from your opinion . . . the references at pages 11 and 12 to the Schwimmer case and the Macintosh case. Neither case has very much to do with the question presented to us now, and the present case does not need their support. I do not deny the truth of the quotations from these opinions. My only feeling about them is that they unnecessarily rub salt into the wounds of a great many very worthy people who, I am convinced, dwell on a higher spiritual plane than I do, and I am not at all sure that another generation may not conclude that their views about war are a good deal wiser than my own. The subject with which we are called on to deal is a delicate one, and I feel that we ought to avoid causing any unnecessary irritants so far as it is reasonably possible." Stone Papers.

Butler was unpersuaded, even though he knew that Cardozo was circulating a concurring opinion expressing views somewhat similar to Stone's. Butler wrote: "I am glad to have your suggestion in No. 55 and have given it consider-

alternatives he confronts. His minimum need—his essential need—is for four additional votes if he is to speak with the institutional authority of the Court. Thus, given the high value of these first four votes, he should rationally be willing to pay a relatively high price in accommodation to secure them. Once majority acquiescence has been obtained, the marginal value of any additional vote declines perceptibly, as would the price which an opinion writer should be willing to pay. However, the marginal value of another vote is never zero, though the asking price may exceed its real value and may have to be rejected.*

---

ation sincerely desiring, if they exist, to find reasons justifying acceptance. . . . In harmony with the thought expressed in your note, the attempt is to avoid, so far as it is reasonably possible, causing any unnecessary irritation. Admittedly the Schwimmer and Macintosh cases as to the points on which they are here cited accurately state the law. They are plainly applicable for the points there decided include the questions raised by these students. Appellants, in the record and in their brief, cite and attempt to distinguish the Macintosh case which quotes from and in part rests on the Schwimmer case. Appellees cite and rely on both. I fear failure now to cite them might, because of the difference on other points reflected by the dissenting opinions, be misunderstood to the detriment of the law." Butler to Stone, November 30, 1934, Stone Papers.

The upshot of the matter was that the case came down four days after Butler's reply with Stone and Brandeis joining in Cardozo's concurring opinion.

* Samuel Lubell has used the analogy of Occam's razor to explain the post 1936 failure of the New Deal. *The Future of American Politics* (2d ed.; New York: Doubleday, 1956). Lubell has argued that Roosevelt won such a huge majority at his second election that it was impossible for him to give one faction of his coalition anything without taking it from another faction in the same coalition. William Riker, *The Theory of Political Coalitions* (New Haven: Yale University Press, 1962), has expanded this kind of observation into what he calls a general theory of political coalitions: it is not rational for a coalition to attract more than the 50.1 per cent needed to win a particular election. Riker adds the qualification that because of the uncertainty inherent in any political situation it is rational for a leader to aim higher than 50.1 per cent, though this remains the optimum figure which he should try not to exceed. Riker thus attacks Anthony Downs's contention—*An Economic Theory of Democracy* (New York: Harper & Bros., 1957)—that a political party, interested only in attaining office, should, to act rationally, do its utmost to maximize its support in the electorate.

I would submit that the marginal cost—marginal value approach is more appropriate as a general theory. While the price any politician would rationally pay for increments of support sharply declines after 50.1 per cent, there is usually a psychological, if not material, advantage in "winning big." This is especially true in a political system where power is fragmented among different

In the judicial process a 5–4 decision emphasizes the strength of the losing side and may encourage resistance and evasion. The greater the majority, the greater the appearance of certainty and the more likely a decision will be accepted and followed in similar cases. One hesitates to imagine how much more difficult implementation of the school segregation decisions would be had there been a four or three or even a two judge minority willing to claim in public that "separate but equal" was a valid constitutional doctrine.

A further bargaining complication may arise when a Justice who at first noted his dissent is persuaded that the majority is right, and, like many converts, is willing to take a firmer stand than some of the original believers with whom the opinion writer has had to negotiate. Here the opinion writer faces a most delicate choice between publication of a more forceful assertion of the doctrine which he is advocating and potential alienation of one or more relatively lukewarm members of his coalition who may view strengthening the majority opinion as a breach of faith or at least cause for a separate statement of views.

There is also the question of with whom to bargain. If a Justice were in the minority and trying to lessen the damage the majority opinion would do to the chances of achieving his objective, the obvious person

---

institutions of government. In such a situation there is a great need for an appearance of consensus. In addition, where party discipline is weak, the threat of the leadership to campaign against, or at least to withhold endorsement of, a candidate at the next primary or general election is one of the chief tools to keep in line a recalcitrant member from a competitive two-party district; the effectiveness of this threat depends in large part on the popularity of the leadership. Clearly a leader who won only 50.1 per cent of the popular vote is not to be feared as much as a leader who won two-thirds of that vote. Moreover, it must be kept in mind that the spoils of victory—offices and policy decisions—are not likely to be divided equally among the members of the winning coalition, nor need they be to satisfy the members.

My statement of disagreement with Riker and Downs may be unfairly put in that their conclusions were based on the peculiar assumptions of the models they constructed, while my conclusions refer to the real world. In any event, I found both their works highly stimulating. It was Riker's analysis that led me to conclude that a marginal theory is more appropriate to the real world than is a minimal or maximal explanation. And, indeed, it was while reading Downs's work that the idea of writing this book came to me. I scribbled the outline—which is essentially that of my final version—on the inside back cover of *An Economic Theory of Democracy.*

whom he would have to influence would be the Justice assigned the task of writing the opinion of the Court. It would not, however, always be necessary to approach the opinion writer directly. The minority Justice might exploit his social relations with a Justice who was also on close terms with the opinion writer and have that third Justice act as an intermediary. Then, too, if the opinion writer were handling a particularly controversial case or were the kind of person who put a very high value on unanimity, it might be most prudent for the minority Justice to wait to be approached rather than make the first overtures himself. The same sort of considerations would apply to a majority Justice who wished the Court to issue a stronger statement than he thought the opinion writer would draft.

If a Justice were in the minority and trying to pick up an extra vote to give the appearance of more solidity to his protest or to turn his minority into a majority, or if the author of the opinion of the Court were attempting to increase his majority, the obvious colleague to approach—again directly or through an intermediary—would be one who had expressed some uncertainty during or after conference or whose voting record indicated ambiguous commitment to the side with which he had actually voted. Having attended the conference and having talked probably with several colleagues in private, a Justice would normally have a good idea of who might be wavering. To give himself the greatest possible advantage in such situations, he might even have one of his staff construct Guttman scales of the voting records of all the members of the Court, though with his intimate day-to-day knowledge of his colleagues' behavior it is not likely that this sort of formal analysis would be of great value.

The writer of the majority opinion who wished to squelch a dissent might also have the option of contacting the dissenter directly or working through an intermediary or, if he strongly suspected that the dissent was being circulated merely for bargaining purposes, of sitting back and waiting to be approached. Probably the most ticklish situation, from the point of view of interpersonal relations, in which a Justice might find himself is when he is with the majority but not writing the majority opinion, and he fears that the opinion writer is about to win over a dissenter by conceding more than the value of the additional vote. Under such circumstances, a Justice would have to proceed most cautiously in order to avoid the twin perils of appearing to be a busybody interfering at every stage of the negotiations and at the other extreme of sulking behind the threat of writing a separate concurrence. Either course might annoy the opinion writer to the extent that he would give up the chance of having that Justice's vote and make even greater concessions to win the former dissenter.

A Case Study in Persuasion

Goldman v. *United States* provides an excellent example of the use of several different kinds of persuasion within the Court. Under review was a conviction of three lawyers for conspiring to violate the Bankruptcy Act. Federal agents, with the co-operation of the building superintendent, entered the office of one of the defendants and installed a listening device. The apparatus failed to work, but the agents, who occupied the adjacent office, utilized a detectaphone—an instrument which can amplify the sound of voices talking on the other side of a wall—and transcribed several incriminating conversations.

At the Saturday conference[69] of the Court in early February, 1942, Chief Justice Stone said that he found the law hazy; it allowed some invasions of privacy but not others. The vice of this sort of eavesdropping, he thought, was that it was totally unrestrained. The federal agents had not asked for a warrant; in fact, if they had merely been searching for evidence, it was unlikely that they would have been able to show the probable cause necessary to obtain a warrant. While he did not think the case was "dead open and shut," he leaned toward reversal. Roberts and Reed took a strong position to affirm. Roberts candidly stated that he did not believe the Fourth Amendment had been intended to prevent police snooping, and Reed felt that the situation was completely covered by *Olmstead* v. *United States,* the famous wiretapping case of 1928. Frankfurter sharply challenged both Roberts' interpretation of the Constitution and Reed's faith in *Olmstead* as a viable precedent, but the conference voted 5–3 to affirm, with Justice Jackson not participating.*

As the senior majority Justice, Roberts assigned himself the task of writing the opinion. He held that use of the detectaphone did not

* The issue of wiretapping was only involved here to the extent that some of the conversations overheard were spoken into a telephone. The wiretapping issue was more squarely before the Court in *Goldstein* v. *United States* (1942), a case which was argued and decided on the same days as *Goldman.* Feelings ran high within the Court on both cases and probably their coming together made the Justices even more sensitive to the issues involved.

violate the Federal Communications Act, nor, under the doctrine of *Olmstead*, did it contravene the Fourth Amendment. He also stated that whatever trespass the agents had committed in installing the unsuccessful listening device did not make inadmissible any evidence later obtained through the detectaphone. For the dissenters Stone undertook to write an opinion, and Murphy gave general directions to guide his clerk in preparing a second dissent.*

Stone quickly drafted his opinion; and by February 27, he had incorporated some minor suggestions by Frankfurter. At this point the draft read:[70]

> Had a majority of the Court been willing at this time to overrule the *Olmstead* case, we would have been happy to join them. But as they have declined to do so, and as we think this case is indistinguishable in principle from *Olmstead*'s, we have no occasion to repeat here the dissenting views [of Holmes, Brandeis, and Butler] in that case with which we agree.
>
> Both courts below found that the trespass by the Government officers in locating the dictaphone did not aid materially in the use of the detectaphone. Hence it is unnecessary to consider whether the use of the detectaphone, if aided by the trespass, would constitute a violation of the Fourth Amendment. The Government did not deny that it would, and we explicitly dissociate ourselves from the declaration in the opinion [of the Court] that it would not.

When Roberts read the second paragraph of Stone's opinion, he agreed to modify what he had said about the trespass and substantially adopted Stone's phrasing: "Both courts below have found that the trespass did not aid materially in the use of the detectaphone. Since we accept these concurrent findings, we need not consider a contention based on a denial of their verity." Having achieved this minor victory, Stone dropped the second paragraph of his opinion.

Meanwhile, when the Chief Justice's opinion came to Murphy's office, his clerk sent it on to the Justice with a report that he had just had a visit from one of Stone's clerks who told him that Frankfurter was champing at the bit to write a searing dissent. The Chief Justice,

---

* In Murphy's case files, one often finds a set of directions from the Justice to his clerk, then a handwritten copy of an opinion draft in his clerk's writing, then a typewritten copy with comments and changes in Murphy's handwriting, then several different printed versions, some heavily edited by Murphy, and others, which had been circulated in the Court, with suggestions from the other Justices.

however, was convinced that it was wiser for the minority to take a beating now without putting up a public fight on *Olmstead*, lest that case become even more entrenched as the survivor of two great battles within the Court. Murphy's clerk added as a countervailing consideration that perhaps Brandeis' arguments in favor of privacy should be repeated every so often.[71]

Murphy may have remembered—he had made lengthy notes during the discussion of the case among the Justices—that at the conference Stone had suggested that *Olmstead* might be overruled, but had not pressed the point; he had also suggested that the two cases could be distinguished. Moreover, the Chief Justice had admitted that historically many different kinds of invasions of privacy had been allowed under the Fourth Amendment.[72] Perhaps because of this recollection Murphy was unsure that Stone was fully committed to overturning *Olmstead*. In any event, he continued work on his own dissent. On March 5, Frankfurter, who by now had been won over to Stone's strategy of avoiding open conflict, tried to dissuade Murphy:[73]

> You have heard my views expressed in Conference, and I am afraid somewhat fiercely, on wiretapping, and you must, therefore, know that I am as uncompromising on that subject as you are, feeling as you do that the issue goes to the very essence of a civilized society. Like you, therefore, I will not yield an inch on my convictions and would accede to no compromising expression of them.
>
> But I do not see that any "compromise" is involved in the way in which the C. J. has formulated dissent from the majority opinion. Of course each man's phrasing has its own distinctive quality, but so far as the substance of the matter goes, I certainly could not dream of improving on what Brandeis and Holmes said in the *Olmstead* case. And so it seems to me that an unequivocal announcement that we would overrule the *Olmstead* case and adopt as our own the views expressed by the dissenters in that case, is an unswerving and unqualified adoption of these views and a reaffirmation of them. And to do it in the way in which the Chief Justice proposes has for me the quality of Doric eloquence. Simplicity and austerity are sometimes the most emphatic way of conveying an idea to the world.

In closing his letter, Frankfurter added a plea for solidarity:

> For the three of us to speak in different language would imply a difference of opinion amongst us. That would attenuate the moral strength of our position. I hope very much, therefore, that it will

commend itself to you to have the three of us speak with one voice and in the way in which the C. J. has proposed.

Murphy, however, stuck to his own plan and circulated a long and eloquent dissent, asserting that government officers had committed a palpable invasion of the defendants' privacy in violation of explicit prohibitions of the Fourth Amendment. In his opinion, he referred to the federal agents as "overzealous officials," and castigated their action as "debasing to government." When he received his copy, Frankfurter made only a few small suggestions and concluded: "You have not only expressed your convictions but you have expressed them, if I may say so, well."[74]

On April 6, after Murphy's dissent was circulated, Justice Jackson, who had been Attorney General when the Goldman prosecution was conducted, sent a memorandum to all members of the Court. Jackson said that in light of Murphy's remarks he felt it necessary to file an opinion to explain his own non-participation in the case:[75]

> By Mr. Justice Jackson
>
> As notation of my disqualification without more would create uncertain implications as to my responsibility for the questionable conduct of the investigation, it is desirable to state the precise facts which lead to my non-participation.
>
> Thirteen days after I was commissioned as Attorney General of the United States this indictment was found. While the prosecution was determined upon and prepared and the detectaphone recordings in question were made prior to my entrance into office and under rules, regulations, and practices of the Attorney General that I found in force, the prosecution was continued under my official responsibility. Under these circumstances it seemed appropriate to refrain from judicial action in the case.

Since he had been Attorney General before Jackson and since, therefore, the action which he was so bitterly criticizing had been conducted under his own official responsibility—though probably without his personal knowledge—Murphy was put in a squeeze. The squeeze was made even tighter because, although the matter was ultimately one for the judgment of each Justice, there was doubt—and Jackson's opinion drew attention to the doubt—that a former Attorney General should hear a case on the bench which was prosecuted under his auspices. The same day as Jackson circulated his opinion, Murphy contacted him and indicated a willingness to reconsider his remarks.[76] Jackson immediately seized the opportunity to seal a bargain. In a letter which began "My dear Frank," he offered a full statement of his feelings:[77]

> This case presents a new question of law on which difference of opinion is to be expected and upon which it is conceivable that one's attitude as a prosecutor and as a judge might differ. However, the Department of Justice under several Attornies General has assumed the law to be as the Court now holds it to be. Even so, any Attorney General was empowered to impose further limitations on investigative methods if he thought good morals or good government required it. None of us did so. . . .
>
> But any discomfort of my own is small compared with the position of those who served under both of us and who looked to us—not as much as they should have, perhaps—for guidance and supervision. . . . My grievance is only academic compared to the gravity of putting words such as I have quoted ["overzealous officials"; action "debasing to government"] into the mouth of every criminal lawyer in the United States to be hurled at the Government as quotations from a former Attorney General and a present Justice, when it attempts to use evidence the Court now holds to be its legal right. . . .

In his next to the last paragraph, Jackson further tightened the squeeze on Murphy by withdrawing his opinion:

> Now that you know how I feel in the matter, I shall leave the result to your own good judgment. Whatever you do, I think the interests of the Court would not be served by carrying the matter to the public. I commit myself not to do that in order to leave you free of any pressures in the matter except those of your own strong sense of justice.

As the final turn of the screw, Jackson noted in his closing sentence: "I am sending a copy of this to the Chief Justice and to our associates so that they may know the way the matter stands."

Murphy was left with no real choice. He might have been able to answer Jackson's argument about how his remarks would reflect on officials of the Department of Justice, past or future; but Jackson's withdrawal of his own opinion and his announcement of this fact to the Court had put Murphy in a position where he had to compromise. In effect, Jackson opened the door to negotiation and then shoved Murphy through it. Murphy's published opinion excused the Department of Justice from any deliberate wrongdoing:

On the basis of the narrow, literal construction of the search and seizure clause of the Fourth Amendment adopted in Olmstead v. United States, Government officials could well believe that activities of the character here involved did not contravene the constitutional mandate. But for my part, I think that the Olmstead Case was wrong.

CO-OPTION

It would be much easier for a Justice to vote and join in opinions with a judge whose policy goals were identical or very similar to his own* than with a colleague with contrary aims. It is possible, under the sort of favorable political circumstances discussed earlier on p. 41, for a policy-oriented Justice to exert influence in the executive process and to have a voice in choosing a new colleague, a colleague who, hopefully, will agree with him on decisions and opinions important to his policy goals. Gratitude, especially if it were coupled with deep intellectual respect, might play a role in increasing the helping Justice's influence with the new appointee, but its role would probably be minor. As Presidents have often painfully learned, gratitude is usually a weak emotion in judges who have what amounts to life tenure. Although gratitude might make social relations easier, certainly it would not be comparable in effect to a basic agreement on policy.

Many members of the Court have become embroiled in appointment politicking. Miller,[78] Fuller,[79] and Brown [80] tried it with varying degrees of success, but the most systematic efforts along these lines were made by William Howard Taft.[81] Probably no judge ever came to the Bench with a clearer conception of the "proper" role of the individual Justice within the Court or the "proper" role of the Court in the American political system than Taft. "Teamwork" was the Chief Justice's overriding value in intra-Court relations, and he saw the protection of property rights through the Fifth and Fourteenth Amendments as the Court's principal task.

Since Harding had promised Sutherland the first place on the Court, Taft had little to do with the former Senator's appointment—except perhaps in a negative way in that both Taft and Sutherland had been

* This relationship might not constitute influence in any formal sense of the term, but by definition the policy-oriented Justice would prefer efficient achievement of his policy objective over merely increasing his personal influence, since the first would be the end and the second only a means.

candidates for the chief justiceship. The center chair had been Taft's avowed lifelong ambition, and Sutherland, so Harding said, was "crazy" for the office.[82] Taft gave a broad hint about his alert interest in the appointing process when, after his own selection, he wrote a gracious letter to George Sutherland expressing the hope that Sutherland would soon join him on the bench. "Our views," the new Chief Justice noted, "are very much alike and it is important that they prevail."[83]

When Justice Day retired, Taft, knowing that Harding was not committed to any candidate, began to work feverishly to find a suitable nominee. After failing to interest John W. Davis, the Chief Justice and Van Devanter decided that "Pierce Butler is our man."[84] Taft then opened an intensive campaign to bring off the nomination. He called on the President and wrote him several letters lavishly praising Butler and criticizing other candidates. The Chief Justice also carried on a lengthy correspondence with Butler, giving him news on events in Washington and plying him with advice on how to advance his cause. Taft's suggestions included not only the best way for Butler to deploy his political assets but also how to exploit his religious assets as well. The Chief Justice believed that Harding wanted to appoint a Catholic (Justice McKenna was expected to retire soon); Taft also knew that Archbishop Hayes of New York was pushing Judge Martin Manton of the United States Circuit Court of Appeals for the Second Circuit. To counter this activity, Taft urged Butler to line up the Catholic hierarchy in the Middle West. Butler protested that he abhorred the thought of involving clergymen in politics, but he did supply the names of one cardinal, two archbishops, and three bishops, plus the bishops in the archdiocese of St. Paul, with whom Harding could consult.

After Harding nominated Butler, the Chief Justice switched his attention to the Senate and once again gave Butler detailed advice on which senators were important and how they might be approached. Taft talked with his own friends on Capitol Hill and arranged a quick judiciary committee meeting to approve the nomination.

When Pitney retired—with an assist from Taft in getting special legislation through Congress allowing full retirement benefits, despite the fact that Pitney had not yet reached the statutory retirement age—the Chief Justice once again plunged into the appointments maelstrom. Several candidates with impressive reputations were under consideration for this vacancy, and the Chief Justice consulted with a number of people, including the President, the Attorney General, and the chairman of the finance committee of the Republican National Committee. For Harding's benefit, Taft gave a rundown on each of the people under consideration. He conceded that Judge Cuthbert Pound of the New York Court of Appeals "has some ability and experience," but that he had shown a preference for dissent over "teamwork" and "solidarity." Judge Frederick Crane, a colleague of Pound, was a popular man. Although not a lawyer of "the greatest ability . . . he would probably be preferable to Pound." Taft dismissed Chief Justice Robert Von Moschzisker of Pennsylvania as an accident—in Pennsylvania the chief justiceship rotated according to seniority, and the judges ahead of Von Moschzisker had died rather promptly. "He is a politician more than a judge."[85] (With his brother Taft was more candid: Von Moschzisker took too broad a view of the police power and state control over the uses of private property.)[86]

Cardozo, Taft continued in his letter to Harding, "is the best judge in New York. . . . [He] is a Jew and a Democrat. I don't think he would always side with Brandeis, but he is what they call a progressive judge." Learned Hand was described as "an able judge and a hard worker. I appointed him . . . but he turned out to be a wild Roosevelt man [in 1912] and a Progressive, and though on the Bench, he went into the campaign. If promoted to our Bench, he would almost certainly herd with Brandeis and be a dissenter. I think it would be risking too much to appoint him."[87]

Taft had many kind words for U.S. District Judge William Grubb, a Yale classmate of Horace Taft; but the Chief Justice's highest praise was reserved for Judge Charles Hough of the U.S. Circuit Court of Appeals. Despite several personal pleas by Taft and his use of intermediaries, Harding refused to appoint Hough because he thought the judge too old. Later, in the course of a conversation with the Chief Justice, Harry Daugherty suggested the name of Edward T. Sanford, U.S. District Judge in Tennessee. Taft jumped at the suggestion and was soon strenuously supporting Sanford. The Chief Justice admitted to a friend that Sanford was not "the strongest man but I so much prefer him to Pound or Crane or the Chief Justice of Pennsylvania that I would now be glad to have him appointed."[88] How much Harding's final decision was due to Taft, or to Daugherty, or to other political considerations will probably never be known, but once again the men whom Taft had opposed were kept off the bench and one of his candidates, although not his first choice, was appointed.

When McKenna retired—also with Taft's assistance, this time in the form of a positive suggestion to the Justice that he was too infirm to perform his duties in a satisfactory manner[89]—the Chief Justice once more took part in choosing a colleague. He visited Coolidge and claimed to have "rather forced" the President to appoint Stone.[90] Fourteen years later, when Stone heard of Taft's statement, he said he doubted that Taft had been influential with Coolidge or that Coolidge had needed anyone to recommend his Attorney General to him.[91] Taft, however, persisted in asserting responsibility for Stone's selection, even after he became convinced that he had made a serious error in the choice.[92]

Stone, in turn, played a major part in Cardozo's nomination. Taking advantage of his close relationship with Hoover, Stone introduced Cardozo to the President. As Stone recalled the incident, "I seized the opportunity to make the President acquainted with the kind of a judge he ought to appoint and prefaced the call by expatiating on that topic at some length."[93] On several later occasions Stone reminded Hoover of Cardozo's fitness[94] and strongly recommended him when Holmes retired. Hoover, however, wavered, fearing to offend the Senate by having three New York men (Stone and Hughes were also from New York) and two Jews (Brandeis was still on the bench) on the Court. Stone then took a bold course of action:[95]

> I was apprehensive lest a selection should be made which would emphasize the Court's conservative tendencies, and feeling that they were already over-emphasized, I feared that great harm might result and that some sort of an explosion would occur not unlike that which actually took place after the decisions in the *A.A.A.* case and the *Tipaldo Women's Wage* case. In a conversation with President Hoover intended to emphasize both the importance of the appointment and Judge Cardozo's fitness I intimated to him that if he feared criticism because of the addition of a New York man to the Court when there were two other New Yorkers already there, I would be willing to retire from the Court. Later, in conversation with Senator Wagner, who was then about to discuss the matter with President Hoover, I made the same suggestion.

It is impossible to determine whether Stone was merely trying to put additional pressure on Hoover or was really tired of the frustrations of

judicial work.[96] Other men and forces were also at work in the appointment and Stone never claimed full—or even much—credit, though
when the nomination was announced Frankfurter wired him: "The
country is your debtor for your decisive help in achieving a great national good."[97]*

Undoubtedly there have been many other instances of Justices working for or against the appointment of specific men. Van Devanter and
Butler acted as intermediaries for the Attorney General in sounding
out Charles Evans Hughes for the chief justiceship in 1930.[98] In the
light of Attorney General Mitchell's long friendship with Pierce Butler, it is not improbable that Butler was acting as more than a passive
instrument of the Hoover administration.

Some judicial efforts have been successful, others may not have been.
Hughes later endorsed Mitchell for Holmes's chair but the nomination
went to Cardozo. Frankfurter, and to a lesser extent Stone, worked for
Learned Hand's promotion to the High Bench in 1942, but F. D. R.
reacted against what he felt was too heavy pressure and chose Wiley
Rutledge instead. Some Justices, like Taft or Stone or perhaps Butler,
have been in an excellent position to influence appointments; other
Justices have not. But, since most members of the Court come to the
bench only after extensive political experience,[99] the average Justice
must be aware of the informal as well as the formal channels through
which influence can be exerted. Most important, it is quite clear that
if a Justice wishes to enter the appointing process—and is able to do
so—he can make ideology a prime factor in determining who will receive his support.

Although many Justices are in a position where they can affect appointments, it does not necessarily follow that any particular Justice
will always, often, or even ever have a voice in the selection of other
members of the Court. Nor does it mean that those Justices who can
exert influence will choose to do so. There are dangers in participating
in the political processes, and a judge may reasonably conclude in many
situations that, all questions of ethics aside, the risk of high costs in
possible requests for a *quid pro quo* from executive officials is not
worth the benefit that may be derived.[100] This sort of assessment is

---

* It should be noted that Justice Frankfurter later changed his mind. In a
letter to me of Sept. 27, 1961, he stated that he had come to believe that the
"decisive help" had been supplied by Senators Borah and Watson.

especially likely to occur when the Justice has good reason to believe that the administration will select the "right" kind of man without assistance from the bench.

II BLOC FORMATION

When it is impossible for a Justice to secure in the foreseeable future majority endorsement of his policy, he has to make a different kind of assessment of strategic plans and tactical maneuvers. In general he would have under such circumstances three major alternatives:

  a) Going along with the majority, trying to minimize through bargaining the damage done by the majority's refusal to accept "true" doctrine or its acceptance of "false" doctrine.
  b) Dissenting alone or with whoever will join him in a particular case.
  c) Trying to form a minority group of Justices into a voting bloc,* at least for purposes of one set of issues.

Alternative *a* may offer the greatest advantages, but only if the members of the majority are willing to compromise. It may happen that they would feel sufficiently secure to refuse to make any significant concessions, thus leaving a policy-oriented Justice with a real choice only between alternatives *b* and *c*. Alternative *b* is cheap in terms of the expenditure of some kinds of resources, since, by playing the role of a lone wolf, the Justice would avoid many of the costs in time, energy, and purity of doctrine involved in arriving at a group decision. On the other hand, this alternative may entail high opportunity costs, forgoing as it does many of the tactics which might gain one, two, or three additional votes to support a particular set of views. There may also be the opportunity cost of winning a particular case, since a bloc of four Justices has thirty-one out of thirty-two chances of winning any vote, and a three-judge bloc has approximately seven out of eight chances—*providing that the votes of the other Justices are distributed randomly*. This condition, of course, is extremely unlikely to obtain; but while the chances of winning are vastly less in the real world than

* Bloc is used here in a more specialized sense than is common in literature on judicial behavior. I use the term to refer to situations in which a group of Justices consciously and usually overtly co-operate with each other to secure a common objective, not to the more general situations in which for any of a variety of possible reasons two or more Justices vote in the same fashion on particular issues. I use the term more in the sense in which it is employed in the legislative process.

such statistics indicate, the chances would still be far better if the minority Justices stuck together and hoped to pick up the additional vote or two needed, than if they divided among themselves according to the nuances of peculiar cases.

Alternative *c* is not always the better choice, despite its potential advantages. Where there is considerable disagreement among the minority Justices on basic issues, the costs of alternative *c* will be high in terms of doctrinal purity as well as in the time and energy needed to come to a group decision. Conversely, since the opportunity costs of alternative *b* in such a situation would be quite low, it would probably be the more rational choice, at least as measured in short-run gains. On the other hand, where there is a high level of agreement among the minority Justices, the group decision-making and doctrinal costs of alternative *c* will be relatively low and the opportunity costs of *b* relatively high, making *c* the preferable choice.

Even assuming a situation in which *c,* the establishment of a bloc, is the more profitable course, it is improbable that any Justice could "form" a bloc among his colleagues. What he could very possibly do is to discover similar outlooks and voting tendencies among his brethren and then use his social and intellectual skills to reinforce ideological affinities and bring about a measure of co-ordination to individual behavior patterns. Most of the tactics discussed in other sections of this chapter would be applicable to bloc "formation." Quite relevant would be another stratagem, the "rump conference"—a device used by Taft as Chief Justice and Stone as an Associate Justice. Taft would occasionally call together Van Devanter and several of his other friends for Sunday afternoon meetings at his home. There the group would thrash over some of the more difficult cases and opinions so that they could present a united front to the rest of the Court. Some years later, to thwart what he thought was Hughes's overefficient disposal of business, Stone held Friday evening meetings at his home to hammer out in advance the important issues scheduled to be taken up at the next day's conference.

Maintaining the group morale needed to keep a bloc together would be a very trying task. A finely developed capacity for moral leadership would be essential where the majority was united and determined in its position. As Samuel Miller explained after the legal tender controversy, "marshalling my forces and keeping up their courage against a domineering Chief, and a party in court who have been accustomed to carry everything their own way, has been such a strain on my brain and nervous system as I never wish to encounter again."[101] Minimum requirements for minority bloc leadership would be a capacity to communicate hope, plus a readiness to compromise—and to do so quickly and amiably—with other bloc members, as well as to accede to the wishes of other bloc members on issues the Justice did not think especially important.

On the other hand, bloc unanimity insofar as published votes and opinions are concerned need be neither an absolute rule nor even necessarily a wise policy. One of the tactics of a bloc should be to conceal as far as possible the fact of its existence, lest other Justices feel it vital to their interests to form a counterbloc and so perhaps nullify the advantages of the first bloc. Thus it might be more prudent if on some, perhaps many, issues, the bloc members vote against each other or at least concur in separate opinions.*

Camouflage can be facilitated in several ways. First, if there are some issues coming before the Court which all members of the bloc consider trivial, the members can agree to open or pitched battle among themselves as a smokescreen. Such divisions can also be arranged where the bloc has lost or where it has a majority which is sufficiently large that defection of one or more of its members will not change the decision of the Court. Separate opinions in these kinds of cases can be based on technical grounds so as both to mask the existence of the bloc and to enhance individual Justices' reputations as skilled craftsmen who are sticklers for procedural niceties.

Third, while it would generally be unwise for bloc members to vote to grant certiorari in cases on which they will be outvoted on the merits, it might help conceal the bloc's existence if the members sometimes vote to bring up a dispute which threatens to push one of the bloc's policies beyond the point where bloc members feel it should go. It would have been shrewd, for instance, for the libertarians on the Roosevelt Court to vote to review *Chaplinsky* v. *New Hampshire.*†

* Cf. Holmes's remark: "Brandeis and I are so apt to agree that I was glad to have him dissent in my case, as it shows there is no preestablished harmony." Holmes to Laski, Feb. 18, 1928, Mark DeWolfe Howe (ed.), *Holmes-Laski Letters* (Cambridge, Mass.: Harvard University Press, 1953), II, 1027.

† The Chaplinsky case came up on appeal not on a Writ of Certiorari, but the Justices vote on whether an appeal raises a substantial federal question in much the same manner as they vote on whether to grant certiorari.

In that case a Jehovah's Witness who had called a local police officer a "goddamned Fascist" and a "damned racketeer" was claiming the protection of the First Amendment—an extension of free speech which none of the Court's libertarians was then willing to support. Similarly, it might be tactically clever for those Justices on the Warren Court who strongly favor workingmen's claims under the Federal Employers' Liability Act to vote to bring up some cases in which they can, in good conscience, decide for the employer. Indeed, one student[102] of the Court has suggested that this might have been done in *Herdman* v. *Pennsylvania R. R. Co.* (1957).

It is improbable that any or all of these stratagems could long conceal either from other Justices or from scholars the existence of a cohesive bloc. Nevertheless, since even a gain in time of a term or two could be important in gaining votes in particular cases for the bloc members, efforts at camouflage may well be worth the effort.

Bloc formation may be equally attractive to a Justice in the majority as to a Justice in the minority, though the addition of each new bloc member tends to increase the number of doctrinal adjustments that have to be made as well as the difficulties of obtaining group agreement. The profit of keeping a majority together, however, may far outweigh these extra costs. Moreover, minority bloc formation, like defense in war, would only be thought of as a temporary measure. The primary aim of a policy-oriented Justice's operations within the Court would be to secure a majority for his policy, and minority bloc formation is, at most, only an expedient step toward that end.

The primacy of this objective means, most obviously, that the Justice would be ready to woo any colleague likely to vote with the bloc in a particular case. It also means that a Justice would have to be very subtle in his planning. Where the votes required to achieve a majority *on a decision* are available but serious questions about overall policy are present, the Justice would have to persuade the bloc members to avoid taking a doctrinaire line either in conference discussion or in opinion writing. The most prudent approach might well be to discuss the case and write the opinion on relatively narrow grounds, hoping that if several such decisions follow each other over a period of years the underlying doctrine will evolve naturally and not prematurely frighten an undecided Justice into rejecting the logical conclusions of the premises he has been accepting. It requires very delicate judgment to decide whether it is better to move when five

81

votes are secured or to play for time, to settle for an immediate but
limited victory or wait until a sixth or a seventh vote can be picked
up—and risk that the majority could also be lost in the interval—
before announcing a controversial principle as the justification of a
decision. If the slower approach is adopted, when the Justice does decide to try to persuade the bloc members to move, two arguments will
be available to defend the newly captured position: first, the substantive reasons behind the principle and second, an appeal to *stare decisis,*
that touchstone of judicial virtue and regularity.

A policy-oriented Justice would also have to plan antibloc tactics.
If he perceived opposing members of the Court uniting on some issues,
he would have to utilize this information to bring together a counter-
group or to break down the unity of the opposing group. One possible
method of accomplishing the latter task would be to press, both in
conference discussions and in written opinions, arguments on which
he knew the bloc members disagreed. Stone told Roosevelt that Hughes
was particularly adept at using this maneuver against the liberals on
the old Court. When a difference of opinion was apparent among the
liberals, the Chief Justice would, so Roosevelt recounted to Harold
Ickes, "get his big toe in and widen the cleavage."[103] Whether or not
Stone's or Roosevelt's or Ickes' judgment and memory were affected
by the bitterness of the Court fight over the New Deal, the statistical
fact remains that, from whatever motivation, Hughes was apt to assign
opinions of the Court to liberals when they were divided among themselves and to conservatives when that group was split.*[104]

III THE SPECIAL CASE OF THE CHIEF JUSTICE

So far this discussion has treated all Justices as equal in authority if
not in power and influence. But the Chief Justice, while usually
thought of by his colleagues only as *primus inter pares,* does have some
authority which other members of the Court do not possess. He presides in open Court and at conference. He speaks first at the conference and votes last. When in the majority he assigns the opinion of
the Court. By a tradition built up since Hughes's time, the Chief
Justice circulates a "special list" of petitions for certiorari which he

* There is another tactic available here, but one which is highly unethical.
A Justice could sow distrust among bloc members by spreading gossip (false or
true). This tactic could also be used—and be no less reprehensible—in almost
all intra-Court relations.

thinks should be denied without conference discussion. Although any Justice may have a petition taken off this list, such action is not often requested. While only indirectly affecting his relations with other Justices, the Chief Justice is expected to make the appointments to staff positions for the entire Court—the clerk, the marshal, the director of the Administrative Office of United States Courts, and so on—with each Justice having the right to appoint his own personal staff.

Justice Miller claimed that the Chief Justice has no more authority than his colleagues care to give him.[105] But, if, as some of the studies of formal groups indicate, there is an expectation that a titular leader will exert both task and social leadership,* it would follow that the Chief Justice generally has an initial psychological advantage over any Associate Justice in a struggle for influence within the Court—though this advantage may be indecisive and short-lived. The Chief Justice, Taft wrote shortly before he assumed the office, "is the head of the Court, and while his vote counts but one in the nine, he is, if he be a man of strong and persuasive personality, abiding convictions, recognized by learning and statesmanlike foresight, expected to promote team-work by the Court, so as to give weight and solidarity to its opinions."[106]

* This distinction is one which has been largely developed out of the work of Professor Robert F. Bales. See his *Interaction Process Analysis: A Method for the Study of Small Groups* (Cambridge, Mass.: Addison-Wesley, 1950). David Danelski first applied this concept of dual leadership functions to judicial behavior in his "The Influence of the Chief Justice in the Decisional Process of the Supreme Court" (paper presented at the 1960 meetings of the American Political Science Association); a shorter version of this paper appears in Walter F. Murphy and C. Herman Pritchett, *Courts, Judges, and Politics* (New York: Random House, 1961), pp. 497–508. Essentially the task leader is concerned with getting the job at hand done. He tends to rivet his attention on efficient solutions of problems which confront the group. The socially-oriented leader provides the warmth and friendliness which make interpersonal relations pleasant or even possible. He raises the self-esteem of other members of the group, easily accepts suggestions, and quickly relieves tensions with a laugh or a joke. While in a laboratory environment it seems that one person seldom exercises both leadership functions, such a dual role is apparently common in ongoing organizations. In the latter kind of situation, the titular leader is generally expected to function in both roles. If the titular leader does so act, available evidence indicates that the group will reject as a usurper any other member who tries to take over these functions. See W. H. Crockett, "Emergent Leadership in Small Decision-Making Groups," 51 *J. of Abnormal Psy.* 378 (1955).

Presiding at conference gives the Chief an opportunity to exercise task leadership by stating his views first on cases and, as Hughes usually did, selecting the issues to be discussed. So, too, at oral argument the Chief Justice may take advantage of his presiding office to give direction to the lines of reasoning which counsel will explore. As presiding officer he may also exert social leadership. He may have the Court dispose of the less controversial decisions before taking up those more likely to cause dissension. By tackling these simpler items first a higher degree of harmony can be established, and this harmony might carry over and protect later discussion from personal rancor. If and when arguments begin to get heated, the Chief may use his authority to ease tension, either by cutting off debate or soothing hurt feelings. Hughes would often end a discussion which was threatening to get out of hand by saying, "Brethren, the only way to settle this is to vote."[107] When Melville W. Fuller was Chief Justice, Holmes once interrupted Justice Harlan's statement of his views with a caustic, "That won't wash!" Harlan, never noted for avoiding a fight, reddened, but Fuller quickly broke in: "But I keep scrubbing away, scrubbing away," using his hands as if rubbing clothes on a washboard. The laughter that ensued allowed the Justices to get back to their work without a bitter exchange of words.[108]

An astute Chief Justice can also utilize his opinion-assigning power to increase his influence on the Court. When in agreement with the majority, the Chief Justice can assign the opinion to the most moderate member, hoping that his mild statement of the doctrine might prevent defections or even gain adherents. The Chief may even assign the opinion to a wavering Justice, hoping that this task—if not further reflection and research—will strengthen the Justice's resolve and perhaps sway the minority. Alternately, the Chief Justice may use the opinion-assigning power to reward his coalition within the Court. He can assign the opinions in interesting and important cases to those Justices who tend to vote with him, leaving the dregs for those who vote against him on issues he thinks important. This authority may also be used as a means of encouraging an elderly or failing colleague to retire. Chief Justice Fuller withheld opinions from old Justice Field to help nudge him off the bench, and Taft tried the same tactic with McKenna.

The advantages of the opinion-assigning power are augmented by the fact that the Chief Justice votes last in conference. Thus, before he finally commits himself, he knows where each Justice stands—at least for the present—and which side will most probably win. If his own views are going to be in the minority, he can vote with the majority and retain the opinion-assigning authority. He may keep the opinion himself—as apparently John Marshall sometimes did*—and so do a minimum of damage to his own deeply felt values. Or the Chief may assign the opinion to the majority Justice whose views are closest to his own. It is worth noting in this regard that during his first nine terms as Chief Justice (1930–38), Hughes officially registered only 23 dissents in 1,382 cases decided by full opinion.

There is an additional potential source of power for the Chief Justice which is usually overlooked by students of the Court. If, in fact, the so-called paradox of voting or the problem of cyclical majorities does occur on the Court,† the Chief Justice in his capacity as presiding officer has a unique opportunity to exploit the situation. The voting paradox might take place in a decision-making body where more

* See letter of Justice William Johnson to Thomas Jefferson, December 10, 1822, quoted in Donald G. Morgan, *Justice William Johnson: The First Dissenter* (Columbia: University of South Carolina Press, 1954), pp. 181–82. According to Charles G. Haines, *The Role of the Supreme Court in American Government and Politics* (Berkeley: University of California Press, 1944), p. 630, in his first five years on the bench Marshall wrote the opinion of the Court in every case in which he participated. In the next seven years he wrote the opinion of the Court in 130 cases, assigning a total of only thirty opinions to his associates.

On at least two occasions, *Ex parte Bollman* (1807), and *Rose* v. *Himely* (1808), Marshall wrote an "opinion of the Court" in which only a minority of the participating Justices concurred. See his apology in *United States* v. *Burr* (1807) and *Hudson* v. *Guestier* (1808).

† Paul David has questioned whether the paradox does in fact occur often in the real political world when only three or four alternatives are open. "Experimental Approaches to Vote-Counting Theory in Nominating Choice," 56 *Am. Pol. Sci. Rev.* 673 (1962); see also his "Reforming the Presidential Nominating Process," 27 *Law and Contemporary Problems* 159 (1962). Gilbert and Sullivan apparently did not think the paradox occurred very often in Victorian England. As they observed in *Iolanthe:*

> I often think it's comical—Fal, lal, la!
> How Nature always does contrive—Fal, lal, la!
> That every boy and every gal
> That's born into the world alive
> Is either a little Liberal
> Or else a little Conservative!
> Fal, lal, la!

than two alternatives—as in complex litigation—were available to the group, and where each actor has different and transitive choice preferences. For preferences to be transitive an actor who prefers alternative a to alternative b and alternative b to alternative c, must also prefer a to c. The voting paradox may occur where:

Actor I prefers a to b, b to c, and a to c.
Actor II prefers b to c, c to a, and b to a.
Actor III prefers c to a, a to b, and c to b.

Here two actors prefer alternative a to alternative b, and two prefer b to c, but two also prefer c to a. Thus each alternative is actually opposed by a majority, although the rules of voting used by most decision-making groups, whether by accident or by some unconscious design, will usually conceal the existence of the paradox and result in a majority choice.

This cyclical problem has been recognized at least since Condorcet, and in recent years a number of economists and a few political scientists have explored more fully its implications for public-policy formulation.[109] One of the most important implications for the power of the Chief Justice is Duncan Black's conclusion that, where the paradox does occur, the time at which a given alternative is put to the vote is crucial in determining its acceptance or rejection, since most rules for voting would provide an opportunity for expression of second choices.[110] The internal procedures of the Court are sufficiently loose so that the Chief Justice might manipulate rather easily the order in which issues were voted on and thus change the outcome.

For example, assume that in discussing a case the Justices divide in support of three alternatives: a, b, and c. Alternative a might well be a decision to affirm the entire judgment under review; alternative b could be a decision to affirm one part of the judgment and to reverse a second part; alternative c could be a decision to reverse both issues before the Court. Conference discussion has brought out that the division is:

Prefer a: Chief Justice and Justices 1, 2, 3 (Group I).
Prefer b: Justice 4 (Group II).
Prefer c: Justices 5, 6, 7, 8 (Group III).

The conference discussion has also brought out the following preference rankings:

Group I prefers *a* to *b*, *b* to *c*, and *a* to *c*.
Group II prefers *b* to *a*, *a* to *c*, and *b* to *c*.
Group III prefers *c* to *b*, *b* to *a*, and *c* to *a*.

The Chief Justice knows that the first alternative voted on, whichever it is, will be defeated, and on the next vote supporters of the defeated alternative will have an opportunity to express their second choice. Thus he suggests a vote first on *b*, which is, of course, defeated by 8–1. Next he puts his own preference, alternative *a*, to a vote, and it carries 5–4 since Justice 4 prefers *a* to *c*. If, however, the Chief Justice had first put *a* to a vote, it would have been defeated and *b* would have become the winner if the Group I Justices next voted their second choice.*

Neither singularly nor together do these special powers insure the Chief Justice sufficient influence to persuade the other Justices to endorse his policy goals. Much of his initial advantage is postulated on the belief that his accepted, i.e., legitimate, role is one of leadership. This may or may not be true. It would not be too much to say that the severe and efficient Hughes did dominate the conference.[111] Only rarely were matters discussed which he did not want brought up, and the Justice who dared debate with the Chief usually found himself in a very painful position since Hughes came into the conference armed both with heavily marked volumes of the U.S. Reports and a photographic memory. He also had a keen sense of humor, though he used it infrequently. Nevertheless, apparently no other member of the Court had the temerity to try to exert social leadership.

* Another important implication of the paradox of possible use to any policy-oriented Justice, not just the Chief Justice, is Black's theorem that it may be possible for an actor to achieve a decision more favorable to his cause by voting at one stage of the proceedings otherwise than in accordance with his schedule of preferences. *The Theory of Committees and Elections* (Cambridge: Cambridge University Press, 1958), pp. 44–45. The applicability of this theorem to the legislative process has been demonstrated time and again. For instance, conservative Republicans opposed to federal aid to education or home construction have nevertheless supported amendments to such bills requiring that funds be spent only for projects which are to be racially integrated. Since these bills normally need overwhelming southern Democratic support to pass, adoption of the race rider can split the proponents and defeat the measure. However, lack of empirical data makes it difficult to judge how applicable this theorem would be to decision-making on the Court, except where the Justices were acting in a quasi-legislative capacity, trying to agree on the rules of procedure for the various federal courts.

When Stone succeeded Hughes, it is not unlikely that the Associate Justices had come to expect the Chief to act both as a task and a social leader. But Stone did not play either role, at least not in a fashion comparable to that of either of his immediate predecessors. Since he had felt frustrated by Hughes's methods, the new Chief Justice refused to cut off discussion—indeed, he joined in angry wrangling with his associates, something which Hughes considered beneath his station. Long, acrimonious harangues, which often stretched from Saturday until Wednesday, marked the Stone conferences.*[112]

Harlan Stone held the center chair for five years, and his legacy to his successor was in all probability a changed concept in the minds of the Associate Justices of the Chief Justice's role. Thus if Vinson, assuming he had had the desire as well as the intellectual ability and social charm, had tried to return to the kind of leadership which Hughes had exerted, he might well have alienated his associates by violating their expectations of his proper role. It is quite possible that for the immediate future Stone destroyed any aura of legitimacy surrounding the Chief Justice's position of leadership within the Court. This does not mean, of course, that such an aura could not be re-created. Hughes, for example, built up an expectation of task leadership which Taft never exercised, and he did so with Van Devanter, the old task leader, still on the bench. John Marshall, of course, had to start with even less of a tradition than did Hughes and for almost twenty-five years achieved a degree of success which startled and dismayed his enemies.

Even where an expectation of leadership by the Chief Justice has been inherited or built up, the advantages conferred are not necessarily decisive. Like that of any Associate Justice, the influence of the Chief is materially affected by the caliber of his colleagues as well as by their willingness to let him select the issues to be discussed at conference and oral argument. Both friendly and critical students of Marshall's reign agree that after 1825 he pretty well lost control over his

* Justice Murphy's notes on the conferences from 1941 to 1946 indicate that discussion generally followed the lines that Stone's opening remarks mapped out, though not necessarily reaching the result which the Chief thought was required. But, beyond doubt, if any one Justice's questioning at oral argument forced counsel to argue certain issues more than or rather than others, it was those posed by Frankfurter. On the other hand, it is not unlikely that the sheer number of Frankfurter's questions to counsel dissipated much of their shaping effect on the thinking of other members of the Court.

Court as younger and more energetic men with different policy ideas replaced the older Justices.[113] Hughes exploited his authority with superb skill, yet he could not prevent his Court from splintering into angry factions or keep some of his colleagues from engaging in a wasted and almost suicidal war against the twentieth century. Nor could Hughes's great talents conceal the drastic nature of the reversal which the High Bench executed when it capitulated to the New Deal—though he was largely successful in masking the extent of his own vacillating course during the period 1935–37.[114]

The Chief Justice's advantage vis-à-vis his colleagues of voting last varies with the seniority of the individual Justice. A knowledge of the Chief's voting record and of his tentative views on the case at bar can give the senior Associate Justice an accurate idea of the Chief Justice's true feelings. Thus, since seven Justices have voted before him, the senior Associate Justice is also in a good position to adopt deceptive poses similar to those open to the Chief Justice. He may vote with the majority and hope that the Chief (if he, too, is with the majority) will pick him to write the Court's opinion, or that the Chief Justice will dissent and leave him the authority of assigning the opinion writer. To lesser extents down the seniority list, similar opportunities are open to other Associate Justices.

Any advantage to the Chief Justice when—or if—the voting paradox occurs depends on his ability immediately to recognize the situation and to discern the preference schedules of the other Justices. Second, the Chief Justice's advantage depends on a Justice's—or several Justices' —willingness to vote his second preference rather than to insist stubbornly on going on record for his first choice, no matter what the Court decides or cannot decide. Third, since any Justice is free to change his vote after conference and since bargaining is always possible, exploitation of the voting paradox can never insure that the Chief Justice will still have a majority when the decision is finally announced. Last, his advantage here also depends on the other Justices being unaware of the situation, lest they demand strict adherence to a particular order of voting.

In short, the chief justiceship supplies numerous opportunities to exert influence; it offers no guaranty that the incumbent can utilize these opportunities to achieve his policy goals. When the votes are tallied, the Chief's counts no more than that of any associate.

IV PROFESSIONAL REPUTATION

This chapter has tended to emphasize opportunities within the Court for persuasion by negotiation and accommodation. There are also situations in which a Justice should not compromise except on inconsequential details. The ethical reasons which sometimes necessitate this sort of stand will be discussed in chapter vii. At this point it is sufficient merely to note that a Justice may be unable in conscience to dilute his views or keep them to himself. What should be brought out here is that a concern for professional reputation may make such an occasional stand strategically wise and perhaps even necessary.*

To make the most of having to share decision-making authority with eight other men, a Justice would have to be willing generally to compromise—unless, of course, he found himself in the very unusual position of being in a strong majority in all cases, or at least all cases which he considered significant—assuming that his colleagues were men of comparable skill, learning, and intelligence. On the other hand, a Justice who was always ready to give in, to accept a half-loaf, could by that very fact weaken his bargaining position. If he habitually accommodated himself to others on all issues, his colleagues might well cease to take him seriously. To maintain the respect of the Court, a Justice would have to use some sanctions at various times. In a similar fashion, Franklin Roosevelt was anxious to veto legislation to prevent congressmen from thinking him soft. It is hardly a novel observation that a successful policy-maker must be feared as well as loved.

* For the effect of such an approach on relations with lower courts and the other branches of government, see below, chaps. iv and vi.

4 Managing the Judicial Bureaucracy

The Queen of Hearts in *Alice in Wonderland* went about shouting "Off with his head!" But, as Alice quickly noted, heads did not roll. Like most real bureaucracies that of the fantasy queen exhibited a marked independence. In politics what may appear to be a neat, hierarchical system often turns out on close examination to be a confused congeries of mutual controls, more analogous to the reciprocal (and not always effective) checks of a competitive price system than to the disciplined chain of command of a military organization. So, too, in its relations with the Supreme Court, the judicial bureaucracy, composed of lower federal and state court judges, functions with a considerable degree of autonomy. As chapter ii pointed out, the independence of inferior court judges and the vagaries of the judicial process itself provide frequent opportunities—legal and moral—for the exercise of wide discretion in interpreting and applying Supreme Court policy.

A Justice who is ambitious for the success of his particular policy goals must include in his strategic planning means of coping with a problem common to executives in politics, business, and the military: bureaucratic resistance. Like all leaders, a policy-oriented Justice must not only formulate policy and secure his peers' endorsement of that policy, but he must also take steps to insure that subordinates down the line will accept and apply the policy decision.

I STRATEGIC ALTERNATIVES

The same simple strategies are available to a Justice in dealing with lower court judges as in dealing with his associates on the Court, with the addition of one further and important alternative. Not only can he try to influence the behavior of lower court judges through intellectual or emotional persuasion, through personal or professional esteem, through threats or uses of sanctions, or through selection of new personnel, but he may also appeal to his authority, especially when he speaks for the Court, since he and his tribunal are at the highest level of the judicial hierarchy insofar as federal questions are concerned. These simple strategies are all subject to restrictions similar to those involved in dealing with associates.

It is true that a Justice, if he can muster a majority of the Court behind him, can usually apply more impressive sanctions against recalcitrant lower court judges than against stubborn colleagues, but used alone these would hardly be likely to engender widespread acceptance of his policies. There are just too many judges and too many cases. It is also true that, because of their relative positions in the judicial hierarchy, lower court judges may be even more open to a Supreme Court Justice's efforts at persuasion on the merits than his associates would be. But lower court judges are apt to have different orientations, different loyalties, different values, and different interests and policy objectives than Supreme Court Justices, and intellectual or emotional arguments alone, no matter how convincing their rhetoric and how close their appeal to self-interest, are not likely to bridge all or possibly even most of these gaps.

Lack of personal contact would make it difficult to increase personal though not necessarily professional esteem; distance would also markedly hamper efforts at negotiation, though tacit bargaining would still be possible. The political tradition which subjects nominees to federal district judgeships to a veto from the local senator of the President's party—where, indeed, this tradition does not make the nomination itself a senatorial prerogative—would greatly inhibit a Justice's ability to influence such appointments on a large scale. Appointments to state courts, of course, are largely beyond the reach of a Justice's influence, except perhaps in his own home state.

In spite of the importance of authority in the judicial process, it would not be prudent for a Justice to rely on a simple strategy based solely on command. As Neustadt has pointed out in his study of the presidency,[1] an executive directive must meet each of a number of conditions before it will be successful in overcoming bureaucratic resistance. Modified slightly to take account of institutional differences, these conditions are relevant to the efficacy of policy-making by the Supreme Court.

The first condition is an unambiguous commitment to a policy, an unambiguous commitment unambiguously stated. The second condition is that the publicity attached to the commitment is so widespread that evasion or resistance would be discovered and thwarted. Third, the judge or judges expected to apply the policy must have the authority and power to do so and be reasonably safe from political reprisal for actually carrying out the Court's decisions. Fourth, there should be no doubt about the Court's authority to hand down any particular decision or to formulate the general policy involved; that is, all the technical requirements of jurisdiction and standing to sue should be met.

The fourth condition would normally be fulfilled. An alert Justice would probably be able to prevent the Court from deciding a case which represented a significant step toward his policy objective until all jurisdictional and standing requirements had been satisfied. Certainly, a majority of his colleagues would hardly be anxious to take and decide a case which did not meet these requirements. All of the other three conditions of command, however, will not always be fulfilled, at least not without considerable additional activity by one or more of the Justices.

A Justice may have to settle for an ambiguous commitment by the Court to his policy either because he cannot secure unequivocal endorsement by a majority of the Justices or because a careful spelling out of the policy would excite a strongly negative and dangerous reaction from other government officials or from interest-group leaders.* There may not be enough publicity given either to the Court's decisions or to the very similar cases coming later before lower courts to create a real risk of reversal or perhaps even appeal. Following the Court's policy directives may well result in the lower court judge being "punished" either by his fellow citizens or by other public officials; and since judges are usually completely dependent on executive or occasionally legislative officers to carry out their decrees, state or federal officials may, by action or inaction, prevent a judge from effectively applying the Court's policy.

* When he was sure of his goal but uncertain about the best means of obtaining it, a Justice might deliberately try to be vague in an effort to encourage judges to exercise a wide range of discretion and so provide him with an empirical basis for later choice.

Thus a Justice would once again have to devise a strategy which would combine several of the simple approaches. Because of the position of the Supreme Court in the judicial system, command would be the principal ingredient in a plan directed toward obtaining lower court compliance, but it would have to be leavened by other strategic elements. Having been trained in the common law tradition, the overwhelming majority of judges would be predisposed to obey Supreme Court mandates, but a policy-oriented Justice would want much more than obedience to individual decrees. He would also want lower court judges to apply his policy to the hundreds or even thousands of cases which would never get beyond the trial or intermediate appellate court level.

The general trend of American society has been away from authoritarian control and toward manipulation by persuasion;[2] as products of this changing environment, judges would undoubtedly respond positively to a policy supported by closely reasoned statements justifying the choice in terms of accepted principles of jurisprudence and constitutional interpretation. Professional esteem would increase the receptivity of lower court judges to arguments on the merits, and personal esteem might make judges more ready to read such arguments with sympathy.

Where a judge or group of judges remained unconvinced—and all the conditions of command were not present or where the situation was sufficiently complex for the judge or judges to assert that the Court's policy was not applicable—the Justice might have to resort, or persuade his associates to resort, to the use of sanctions or to bargaining. If the Justice could in fact influence the appointment process so as to bring to the lower bench judges who were already inclined to support his policy, his task would obviously be much easier.

As in dealing with associates, the major strategic problems for the Justice would arise in determining what strategy-mix would most efficiently further his policy objectives and then integrating this into a general, co-ordinated plan of action. The main factors which determine the most prudent course are similar to those affecting strategy selection for intra-Court operations.

The personality of the Justice would be critical—not every Justice could make fruitful use of all of the possible strategic and tactical alternatives—as would the size of the Justice's majority on the Court and the degree of his associates' commitment to his policy. The character of the judges who will have to apply that policy would be important, as would be the question whether they were largely federal or state judges, since a Justice could more easily persuade his colleagues to exercise closer control over the former than the latter. In addition, a successful strategy designed to cope with the problem of bureaucratic resistance would have to be even more flexible than one centered on the Court itself, since responses from such a large group are likely to be far more varied than from eight men.

Another significant factor would be the nature of the policy itself and the actual and expected reactions from the political environment generally and perhaps in specific areas, if the impact of a case or set of cases were to be restricted for some time to a given region. A Supreme Court Justice must remember that local pressures can come down hard on a federal judge who lives, and must continue to live as long as he retains his position on the bench, in a particular community, and that, as a subordinate federal official, a lower court judge may be more apprehensive about congressional or presidential reactions than would a Supreme Court Justice. A policy-oriented Justice must also keep in mind that community pressures can come down even harder on a state judge than on a federal judge. A state judge lacks the tie with the Supreme Court of being a *federal* official, and he often must run for re-election or be subject to reappointment by other state officers.

A last factor is that of the prestige of the Court and the reputations of the Justices both for skill in their craftsmanship and for determination in seeing that their judgments are followed. When both are high the strategy choices may be bold; when one or the other is low, it would be prudent for a policy-oriented Justice to divert a large share of his resources to building up or restoring prestige and reputation—a remedy as easy to prescribe as it is difficult to carry out. The first step in such a task would be for the Justice to insure that his own work met the most exacting professional standards. His second step would be to try to influence his associates so that their work met the same standards.

II TACTICS

Once a Justice has decided on the kind of mixed strategy best suited to his policy and to the facts of the political and judicial environment within which he must act, he would again have to assess the tactics available to exploit each of the elements of his strategic plan—and to co-ordinate those tactics into an operational scheme which would maximize his chances of achieving both the immediate goal of lowering bureaucratic resistance and the larger purpose of securing the policy objective.

COMMAND

The first and most important step in exploiting the authoritative position of the Supreme Court would be for a Justice to try to meet the conditions of command. Since the Justices' craftsmanship would almost always satisfy the fourth condition, the main problems would center around the other three conditions. The task of securing an unambiguous commitment by the Court raises problems of tactics in dealing with associates, and these matters were discussed in the preceding chapter. The task of preventing political action which would frustrate judicial policy or of securing the political action necessary to carry out judicial policy involves tactics discussed in chapters v and vi. We note here that some of the more obvious possibilities include: (1) a coincidence of interest which moves another branch of the federal government to the aid of the Court—as in Little Rock in 1957 or Oxford in 1962; (2) persuasion by a variety of tactics to convince other federal officials that they should act to support the Court; or, (3) throwing the prestige of the Supreme Court onto the scales in an effort to force other federal officers to act out of a feeling of moral obligation or out of the fear that their constituents would expect them to assist the Court.

The problem of publicity of the Court's policy can be eased by clearly written opinions, by timing decisions so that newspaper attention can focus on one or two important cases at a time,[3] by public speeches before professional associations or citizens' groups, as well as articles by friends in popular or professional journals.* On the other hand, there is little a Justice can do to find out about, let alone publicize, a case never brought before the Court if one of the parties or some interest group which knows how to utilize the judicial process does not seek review.

A Justice can choose between a number of courses of action in order to minimize any damage which might be done by threats of political retaliation against lower court judges. Because of problems of re-election or reappointment, state judges would normally be more vulner-

* These tactics are discussed in greater detail in chaps. v and vi.

able than federal judges to such threats, but an ambitious federal judge who wanted to be promoted to a higher court or to another government post might not be completely immune. In neither case, however, need a Supreme Court Justice assume that the existence of a threat would automatically deter judges from carrying out the Court's policy. Judges, as Holmes once remarked, are expected to be men of ordinary firmness of character,[4] and most of them probably have more than ordinary firmness. Especially where the Supreme Court's prestige and reputation were high, a threatened judge might draw courage from his loyalty to the Court and from his pride in the ideals of his profession. Well-written opinions which maintain or increase professional esteem would be important in reinforcing loyalty to the traditions of the bench; so would opinions which would convince the judge that he should follow the Court not only because it was generally his duty to do so, but also because the particular policy in question was in the best interests of the country. Personal esteem might act as a further reinforcement as well as a factor predisposing a judge to accept the correctness of the reasoning of the Court.

A counterthreat of use of judicial sanctions might negate the effects of threats of political retaliation in one or both of two ways. First, if the Justice can get the Court to present a potentially recalcitrant judge with the possibility of an equally or more painful punishment than the threatened political one, the judge may be moved to prefer the lesser to the greater injury and carry out the Court's policy. Or, the fact that he is threatened with Supreme Court sanctions may put the judge in a strong position to thwart the action of those who are threatening him. If he can persuade them, or their successors in office, or his own constituents—if he must run for re-election—that he was only acting under duress, then they might be less inclined to carry out their threats.

PERSUASION ON THE MERITS AND PROFESSIONAL ESTEEM

Where the interests of lower court judges coincide with those of a Supreme Court Justice, the Justice need do nothing to influence the judges' behavior, except perhaps to inform them of the situation and alert them to the necessity for action. Where their interests are indifferent, the Justice can expect that, when he speaks for the Court, his authority will be generally a decisive influence on the judges' behavior. When their interests are in conflict, the Justice must reinforce command with persuasion, with threats, with bargaining, or somehow have new judges put on the bench whose interests coincide with or are indifferent to his own.

There may be close limits to what intellectual argument on policy questions can do to sway opponents; but in the peculiar situation of the judicial process, lower court judges would certainly be as open to persuasion on the merits of a case by a Supreme Court Justice as would the Justice's colleagues, if not more so given his position in the Court hierarchy. And there is no reason to suppose that lower court judges would be any more—or less—immune to appeals to their emotions than their seniors on the High Bench.

A speech or an article, a private conversation at a professional or public meeting, or an exchange of correspondence might provide occasional opportunities for a Justice to convince judges of the soundness of his views and to impress them with his professional abilities. The major avenue for such influence, however, would be through the opinions he writes for the Court or for a minority of his associates. Here his capacity to engage in thorough research, to organize relevant facts and legal principles, to reason with taut logic, to write with eloquence, and to use persuasive rhetoric would be crucial. These are the basic tools of his profession, and the Justice who had not fully mastered them would be at as serious a disadvantage in allaying bureaucratic resistance as he would be in overcoming opposition to his policies within the Court.

PERSONAL ESTEEM

The Justice's ability to use these tools would increase the professional esteem in which judges hold him and in turn would make them more ready to accept his arguments. So, too, personal esteem might make judges more disposed to read his opinions with sympathy and, given the prevalence of "unit perception" or "facilitative distortion,"[5] to confer automatically on his opinions a high degree of respect. The means of increasing professional esteem are clear, though their fruitful use means long, hard work. The ways of increasing personal esteem are much more varied and far less immediately apparent.

One of the simplest methods is that which Frankfurter has termed "alert deference" to lower court opinions. "Such a system as ours," Frankfurter has said for the Court, "must . . . rely on the learning, good sense, fairness and courage of federal trial judges."[6] Not only are such statements correct, but public reiteration of the fact can be most diplomatic. Emphasis in opinions on the respect which the Court—or an individual Justice—holds for the judicial bureaucracy may do much to smooth friction, and a general policy of respect can be made more effective by occasional notations of individual esteem.

In *Betts* v. *Brady* (1942), for instance, the Court refused to rule that an indigent defendant had been denied due process in not having an appointed counsel to represent him.* For the majority, Justice Roberts incorporated the reasoning of the Chief Judge of the Maryland Court of Appeals and mentioned the Chief Judge by name fifteen times in an eighteen-page opinion. In *Feiner* v. *New York,* Chief Justice Vinson, in affirming a questionable breach-of-the-peace conviction, went out of his way to emphasize the persuasiveness of the findings and opinions of the New York courts. In a separate concurrence, Frankfurter added that "only unfamiliarity with its decisions and the outlook of its judges could generate a notion that the New York Court of Appeals is inhospitable to claims of civil liberties. . . ." In *Akel* v. *New York,* Frankfurter, in denying a petition to set bail for a defendant pending his filing an application for certiorari, mentioned as one of the main factors in his decision the similar refusal of "a judge as solicitous as is Judge Stanley H. Fuld to safeguard the interests of defendants in criminal cases. . . ."

Occasions do arise—and they often arise—where a Justice will feel obliged to urge or join in a decision to reverse lower court decisions. The upsetting personal effect of reversal on judges can be minimized if the reversal is accomplished with tact and graciousness. Even in disagreement, respect can be paid to the lower court decision, and the blow can be softened by such concessions as "the law is in need of clarification," or "the trial judge might well have concluded as he did." According to Judge Calvert Magruder, one of the marks of respect apparently most appreciated is a full explanation of the reasons for the Court's action and a careful mapping out of guidelines for future decision-making.[7]

As a different kind of gesture of respect for and faith in lower court judges, the Supreme Court can entrust them with special responsibility. The implementation order in the school segregation decision may be a case in point, though some district judges in the South have not been overly pleased with this "expression of confidence." But perhaps this

* The holding of *Betts* was, of course, reversed by *Gideon* v. *Wainwright* (1963).

tactic, if it was deliberate, was wiser than intended. Sociologists have noted the tendency in conflict situations for men to turn their aggressions against their immediate superiors rather than against more responsible, but also more distant, higher echelons.[8] Thus in relegating to the various courts of appeals the onerous task of supervising school desegregation, the Justices may have inadvertently encouraged district judges to displace their aggressions and thus diverted some of their hostility from the Supreme Court to circuit judges.[9]

Consultation is another means of smoothing interpersonal relations. Sociological evidence conflicts on the question of whether consultation increases the efficiency of production in industry, but it does seem to increase job satisfaction.[10] Efficiency in the sense of economical use of time by lower court judges is not directly related to this discussion, though it is an important aspect of judicial administration. Efficiency in the sense of wholehearted and cheerful co-operation in the execution of Supreme Court policies is a central concern for the policy-oriented Justice, and seeking the advice of lower court judges might be a fruitful way of reducing friction.

The Judicial Conference of the United States provides a formal means of consultation and co-operation among federal judges. By statute the Chief Justice annually summons a meeting of the Chief Judge of the Court of Claims, the Chief Judge of each circuit, and a district judge from each circuit. The purpose of this meeting is to review and analyze, and if possible improve, the conduct of judicial business during the previous year and to advise Congress on needed legislative action. Since he presides over this conference, the Chief Justice has a unique advantage in dealing with lower court judges, though he is hardly the "commander in chief" which congressional foes of the conference once feared he would become.[11] While they are usually invited only to attend social functions, other members of the Court can still use these occasions to discuss mutual problems with other judges and in so doing to engage (as can the Chief Justice) in the informal sort of explaining-persuading-politicking so common in other fields of American business and political life.

Moreover, each judicial circuit has its own conference, and the Justice assigned to each circuit is always invited to attend and even sometimes to preside. At neither the national nor the circuit level does the conference guarantee improvement of the Justice's relations with his bureaucracy. Indeed, mismanaged direct personal contact can do even more damage than more distant interpersonal relations. However, the conferences do provide opportunities which an astute Justice may utilize to build up a feeling of teamwork and understanding.

Although there is no formal machinery for co-ordination between state and federal judges, there is ample opportunity for informal discussion. Bar association meetings provide one common meeting ground. The state chief justices have their own annual conference, and there is no reason why some form of contact between the two national judicial organizations could not be arranged—as indeed it was in regard to the joint efforts to revise existing federal habeas corpus regulations.[12]

Informal contact can be equally if not more important than formal meetings. When Taft became Chief Justice neither judicial conference existed, but he still felt it to be part of his job to work to minimize the conflict between the various court levels. During his first term on the bench he sent a personal letter to the chief justice of every state, noting that he had instructed the clerk to send to every state supreme court the opinions of the U.S. Supreme Court. In return, he requested that reports of state decisions be forwarded to Washington. "I feel," Taft explained, "as if the Judges in the Courts of last resort in this country should be brought more closely together, and that [an exchange of opinions] would facilitate a mutual understanding."[13] As Taft's letters indicated, there may be certain interests and outlooks which judges of courts of last resort share—controlling lower court judges being an important one. A Justice might emphasize these common interests to build up good will.

In the fall of 1921 Taft also sent a cordial personal letter to practically every federal district judge asking for suggestions on needed reforms in judicial procedure. Furthermore, he wrote to every senior circuit judge requesting information and advice on overcrowded dockets. "I am very anxious," Taft told his fellow jurists, "to introduce teamwork among the Federal Judges of the country, and I call on you to help me in this matter."[14] Every reply was promptly acknowledged and individual suggestions were frequently discussed. And, of course, Taft was influential in persuading Congress to establish what has become the Judicial Conference.* The need for judicial reform is clearly perennial, and a shrewd Chief Justice—here again the Chief Justice would have a decided advantage over his colleagues—could

* See below, chap. v.

have a constant excuse to seek the opinions of lower court judges. Moreover, he could also work for tighter organization of the Judicial Conference and so extend his own influence formally as well as informally.

The Taft Papers contain literally hundreds of other letters from the Chief Justice seeking advice from lower court judges—especially from Augustus Hand of the Second Circuit and Arthur Denison of the Sixth—on matters relating to judicial procedure, congressional legislation, or personnel affairs within the judiciary or the Department of Justice. Stone, too, often discussed problems with lower court judges, especially with Learned Hand.*

Hopefully, consultation and emphasis on teamwork would create a sense of loyalty and commitment on the part of lower court judges to whatever final policies were worked out. A sense of personal loyalty added to institutional loyalties would increase moral pressure against resistance. Internal compulsion can be far more powerful than external force in shaping behavior patterns. As Erich Fromm has observed, "In order that any society may function well, its members must acquire the kind of character which makes them *want* to act in the way they *have* to act as members of the society or of a special class within it. They have to desire what objectively is necessary for them to do."[15]

As in all interpersonal relations, charm is important in dealing with judicial colleagues. No less than a new Supreme Court appointee, a new judge when he comes to the lower bench must experience a feeling of entering a strange and awesome world. A friendly, encouraging letter of welcome from a Supreme Court Justice may predispose the new judge to look in later years with greater tolerance at what might seem to him odd Supreme Court policies and practices. There is no reason why a Justice could not (as congressmen usually do with regard to their constituents) have one of his staff keep a file on the careers of at least federal judges and state supreme court justices, so that the Justice might at the right moment offer congratulations or commisera-

---

* Compare the request for advice which Chief Justice Chase sent to U.S. District Judge William Giles when the Court was confronted with the problem of increased circuit-riding duties and a decrease in the number of the Justices: "I shall be glad," the Chief Justice wrote, "to have your opinion, to which . . . association with you has taught me to give great weight." Quoted in David Hughes, "Salmon P. Chase: Chief Justice" (Ph.D. diss., Princeton University, 1963), p. 270.

tions. Taft and Stone often wrote such letters, though neither seems to have been very systematic about it.*

When disagreements arise between a Supreme Court Justice and a lower court judge, a warm note may help smooth future relations. As Chase wrote a district judge with whom he was having problems over distribution of court patronage as well as on substantive issues of law growing out of Civil War and Reconstruction policies, "We may differ on legal questions and on matters outside our judicial duties, but I fear no difference which will make me anything else than your sincere friend."[16]

An ambitious Justice might follow the old military maxim that loyalty down begets loyalty up—"Take care of your men and your men will take care of you" is basic advice to young lieutenants. Federal district judges face many problems with which they cannot cope without additional legislation; and although they usually have direct access to one or two senators or congressmen, without outside help they are seldom able to capture the attention of Congress or the executive department to an extent sufficient to remedy their problems. A Justice who uses his own political contacts with larger bar, congressional, administrative, and public audiences to assist lower court judges may be able to build up a useful rapport.

Federal district and circuit judges have usually been heavily overworked and grossly underpaid. The efforts of Chief Justices like Chase[17] and Taft[18] to raise judges' salaries must have built up a reservoir of

---

* Justice John Marshall Harlan the elder, for all his bluster and occasional table-pounding, sometimes went out of his way to keep on good terms with judges in his circuit. In May, 1903 he wrote Judge Horace Lurton to apologize for not being able to visit the circuit that year. "I very much fear," Harlan said smoothly, "that you and your colleagues of the Circuit Court may come to consider that I am a very poor circuit justice, but in considering that matter do not forget that the bench in my circuit is so strong that a circuit justice is rarely ever necessary and is something like a fifth wheel." Harlan to Lurton, May 4, 1903; Horace Lurton Papers, Library of Congress. Later in the same month, Harlan showed his interest in the work of the circuit by asking Lurton if he might be allowed to write the opinion in two or three cases. May 21, 1903, *ibid.* A few months earlier, Harlan confided to Lurton (who was anxious for promotion to the Supreme Court) that the President had asked his opinion of Lurton. "What was in his mind," Harlan told the Circuit Judge, "I do not know, nor did I deem it proper to inquire. I need only say that I said of you to him all that your warmest friend could have wished to be said." Dec. 16, 1902, *ibid.*

good will in the judicial bureaucracy. Old as well as new federal judges should have been grateful for Taft's tireless lobbying for the Judiciary Act of 1922, which provided for the appointment of twenty-four additional judges to ease the existing work load. His equally strenuous efforts to persuade Congress to establish a more flexible system of setting rules of court procedure must have increased his store of good will with harassed trial judges. So, too, Charles Evans Hughes's intervention in favor of legislation providing clerks to aid district judges must have been appreciated, as well as Taft's attempts on two different occasions to secure special legislation to enable district judges who were ill but under the statutory retirement age to step down with full retirement benefits.[19]

SANCTIONS

Application of sanctions against judges may be a relatively poor way of obtaining their co-operation, but in some situations, for example, where the judge is being threatened with political retaliation if he applies the Court's policy or where out of sheer stubbornness or strength of conviction he refuses to obey a specific decree, a Justice may have no alternative. Reluctant obedience may be better than disobedience. Moreover, the willingness and ability of the Justices to use their sanctions adroitly, or threaten to use them, when faced with recalcitrance is one of the factors by which the Court's institutional reputation is measured. In this sense, any invocation of sanctions would affect the readiness of judges, at least those who were aware of what had happened, to follow broad Supreme Court policies as well as to obey a particular mandate.

Review and reversal are highly selective weapons in discouraging lower courts from ignoring, neglecting, or undermining Supreme Court policy. The Court may not be able to reverse more than a minute percentage of lower court decisions, but a Justice who can muster three other votes can bring up at least the most important cases bearing on the policies which he considers vital, providing, of course, that a losing litigant requests review.

Since judges enjoy no more than other men the prospect of public reprimand, review and reversal can be even greater deterrents if they are backed by scathing sarcasm directed at the offending judge. Coming as an exception to a general policy of respect for lower court judges such a threat would further increase the force of a reprimand. In 1954,

Frankfurter wrote the opinion of the Court reversing a contempt conviction which District Judge Alexander Holtzoff had imposed on an attorney for alleged misconduct during a criminal trial. Conceding that a trial judge had to be accorded a great amount of discretion in administering justice and controlling lawyers, Frankfurter nevertheless noted that a judge should not "give vent to personal spleen or respond to personal grievance." He then went on to deliver a severe lecture to Holtzoff: "The record [of the trial] is persuasive that instead of representing the impersonal authority of law, the trial judge permitted himself to become personally embroiled with the petitioner. . . . For one reason or another the judge failed to impose his moral authority upon the proceedings. His behavior precluded that atmosphere of austerity which should especially dominate a criminal trial and which is indispensable for an appropriate sense of responsibility on the part of court, counsel and jury."[20]

Similarly in 1962 the Court administered to Federal District Judges Sidney Mize and Claude Clayton of Mississippi a rebuke which one newspaper called "as deserved as it was stinging."[21] A special three-judge district court had been convened to hear a suit by several Negroes for an injunction against the enforcement of state laws requiring segregated facilities in intra- and interstate commerce. These were the regulations that Mississippi was using to justify imprisoning "Freedom Riders." The special court, with Circuit Judge Rives dissenting, applied the doctrine of equitable abstention, denying relief pending state court construction of the statutes. In a terse but pointed and unanimous *per curiam* opinion, the Supreme Court insinuated that the two district judges were ignorant of fundamental law: "We have settled beyond question that no State may require racial segregation of interstate or intrastate facilities. The question is no longer open; it is foreclosed as a litigable issue."[22] The Court went on to hold that such statutes were so clearly unconstitutional that there was no need to have the case heard by a three-judge court.

In the same term, Chief Justice Warren was equally sharp in his criticism of the handling of a criminal case by the courts in the District of Columbia. Richard E. Leigh, convicted for his fifth forgery offense, had been imprisoned in December, 1960; but despite his timely efforts to appeal, seventeen months later the Court of Appeals for the District of Columbia had not yet even decided whether or not Leigh had raised a point which could validly be reviewed on appeal. Moreover, notwithstanding the long delay and the fact that the offense had involved only $170, both the trial judge and the Court of Appeals refused to release the prisoner on bail pending determination of the legal issues raised by the appeal. Noting first that there was "clear precedent" which established a right of appeal in such cases, the Chief Justice went on to reproach the Court of Appeals for its dilatory attitude: "There is no adequate reason why initial appellate review of applicant's case should not have been completed by this time [May, 1962]."[23]

A threat of reversal can also be worked into the dicta of an opinion. The Little Rock opinion, for example, contained a veiled warning which must have been as clear to judges as to other students of constitutional law that the High Bench would not look with favor on the so-called private schools plans which many southern state legislatures had endorsed as the last hope of avoiding desegregation. The Court said: "the prohibitions of the Fourteenth Amendment extend to all action of the State denying equal protection of the laws; whatever the agency of the State taking the action, or whatever the guise in which it is taken."[24] As important as the tone of the statement were citations to two decisions by courts of appeals which held unconstitutional state attempts to continue segregation by leasing state property to private corporations.

Personal contact provides another alternative avenue of influence. On several occasions Taft wrote directly to trial judges warning them that they were being less than diligent in their work, and Hughes arranged with a circuit judge so as to be quoted in favor of a procedural reform in the eighth circuit.[25] Taft and Hughes directed their intervention to problems in judicial administration; intervention in decisional matters would be vastly different, and would probably increase—if not multiply—bureaucratic resistance. A tactful hint at a bar association meeting or at one of the judicial conferences could be far less objectionable and would also eliminate the possibility of a blackmail threat to publish the correspondence. A Justice might find it more expedient to speak to one of the colleagues of the recalcitrant judge or, if he is a federal trial judge, to one or more members of the Court of Appeals for his circuit.

In the last century when they rode circuit and actually held trials with district judges, the Justices could be more direct in dealing with federal judges. In the early days of the Civil War, Chief Justice Taney instructed a district judge in Maryland not to hold treason trials alone because there could be no appeal from a conviction unless two judges sat on the case and disagreed.[26] Faced with equally difficult problems after the war, Chief Justice Chase freely intervened in the work of trial court judges. In 1866 he advised Judge Brooks in North Carolina: "If I were you and if conflict with military powers should occur, I would submit for the occasion, referring the matter to the President. Of course I should take care to avoid all unnecessary conflicts."*[27] Two years later, Chase instructed a district judge in Virginia that he was authorized to hear habeas corpus petitions "in an adjourned term"[28] only with the permission of the Chief Justice. Under the circumstances, Chase said, it would be best to postpone the case until the two could hear it together.[29] In 1871, the Chief Justice tried to speed a Supreme Court decision on the Ku Klux Klan Act by urging Judges Bryan and Bond in Virginia to disagree in a case which came under the statute then pending before them.[30]

The end of circuit riding deprived the Justices of much opportunity for close personal contact but it hardly stripped them of means of overcoming resistance in the form of heel-dragging or disobedience to a specific mandate. If the judges involved are state officials, the Justices can point out to the frustrated litigant the means by which he can have his rights protected in a federal tribunal. Thus, in 1957 after years of procrastination by the Florida supreme court against Virgil Hawkins' efforts to break down racial barriers at the state law school, the U.S. Supreme Court noted in refusing further review that the denial was "without prejudice to the petitioner's seeking relief in an appropriate United States District Court."[31] Hawkins' lawyers got the point and in a little more than a year won a compromise victory, though not without some additional bureaucratic resistance, this time by a federal district judge.[32]

The Justices can exert a greater degree of control over federal than over state judges both because of the smaller number of people involved and because of tradition. Since the time of John Marshall,[33] the Supreme Court has claimed authority to supervise the administration

---

* It is hardly chance coincidence that Taney was opposed both to the treason trials and more basically to the war itself; nor was it likely to have been mere happenstance that the course which Chase advised Brooks to follow was that along which he himself tried to steer the Court in its troubles with the Radical Republicans in Congress.

of justice in lower federal courts, a claim whose legitimacy Congress has recognized by conferring on the Justices a broad rule-making authority. Furthermore, in exercising this traditional power the Court frequently has set standards for federal tribunals which go beyond the explicit criteria of statute law or formal rules. The Court has not yet claimed such supervisory authority over state judges, but the Justices are not as limited as normal practice might indicate. The Court's tactful formula used in reversing and remanding state court decisions is a diplomatic device, not a rigid legal requirement. The Judiciary Act of 1789 provided:[34]

> . . . the Supreme Court, *instead of remanding the cause for a final decision as before provided,* may at their discretion, *if the cause shall have been once remanded before,* proceed to a final decision of the same, and award execution.

The act of February 5, 1867 eliminated the words in italics and thereby the necessity for one unsuccessful remand.[35]

On several occasions when faced with lower court recalcitrance, the Supreme Court did proceed to enter or direct the entry of a final decree. In *McCulloch* v. *Maryland,* for example, the Court "Adjudged and Ordered":

> that the said judgment of the said Court of Appeals of the State of Maryland in this case, be, and the same hereby is, reversed and annulled. And this Court, proceeding to render such judgment as the said Court of Appeals should have rendered; it is further Adjudged and Ordered, that the judgment of the said Baltimore County Court be reversed and annulled, and that judgment be entered in the said Baltimore County Court for the said James W. M'Culloch.

The Justices followed a similar course in *Martin* v. *Hunter's Lessee* (1816) and *Gibbons* v. *Ogden* (1824). A less well-known case, *Tyler* v. *Magwire* (1873), gives an excellent example of the use of this power to counter lower court disobedience. Five years earlier, the U.S. Supreme Court had heard the Tyler case—a dispute over title to a tract of land along the Mississippi River—and had remanded the cause for "further proceedings" after deciding for the plaintiff. On remand, however, the Missouri supreme court dismissed the suit. This action, as Justice Clifford noted for the U.S. Supreme Court, "in effect reverses the judgment and decree which the mandate directed [the state judges] to execute. Argument to show that a subordinate court is bound to

108

proceed in such an event and dispose of the case as directed, and that they have no power either to evade or reverse the judgment of this Court, is unnecessary, as any other rule would operate as a repeal of the Constitution and the laws of Congress passed to carry the judicial power conferred by the Constitution into effect." Having framed the issue so starkly, the Court had no recourse but to take firm action. The majority opinion then went on to say that because it was "quite clear" that it would be "useless to remand the case a second time," the Court had to enter its own decree:

> ORDERED, ADJUDGED, AND DECREED, that so much of the decree of the Supreme Court of the State as dismissed the petition of the plaintiff be, and the same is hereby, reversed with costs. And it is further ordered, adjudged, and decreed, that the tract of 4×4 arpents claimed by the plaintiff . . . justly and equitably belongs to the plaintiff as alleged in his petition. . . .
>
> Wherefore, this court proceeding to render such decree in the case as the Supreme Court of the State should have rendered, it is ORDERED, ADJUDGED, AND DECREED, that the said tract of land . . . is hereby decreed to the plaintiff, and the rights, title, and interest of each and every one of said defendants, in and to said tract of land, is hereby divested out of said defendants, and each of them.
>
> AND IT IS FURTHER ORDERED, ADJUDGED, AND DE-CREED, that the plaintiff recover the possession of the said tract of land as herein meted and bounded, and that a writ of possession issue for that purpose in the usual form, directed to the marshal of this court, duly executed by the clerk, and under the seal of this court.

As revised in 1948, the sweeping authorization of the acts of 1789 and 1867 is found as Section 2106 of Title 28 of the *U.S. Code:*

> The Supreme Court or any other court of appellate jurisdiction may affirm, modify, vacate, set aside, or reverse any judgment, decree, or order of a court lawfully brought before it for review, and may remand the cause and direct the entry of such appropriate judgment, decree, or order, or require such further proceedings to be had as may be just under the circumstances.

It may be questioned whether this new wording allows the Court only to direct a state tribunal to make a specific judgment or whether it still permits the Justices to "enter" a final judgment themselves. Hart and Wechsler conclude that in conjunction with the All Writs Act (which I will discuss next), Section 2106 "would presumably confer no less authority than the Court had before the 1948 revision,"[36] and the Justices have indicated that they retain their old, plenary authority.*

Even if the Court could only direct a state court to enter a specific decree, the Justices' authority would still be sufficient to terminate most disputes since the Court also possesses power to issue a mandamus and to punish for contempt. The first Judiciary Act permitted the Supreme Court to mandamus only *federal* officials,[37] but this restriction has since been removed. The All Writs Act of 1948 provides: "The Supreme Court and all courts established by Act of Congress may issue all writs necessary or appropriate in aid of their respective jurisdictions and agreeable to the usages and principles of law."[38]

Disobedience of a mandamus would be punishable—just as would flagrant disregard of any Supreme Court order—as contempt of court. These are clearly extreme powers and neither has been or is likely to be frequently used. As Justice Jackson said for a unanimous Court in 1949, "As extraordinary remedies, they are reserved for really extraordinary cases."[39] The Court has rarely mandamused federal judges,[40] and has never yet mandamused a state judge. Nor has the Court yet held either a state or federal judge in contempt, although in the nineteenth century federal circuit judges on several occasions imprisoned state judges for disobedience.†[41]

* In *NAACP* v. *Alabama* (1964), a case which, because of the determination of Alabama judges to drive the NAACP out of the state, was before the Court for the fourth time, the Justices came close to asserting that they could still enter judgment themselves, even though the litigation had originated in a state tribunal. Speaking for a unanimous Court, Justice Harlan wrote: "In view of the history of this case, we are asked to formulate a decree for entry in the state courts which will assure the Association's right to conduct activities in Alabama without further delay. While such a course undoubtedly lies within this Court's power [citing *Martin* v. *Hunter's Lessee*], we prefer to follow our usual practice and remand the case to the Supreme Court of Alabama for further proceedings not inconsistent with this opinion. . . . Should we unhappily be mistaken in our belief that the Supreme Court of Alabama will promptly implement this disposition, leave is given the Association to apply to this Court for further appropriate relief."

There is no question of Supreme Court authority to enter a final order in a dispute originating in a federal tribunal. The Justices have exercised such power by virtue of their status as supervisors of the administration of federal justice. *Yates* v. *United States* (1958).

† Some questions have been raised about the circumstances under which the Supreme Court can legitimately mandamus a state court. See Henry Hart and

BARGAINING

Schelling's concept of the mixed-motive (rather than the zero-sum) game[42] may be helpful in analyzing the bargaining possibilities in inter-court relations. There may be present in the judicial process elements both of competition and co-operation. A Supreme Court Justice may succeed in obtaining his Court's endorsement of a particular policy; some lower court judges may strongly prefer opposing policy alternatives. Certainly this is a classic description of a conflict situation. On the other hand, whatever their differences, the competitors in this situation are all judges, partakers of the holy mysteries of the cult of the robe, competitors for power, whether they wish it or not, with legislative and executive officials. Judges have to keep in mind that the power which the Supreme Court loses may not accrue to their courts but to Congress or the executive department, or to some independent regulatory agency, or to state governors or legislators. For their part the Justices have to remember that a prolonged conflict with lower court judges may strengthen rival agencies of government and weaken the whole court system. Furthermore, a large-scale clash within the judicial system may encourage opposition to the Court's policy in other branches of government. The situation is further complicated by the dual character—state and federal—of the Supreme Court's bu-

---

Herbert Wechsler, *The Federal Courts and the Federal System* (Brooklyn: Foundation Press, 1953), pp. 420–21. See also *Ex parte Texas* (1942); Comment, "Jurisdiction of the Supreme Court To Issue a Mandamus to a State Court," 20 *Tex. L. Rev.* 258 (1942). The U.S. Supreme Court in *Fisher* v. *Hurst* (1948), refused to issue a mandamus to the Oklahoma supreme court but on the grounds that the original mandate had not been disobeyed; neither the majority nor dissenting opinions questioned the Court's authority to issue the writ if disobedience had been shown.

Chief Judge Magruder's opinion in *In Re Josephson* (1954) has an excellent historical summary of the statutes and practice regarding the use of mandamus by the Supreme Court to control lower federal courts. Magruder concluded that the All Writs Act had "withdrawn from the Supreme Court its special appellate power to supervise proceedings in the lower federal courts by means of the writ of mandamus. . . ." Nothing would seem further from the truth; it is difficult to imagine a more blanket authorization than that provided in the All Writs Act. In 1951, Richard F. Wolfson concluded (though without specific mention of the All Writs Act) that the Court's mandamus authority was "practically limitless"; the problems in its use were problems of discretion rather than authority. "Extraordinary Writs in the Supreme Court since Ex Parte Peru," 51 *Col. L. Rev.* 977, 991 (1951).

111

reaucracy. In a sense these two branches of the judicial department are also competing for power with one another as well as with the Supreme Court and the other agencies of government.

The presence of elements both of conflict and co-operation makes it rational for the judges to play for lower stakes than if they were participants in a simple two-sided game. In this situation, the winner in an all-out struggle may not take all but in fact may lose something. Thus bargaining, with each set of judges giving something and gaining something, might be a more prudent course for both sides than open conflict, even though there would always be a risk that it would not result in a net gain for either's policy objectives. Generally, a Justice would find bargaining a particularly attractive alternative where lower court opposition to his policy would receive heavy support from powerful interest groups and from the legislative or executive department, or where his Court was under serious attack from an aggressively led branch of government, or where the cases involved were important but not crucial to his policy objective and he wished to concentrate his other resources on the settlement of different problems.

Distance makes negotiation between courts more difficult than between associates, but tacit bargaining would still be quite feasible. A reversal situation is replete with opportunities for diplomacy as well as tacit bargaining. The vague remand formula for returning reversed cases to state courts, "Reversed and remanded for proceedings not inconsistent with this opinion," and the frequently equally inexplicit directions to federal judges, both give these officials an opportunity to bring their policies closer in line with those of the Supreme Court, without necessarily forcing them into a tight mold of uniformity.

The doctrine of equitable abstention has a similar potential.[43] Under this doctrine, federal courts, even where their jurisdiction is clear beyond doubt, are instructed not to rule on the constitutionality of ambiguously worded state statutes or orders until state courts have first had an opportunity to pass on the regulations. Use of this device gives state judges a chance to declare the acts invalid or to construe them so as to moot a constitutional challenge. The Justices thus avoid a federal-state clash at the price of losing an immediate opportunity to formulate a constitutional rule for the nation. State officials lose part or all of their policy but gain in that they themselves withdraw, thus avoiding both an absolute veto from the Supreme Court and a blow to their pride in being told what to do by federal officers.

112

In a diplomatic way, the Justices may also inform judges that they understand and sympathize with lower court problems but at the same time expect a modification, if not a complete reversal, of policy. In 1927, when faced with a mandamus petition against an overworked district judge who had been ignoring two of the equity rules which the Supreme Court had prescribed for federal courts, Taft provided an excellent example of strong but tactful long-distance negotiation. In his opinion for a unanimous bench, the Chief Justice pointed out that the charge against the judge was essentially correct. Then he continued:[44]

> We are not inclined to infer that there has been any deliberate abuse of discretion in this matter or to hold that there may not sometimes be such a congestion in the docket as to criminal cases as would justify a district judge in not literally complying with the requirements of the two rules in question. There has been an emergency due to a lack of judges in some districts which we can not ignore. We shall therefore deny leave to file this petition, but are content to state our views on the general subject, with confidence that the district judge will be advised how important we think these two rules are, and that we intend, so far as lies in our power, to make them reasonably effective. . . .

STAFFING THE COURTS

As in appointments to the High Bench itself, having a voice in the selection of lower court judges would allow a Justice to reduce the amount of bureaucratic friction to which his policy might be exposed. It takes, of course, a peculiar set of political circumstances for a Justice to be able to exert a major influence in the appointing process—close ties with the President and the Attorney General and his deputies as well as a situation in which these officials are both willing and able to accept the Justice's advice. A Justice would have to possess a peculiar set of skills in order to take full advantage of favorable circumstances. Apparently many Justices* have played at least a sporadic role in

---

* There are scattered letters in the Chase, Sutherland, and Stone Papers indicating that they occasionally offered advice to executive officials—or their advice was solicited by executive officials. Reading the letters of the latter two Justices has left me with the impression that they considered it part of their job to give such advice when it was sought—if not to offer it when it was not sought. It is also probable that Chase, Field, and Miller tried to influence judicial appointments. See Charles Fairman, *Mr. Justice Miller and the Supreme Court*

choosing lower court judges, but William Howard Taft has left the most complete record of operations directed toward this goal.

Shortly after he became Chief Justice, Taft told a friend that he thought he had "established a very pleasant relationship with the Attorney General and with the President. The Attorney General assures me that he expects to talk with me all the time about the selection of Judges, and I am very sure of what he says. . . ."[45] Taft was soon writing Daugherty on a "Dear Harry" basis[46] as he bombarded the executive department with suggestions for court appointments. Hardly a vacancy occurred anywhere on the federal bench without the Chief Justice actively intervening.

Before making his recommendations, Taft often solicited the advice of lawyers, politicians, newspapermen, family, and friends. While his own candidates did not always get the nomination, Taft was usually able to block the appointment of people to whom he objected. It was inevitable, however, that the Chief Justice's standards would differ from those of the senators and that the President would have to choose between the two. Furthermore, as Taft himself realized, his persistence in injecting himself into the appointing process (often without invitation[47] despite what he thought was an understanding with Daugherty) irritated the President. This irritation was undoubtedly aggravated by newspaper reports that Harding had given the Chief Justice authority to select judges. "I think," Taft mused in early 1923, that the President "has grown a little sensitive about the constant reports that the matter is in a way delegated to me."[48]

During Harding's last months in office, the Chief Justice was aware that his influence was waning,[49] and, when Coolidge became President, Taft tried to re-establish his advisory position. He went to Harding's funeral with Coolidge, and on the funeral train he discussed an appointment problem with the new Chief Executive. When they returned to Washington the Chief Justice called on Coolidge at his hotel to complete the conversation. "I hope," Taft wrote the President a few days later regarding a South Carolina judgeship, "that you will permit me to write you on questions of this sort, where I may have any means of information, because of my intense interest in securing

---

1862–1890 (Cambridge, Mass.: Harvard University Press, 1939), pp. 341, 370–71; Carl Brent Swisher, *Stephen J. Field* (Washington, D.C.: Brookings Institution, 1930), chap. 12; David Hughes, "Salmon P. Chase: Chief Justice," esp. chap. iii.

a good judiciary, and my earnest desire to help you in your manifold labors when I can be of assistance in a field like this one."⁵⁰

Coolidge did not reply to this letter, but in answer to another note regarding a Missouri judgeship, the President apologized for his oversight and indicated that Taft had scored an initial success. "When your notes come to me, sometimes I put them aside in my desk for my private information, so that I am afraid they do not get the proper acknowledgement. You will know, of course, that they are all the more welcome for being of that nature."⁵¹

By the beginning of Coolidge's second term, Taft again felt his influence ebbing, and for almost two years he largely stayed out of appointing politics. He blamed his loss of power on Attorney General Sargent—"stupid and slow"⁵²—and on "the vicious disposition of [Republican] Senators to use appointments to the Bench for their own political purposes."⁵³ Soon, however, the Chief Justice was lured back into the struggle and was once more fighting, though not always successfully, to get the "right" men appointed or promoted.

Two case studies can illustrate the role Taft attempted to play in the appointing process. One of these cases involved both the Harding and Coolidge administrations, the other only that of Coolidge. While it is impossible to characterize either as typical of the appointing process itself, each is quite typical of the sort of activity in which Taft was constantly engaged.

The Problem in St. Louis.—The Judiciary Act of 1922 established a new district judgeship in St. Louis, and the filling of this vacancy created a thorny problem. Senator Selden P. Spencer, a Republican from Missouri, began to push as his candidate a state circuit judge named Vital Garesche. Taft, however, distrusted Garesche. Moreover, he had his own candidate for the position. Almost nine months before the 1922 legislation was enacted, the Chief Justice had promised President Lowell of Harvard that he would support George Hitchcock. Hitchcock, Taft wrote, "would make a first class judge. It would gratify me much if he could be appointed. . . . I am not infrequently consulted, and if I am, I can put in a very strong word for him, as I shall be delighted to do."⁵⁴

When the Chief Justice heard of Spencer's candidate, he took immediate action. On January 6, 1923, he sent Harding a letter warning him that there was a complex piece of bankruptcy litigation pending in St. Louis and that the next district judge would have to appoint a receiver to handle very large sums of money. "I have observed," Taft cautioned, "great activity on the part of men, who are interested in that litigation, to secure Garesche's appointment." The Chief Justice enclosed a clipping from the *St. Louis Star* and communications from several people in St. Louis, including a letter from U.S. Circuit Judge William S. Kenyon, who stated that Garesche was "a political judge, he is a man who uses his influence on the Bench to secure support, and he is a man to punish his enemies." Taft ended his own letter with an apology for intrusion into the affairs of the executive department: "Of course, you have more evidence on the subject than I have, but I venture to think that some people tell me more frankly the situation than perhaps they do you, and I have thought it my duty to bring this matter to your attention."

Two weeks later the Chief Justice wrote a similar though shorter letter to the Attorney General. For some reason, perhaps Taft's intervention, Spencer's pressure was checked; but when Harding died the vacancy was still unfilled.

Spencer lost no time with the new President. He went on the funeral train with Coolidge and reopened the possibility of an appointment for Garesche. Unfortunately for Spencer, Taft was riding on the same car, and he took Coolidge aside and stated his case against Spencer's man. It was to press his argument against Garesche that Taft visited Coolidge at the Willard Hotel on their return to Washington.[55] When the interview was over the Chief Justice was certain that Garesche would not get the nomination.

Spencer, however, was busily claiming that Garesche would be the new federal judge; and Casper Yost, editor of the *St. Louis Globe-Democrat,* wrote Taft a worried letter on September 15, 1923. In his reply the Chief Justice gave a full account of his conversations with the President, and he reassured Yost that "from his remarks I inferred that the situation was not that which Spencer would like to have it understood to be." Taft observed with approval that Yost had personally written Coolidge, and added: "I think the more people that you send him to protest against the appointment, with a full explanation of the character of the candidate, the better it will be."[56]

Meanwhile, Taft had written a number of his other friends about Garesche, and he forwarded their replies to Warren F. Martin, Special Assistant to the Attorney General. But the Chief Justice knew that to attack Garesche was not sufficient. He had to press his own candidate.

He had already spoken to Coolidge about Hitchcock, and on October 6, 1923, he forwarded the President an endorsement of Hitchcock by Federal Judge Walter Sanborn of the Eighth Circuit, whom Taft described as "the Senior Circuit Judge of the country, and one of the best Judges we have had."

There the matter stood for another three weeks. Then Harry Daugherty got in touch with Taft to ask his views on a man named Hogan, the son-in-law of a prominent Missouri politician. Taft, in turn, wrote to Yost and to U.S. District Judge Charles B. Faris[57] requesting advice about the new candidate. Yost quickly replied that, in his opinion, Hogan was "morally better than Garesche [but] he is even less competent."[58] Yost also reported that he had heard that Spencer was saying that Hitchcock was "personally offensive." Since this objection from a member of the President's party would block senatorial confirmation, it made, if true, any additional efforts to secure Hitchcock's nomination futile. As other possibilities, Yost included the names of four local lawyers, Davis, Grimm, Hamilton, and Hill, whom he thought highly qualified for the judgeship.

The Chief Justice told Yost that he had sent this information "to a place where it would do the most good,"[59] probably to the Attorney General, for on the same day Taft gave Daugherty some confidential material on Hogan, concluding that "he is even worse than Garesche." Taft also included some comments about three "good" candidates, Davis, Hamilton, and Grimm. Taft must have had some source of information other than Yost about these lawyers because on the day before he received Yost's comments on them he had written to Yost, to Judge Faris, and to T. J. Akins, also of St. Louis,[60] asking their opinions of the three men. A short time thereafter, Taft corresponded with former Governor Herbert S. Hadley—who had been one of Roosevelt's floor managers at the 1912 Convention and was now Chancellor of Washington University at St. Louis—regarding Hitchcock and the four Yost had mentioned.[61]

On November 16, Taft wrote again to Faris and Yost and told them of a conversation he had had the day before with the Attorney General. It now seemed that the President would appoint neither Garesche nor Hitchcock. Daugherty mentioned as a fresh possibility Forrest Donnell, who had earlier been Spencer's partner. The closeness of this relationship worried the Chief Justice. Yost, however, was most reassuring. He stated that Donnell had "a reputation for integrity and ability.

... I do not believe that Donnell could be used by Spencer or any one else."[62]

In spite of his frequent statements that he was certain the President would not name Garesche, Taft periodically reminded Coolidge of Garesche's lack of fitness. In November, Taft sent the President an editorial from the *St. Louis Post-Dispatch* attacking Spencer's candidate and in December the Chief Justice forwarded a letter which Harding had written explaining why he had decided against Garesche.[63]

Just after Christmas, Congressman C. A. Newton of Missouri confided to Taft that Senator Spencer had "stated that he can not agree to the appointment of any man whose name has been mentioned because he wants the man who gets the appointment to feel that he owes the appointment to him, the Senator. . . ."[64] Taft could only answer stoically: "I have done everything I could and there is nothing left for me to do now but to wait and pray."[65] In the privacy of his family, the Chief Justice was less restrained. He exploded to Horace Taft that Spencer was "full of pious unction, unscrupulous, a liar, immoral, certain never to be returned from Missouri again, but earnest and desperate in demanding the appointment of a United States Judge whom he can control in St. Louis, and rejoicing in the importance that the present financial crisis [a bill for immediate payment of World War I bonuses was before the Senate and the vote was expected to be very close] gives to every Senatorial vote." Drawing perhaps on his own unhappy experiences in the White House, Taft added despondently that "every President finds it necessary, to accomplish the greater thing, to yield to the blackmailing of unscrupulous Senators."[66]

The Chief Justice was overly pessimistic. Judicial virtue was not to be trampled underfoot, at least not in this instance. Spencer could block Hitchcock's appointment, but he was not able to get Garesche nominated. Instead, Charles Davis, a state circuit judge and one of the men Yost had suggested as highly qualified, became the compromise appointee.

Eastern District of North Carolina.—In 1924–25 Taft played an even more positive part in selecting a new judge for the Eastern District of North Carolina. The incumbent, H. G. Connor, planned to retire in 1925; in late 1924 Colonel Isaac M. Meekins, then counsel for the Alien Property Custodian and a former U.S. Attorney in the Taft administration, wrote the Chief Justice to request his assistance in securing the appointment. Taft remembered—or at least was reminded by Charles D. Hilles, his former White House secretary who was now chairman of the finance committee of the Republican National Committee—that at the 1912 Republican Convention, Meekins had been one of the uninstructed delegates whom the Roosevelt forces had tried to capture. Meekins, however, had stood firmly for Taft despite all sorts of promises and threats.

As did every vacancy on the federal bench, this one caused a scramble, but here the Department of Justice had a freer hand since neither North Carolina senator was a Republican. As Meekins visualized the situation, there were three candidates besides himself: George E. Butler, a local attorney; H. F. Seawell, former U.S. Attorney; and I. B. Tucker, the current U.S. Attorney. The Colonel sent Taft a concise evaluation of each of his rivals. Seawell was a Populist; Butler had been a Roosevelt supporter; and Tucker was sound, but lacked experience.[67]

The Chief Justice quickly endorsed Meekins. He wrote Attorney General Stone on November 23, 1924: "My own judgment about North Carolina is that the best man to appoint is Colonel Meekins. . . . I should be glad to talk to you about this matter when the opportunity offers." A week later Taft reported to Meekins that he had talked with the Attorney General twice about the appointment and there did not appear to be too much agitation. The Chief Justice also stated that he had contacted Hilles "and asked him to write the President. . . . I am going to see the President tomorrow morning, and shall talk with him about it."[68]

On the same day that Taft reported to Meekins, Hilles told the Chief Justice that a letter from George Wickersham, who had been Taft's Attorney General during Meekins' tenure as U.S. Attorney, would help, and suggested that Taft should arrange this. Hilles also said that he had been in touch with Congressman Bertrand Snell, chairman of the House Rules Committee and an Amherst classmate of Harlan Stone. "I think," Hilles wrote, "that Snell will help us."[69]

Back in North Carolina, U.S. Attorney Tucker was shaping up as the most formidable opponent. Assistant U.S. Attorney General Rush Holland was backing Tucker,[70] as were State Circuit Judge Henry Grady and several influential political leaders including North Carolina National Republican committeeman John J. Parker—though Meekins had obtained a statement from Parker expressing no objection to his candidacy.[71]

Judge Grady and Sophia Burber, who had been Judge Connor's private secretary for twenty-one years, each wrote Taft endorsing Tucker's candidacy and asking the Chief Justice's assistance.[72] Taft candidly replied to both that he had already recommended Meekins.[73] To Grady the Chief Justice added the righteous reminder that "these appointments are made by the President and recommended by the Attorney General. I can only indicate my judgment when called upon."

After finishing this letter to Grady, the Chief Justice dictated another to George Wickersham asking him to write Coolidge in support of Meekins. A few days later, Taft, at Meekins' request,[74] called Warren F. Martin, Special Assistant to the Attorney General, and got him to arrange a meeting between the candidate and Senator F. M. Simmons of North Carolina. The Chief Justice also told Meekins, who was then in New York, to go to see Wickersham so that the former Attorney General might refresh his memory and compose a stronger letter to the President.[75] Meekins and Wickersham had their conference, and Wickersham sent a laudatory endorsement to Coolidge.[76]

Taft saw Stone again about the appointment around New Year's, and put the Attorney General in touch with Wickersham, who straightened out several questions about Meekins' service during the Taft administration.[77] In early January, 1925, Meekins was nominated for the judgeship, and, with the endorsement of North Carolina's Senator Lee Overman, his appointment was swiftly confirmed by the Senate.*

* On December 7, 1924, *The Charlotte Observer* carried a page one story that Taft was trying to get Meekins appointed. After the nomination was announced, H. F. Seawell wrote to the Chief Justice taking him to task for his opposition. Seawell asked: "Must I expect your personal opposition to any of my ambitions to serve my country and the generation in which you and I live?" Jan. 23, 1925, William Howard Taft Papers, Library of Congress. Taft answered that Seawell was mistaken about his attitude. He had not opposed anyone in North Carolina; he had simply supported the man whom he had thought best for the job. If another vacancy occurred, the Chief Justice promised, "you could become a candidate without any adverse recommendations from me, should I be consulted. . . ." Jan. 20, 1925, *ibid.* There is an obvious discrepancy in dates here. Taft's secretary probably meant Jan. 30, 1925.

Ideology, Publicity, and Influence

Taft's announced criteria for supporting a judicial candidate were integrity and professional competence, but ideology could well play a role in the Justice's selection, as indeed it may have in Taft's. Bringing to the bench men who agreed with his policy objective would reduce some of the Justice's problems with the lower judiciary, and having a voice in the promotion of judges already on the bench could further reduce his problems. As in all organizations, there is a danger in the judicial process of conflict not only between the formal strata of authority but also between formal and informal hierarchies. That is, it may happen that lower court judges would respect more, and prefer the views of, one of their own number, a Learned Hand or a Benjamin Cardozo, for example, to those of the Supreme Court.

An astute Justice who has influence in the appointing process might use that influence to reduce this latter kind of conflict by trying to reward with promotion those judges who have enthusiastically followed his policies and by trying to prevent the promotion of those who have been less eager to carry out his wishes. To be most effective in this respect the Justice's influence in judicial selection would have to become known, at least to federal judges. Thus, while news leaks about Taft's work in staffing the courts may have irked the White House, these leaks may have helped motivate ambitious lower court judges to conform closely to the Chief Justice's conservative standards of judicial statesmanship.

III INCREASING FRICTION

Chapter i stated, as one of the assumptions on which this book was based, that a Justice would identify his own policy goals as tied to the preservation of the power of the Court. That chapter also pointed out, however, that it would often be difficult for a Justice to work to overturn a specific decision or set of decisions without injuring or risking injury to the prestige of the Court. Stirring up resistance among lower court judges so that a policy to which he was opposed would become practically unworkable is an obvious means a Justice might consider using to move his brethren to adopt his own policy.*

* One method of stirring up such resistance would be to emphasize in a separate opinion the unfairness of the burden which the majority is about to place on trial and appellate judges.

It is evident that any such strategy is fraught with danger. It is dangerous to the Justice's position within the Court since his colleagues may take such a pronouncement as an act of institutional disloyalty. It would be dangerous to the possible future success of his own policies, since once stirred up bureaucratic resistance may not immediately disappear after it has performed the function which the Justice intended. Moreover, it could be dangerous to the prestige and general power of the Court in encouraging not only additional bureaucratic opposition but also attacks from disaffected interested groups and rival government officials.

If a Justice were to decide that he could utilize such an approach without injuring the Court—or his position within the Court—he would have to act most cautiously, and he would probably think it best to operate as informally as possible. Chief Justice Chase followed a course after the Test Oath cases—cases in which he had been in the minority—which narrowly skirted the edge of encouraging resistance. Instead, he merely urged a narrow interpretation of the majority opinion. In reply to a query from District Judge Robert A. Hill of Mississippi, the Chief Justice wrote: "The decision of the majority of the Court is law until reversed and you do right in conforming your action to it. [But] I do not regard it as denying the right of Congress to require the oath as a prerequisite to entering on the duties of an officer where the appointment has been made [under] the act: but only as denying the right to impose the oath as a condition of continuing to occupy an office. . . ."[78]

5 The Political Checks: Securing Positive Action

In analyzing the problem of minimizing the effect of political checks on his policy-making power, a Justice would have to make plans for two different kinds of general situations. In the first, he would need positive congressional or executive action to achieve his policy objectives; in the second, he would find it necessary either to prevent Congress or the executive department from acting to impair the chances of attaining his goals or to lessen the danger to his policy from action already taken by one of these other branches of government. This chapter will be concerned with the task of securing positive action, the next chapter with that of preventing or reducing the effects of hostile political action.

I CONGRESS

Where achievement of his policy goals would require positive congressional action, a Justice might be fortunate enough to find that a coincidence of interest had already or was in the process of moving Congress to do what the Justice wanted. Or, the Justice might find an older congressional statute which he could reasonably interpret to embody his policy preferences. In a series of cases in the 1940's and 1950's, for instance, the Court held that Congress in the Railway Labor Act of 1934 had forbidden railroad brotherhoods to discriminate against the job rights of members of minority races.[1] Three of the Justices protested in vain that their more egalitarian brethren had in effect enacted a limited FEPC statute. A sufficient number of additional examples, such as the Court's reading of the "rule of reason" into the Sherman Act[2] and its conclusion that Congress in the Smith Act had meant to preclude the states from punishing sedition against the United States,[3] could be listed to show that this sort of strategy is often feasible. But in using this approach a Justice would have to be wary that a working majority of Congress was not actively opposed to his policies or could not be pressured into opposition by an active interest group. A new law abruptly and summarily reversing a piece of statutory interpretation could do serious harm to his policy.

Under the best of conditions, securing new congressional legislation is a most difficult task. A Justice could seriously hope to do so only when the interests of a working majority of congressmen coincided with or were indifferent to or were only mildly opposed to his own. Even close coincidence of interest would not be a sufficient condition to insure congressional action if a well-led minority, protected by seniority, were firmly opposed. If, however, new legislation was vital to the Justice's objective and he had some real chance of success, he would have little choice but to try to move Congress to act.

His strategic alternatives for such a task would be relatively narrow. He could hope to persuade congressmen of the desirability of the sort of action he wanted, or he could place the Court—assuming always in the discussion in this chapter that he could obtain the approval of a majority of his associates—in a position in which it would suffer great harm if Congress did not come to its aid. He would be gambling, of course, that even though members of Congress were not enthusiastic about his policy, they would assist the Court because they felt a moral obligation to do so, or because they feared their constituents would punish them at the polls if they did not rescue the Justices.

Although this latter alternative might be effective in forcing a President's hand, its use would be extremely dangerous in dealing with Congress, where both power and responsibility are badly fragmented. A Justice would probably find this course safe only where public opinion was thoroughly aroused and strongly in favor of his policy. But in such a case it is likely that congressmen would be acting whether or not the Court were risking its prestige, though such a strategy might succeed in spurring members of Congress to move faster.

Persuasion on the merits would under most circumstances be the only strategic alternative really open to a Justice. Fortunately for a policy-oriented member of the Court, a myriad of tactics, ranging from sweet reason to a "trap pass" to lobbying in the grand manner, are available to "persuade" congressmen to act.

REASON AND THE CLIMATE OF OPINION

As a group, senators and representatives are very intelligent, well-educated men, and most of them are no less open than judges to persuasion by intellectually respectable arguments. Carefully written and reasoned opinions would thus again be an important means of influencing official behavior, and the opinion need not be one speaking for the Court. Perhaps the best example of Congress being moved to action was provided by Justice Rutledge's minority opinion in *Yakus* v. *United States*. In this case six Justices sustained the constitutionality of the provision in the Emergency Price Control Act of 1942 which conferred jurisdiction on federal and state courts to try violations of OPA price ceilings but denied these courts power to inquire into the validity of the particular regulations. Instead Congress had provided a separate administrative procedure, ultimately reviewable by the Supreme Court, to challenge the legality of any specific price ceiling. Rutledge filed a long dissenting opinion in which he argued that Congress could control jurisdiction but could not prescribe the grounds on which a court could decide a case once jurisdiction had been granted:

> It is one thing for Congress to withhold jurisdiction. It is entirely another to confer it and direct that it be exercised in a manner inconsistent with constitutional requirements or, what in some instances may be the same thing, without regard to them. Once it is held that Congress can require the courts to enforce unconstitutional laws or statutes, including regulations, or to do so without regard for their validity, the way will have been found to circumvent the supreme law and, what is more, to make the courts parties to doing so. This Congress cannot do.

At the time *Yakus* was decided, the banking and currency committees of both houses were considering renewing the price control law, and Rutledge's eloquent dissent moved a number of congressmen to press for serious procedural revisions. While perhaps the new statute did not meet all of the Justice's objections to the 1942 act, it did establish more liberal procedures for challenging the constitutionality of price regulations and explicitly stated that a decision that a regulation was invalid would be a defense against charges of violating the act.[4]

Congressmen may also be vulnerable to emotional appeals, especially when they suspect that those same appeals may be arousing their constituents. Justice Clark's dissent in *Jencks* v. *United States,* for instance, helped excite Congress to "protect" the records of the Federal Bureau of Investigation. In *Jencks* the Court ruled that a defendant should have access to FBI files to examine earlier statements which prosecution witnesses had made about him to government officials. The majority believed that only if he were allowed this opportunity could defense counsel adequately cross-examine and impeach the credibility of prosecution witnesses testifying about events which had occurred years earlier.

In spite of the fact that several years earlier the most staid of authoritative commentators, the annotation editors of the Lawyers Cooperative Publishing Company, had noted that the trend of American law was in the direction which *Jencks* would actually take,[5] Justice Clark found the decision "a new rule of evidence foreign to our jurisprudence." Directing his remarks to Capitol Hill, he predicted:

> Unless the Congress changes the rule announced by the Court today, those intelligence agencies of our Government engaged in law enforcement may as well close up shop, for the Court has opened their files to the criminal and thus afforded him a Roman holiday for rummaging through confidential information as well as vital national secrets . . . and persons conversant with federal government activities and problems will quickly recognize that it opens up a veritable Pandora's box of troubles.

Foes of the Warren Court quickly picked up Clark's charge, and it was reprinted in literally hundreds of newspaper editorials and echoed and re-echoed in congressional debate.[6] Within three months new legislation modifying *Jencks* was on the statute books.*

Formal speeches provide a means of informing and persuading congressmen by reason and/or emotion. Justices are frequently asked to address law school forums, bar association meetings, academic gatherings, and public ceremonies, and to write for legal and popular publications. These speeches, like official opinions, may be directed more at Congress than at the immediate audience; they may also be invitations,

---

* Although successful here, Clark's tactics may often cost more than they gain. Such an open plea to another agency of government to reverse the Court may conceivably violate prevailing norms of institutional loyalty and destroy a Justice's influence with his associates. We lack, however, sufficient empirical data to know if the Justices in fact do draw a line against outside appeals, much less knowledge as to where such a line might be located. See similar discussion in chap. iii.

as were several of Chief Justice Taft's addresses, for the audience to pressure Congress to take some specified action. Historically, one of the common ways of securing measures to reform judicial procedure has been for a Justice to use the opportunity of a public speech to plead with Congress to adopt new legislation.[7]

Congressmen are amenable to reason and sometimes vulnerable to emotional appeal, but being subject to the check of the ballot box means that they are not always as free as judges to vote according to their convictions or their feelings. Reason and emotion may be completely persuasive to a representative or senator and not move him to take any action other than swallowing an antacid pill to soothe his physical reactions to the conflict in his value system, if he feels his constituents would be aware of, understand, and disapprove of the line of action he wished to take. The general climate of popular opinion must be, then, a prime target of judicial strategy, if congressmen are to be induced to act officially as well as to agree in private.

Once again formal opinions are one way of creating such a climate. Marshall's opinions in cases like *McCulloch* v. *Maryland* and *Gibbons* v. *Ogden* were effective arguments for national supremacy. "All wrong, all wrong," John Randolph lamented, "but no man in the United States can tell why or wherein."[8] By mapping out a vast domain of congressional authority—authority which took precedence over any conflicting state claims—Marshall in effect issued not only an open invitation for Congress to assert its supremacy but also a widely-read justification for such action. Other Justices have tried, though usually with less skill, to emulate Marshall's long-range accomplishments.

Public speeches and writings can also be important influences on the general climate of opinion, a fact which the Justices have realized since they first held court in the last decade of the eighteenth century.[9] A Justice can, as John Marshall did, use available newspaper space to answer critics of Court decisions.[10] He may make more basic appeals, as Brewer so often did, to leaders and members of interest groups to support his general political theory. Repeating a familiar theme on and off the bench, Brewer time and again tried to persuade audiences that the fundamental problem in American politics was the protection of private (i.e., corporate) property from government regulation.

Most broadly, a Justice may write scholarly treatises on public law or explore some facet of history or biography. There is a long American tradition of such writing, stretching from Marshall's biography of

Washington to Story's and Baldwin's opposing commentaries on the Constitution, to Miller's *The Constitution of the United States*,[11] to the first Harlan's lectures on law, through the contemporary legal writing of William O. Douglas. "The crucial point," one close student of the Justices' out-of-Court writings has concluded, "is that these commentaries were not narrow and neutral presentations of case law,* but broad defenses of the constitutional position of the author-Justice."[12]

A Justice's ability to appeal directly to enlightened segments of the public is only one aspect of the public relations of all political life. No policy-maker in his right mind would deny the importance of a "good press." For one thing, a Justice might write his opinions with clarity and verve. It is not impossible to put together opinions which are technically correct and still intelligible to non-lawyers, and a shrewd Justice would realize that his objective can often be promoted more by a facile phrase like "the power to tax is the power to destroy" or "clear and present danger," than by pages of esoteric legalisms. These latter, too, may be important as public relations tactics to gain or maintain a reputation for professional craftsmanship, but sole or too frequent reliance on them may estrange the Justice from a powerful source of support.

For another thing, a Justice might time decisions which were important to his cause so that reporters would have an opportunity to read and digest the opinions and newspapers a chance to give each case some prominent space. Most simply, this would mean not handing down four or five important cases on a single Monday or allowing an important case to be buried under opinions in a dozen or more unimportant decisions.

A Justice might also encourage his friends among reporters and popular writers to support in print his policies, or he might make friends with influential writers. It is not at all unlikely, of course, that a Justice would know many such people and pass on his views to them. Chase, for instance, made persistent efforts to insure that his newspaper acquaintances published his reactions to contemporary problems.[13] Stone's close relations with Felix Frankfurter (who during the 1920's

* I would make one exception. Though by no means narrow, Douglas' *We the Judges* (New York: Doubleday and Co., Inc., 1956) meets all the professional criteria to qualify as a scholarly presentation of the basic principles of American constitutional law.

and 1930's often wrote for popular journals), Irving Brant, and Marquis Childs are matters of public record, as is their sympathy at the time for Stone's constitutional philosophy. On at least two occasions Stone tried to persuade Frankfurter and Childs to write articles for general consumption expounding his (Stone's) brand of jurisprudence, and it is possible he exerted a similar influence on his other friends.[14] Frank Murphy's author friends, at least those with whom he corresponded, were less famous than Stone's, but the Justice did occasionally circulate his published opinions to newspapermen and magazine writers.*

THE "TRAP PASS"

The Justice may feel that while existing statutes could be interpreted in ways which would gain some ground for his policy, full attainment of his goals would necessitate congressional action and that, given the contemporary climate of political opinion, congressmen might feel heavy constituent pressure were the existing statutes not functioning as a safety valve. Under such circumstances a Justice might resort to a tactic similar to the trap pass in bridge and interpret existing statutes so narrowly as to render them ineffective in the hopes of forcing fresh legislative action.

Ten weeks after America entered World War II, the Court decided *United States* v. *Bethlehem Steel Co.,* a case growing out of the government's long efforts to recover allegedly excessive profits on World War I shipbuilding. (Bethlehem had made a 22 per cent profit on the cost of constructing vessels, plus an additional profit from selling itself the necessary steel.) Speaking through Justice Black, a majority of the Justices denied that these gains were illegal under existing statutes. Such profits, Black admitted, "may justly arouse indignation. But indignation based on the notions of morality of this or any other court

---

* As in all matters of political strategy there are dangers in dealing with writers. Since authors are notorious for liking to think themselves intellectually independent, a Justice would have to be most cautious in whom he approached, usually limiting himself to those who would be most apt to agree with him already. There is the further possibility that a writer might use the Justice rather than vice versa, and the even greater danger of a story boomeranging to hurt the Justice, as happened when Stone injudiciously told Marquis Childs of his low opinion of Justice Black.

cannot be judicially transmuted into a principle of law of greater force than the express will of Congress." In closing Black added:

> The problem of war profits is not new. In this country, every war we have engaged in has provided opportunities for profiteering and they have been too often scandalously seized. . . . To meet this recurrent evil, Congress has at times taken various measures. . . . It may be that one or some or all of these measures should be utilized more comprehensively, or that still other measures must be devised. But if the Executive is in need of additional laws by which to protect the nation against war profiteering, the Constitution has given to Congress, not to this Court, the power to make them.

The Court thus dumped the whole question of the legality of war profiteering back into the lap of Congress and compelled legislators to take another long, hard look at the problem. With American casualty lists mounting and with millions of young men being torn from their families and jobs by the draft, war profiteering was not an issue on which many congressmen who were fond of their jobs could remain neutral, whatever their views on the merits of the problem. The congressional reaction in passing the Renegotiation Act of 1942 was as rapid as it was predictable.*

In a similar fashion, Frankfurter may have tried (but if so he failed to persuade his colleagues) to interpret narrowly the Jones and Federal Employer Liability acts and, by refusing to correct judicially the injustices inherent in these antiquated statutes, to force Congress to adopt more modern—and effective—employer liability legislation to protect injured workmen. As he noted in 1949, protesting against a decision interpreting the statutory term "accident" to include an occupational disease:[15]

> I think I appreciate the humane impulse which seeks to bring occupational diseases within such a [statutory] regime. But due regard for the limits of judicial interpretation precludes such free-handed ap-

---

* There is a strong possibility that here, as in some of the other examples cited in this book, at least a few of the Justices were quite aware of the power implications of their actions. John P. Frank, Justice Black's biographer and former clerk, has stated that Black's opinion "was so written as to come close to inviting Congress to take comprehensive action to control profits." *Mr. Justice Black: The Man and His Opinions* (New York: A. A. Knopf, 1948), p. 205. Certainly Black has never been noted as a man favoring an unregulated economy, nor is he habitually unable to interpret statutes broadly when he feels strongly about an issue.

plication of a statute to situations outside its language and its purpose. To do so, moreover, is, I believe, a disservice to the humane ends which are sought to be promoted. Legislation is needed which will effectively meet the social obligations which underlie the incidence of occupational disease. . . . The need for such legislation becomes obscured and the drive for it retarded if encouragement is given to the thought that there are now adequate remedies. . . . The result of the present decision is to secure for this petitioner the judgment which the jury awarded him. It does not secure a proper system for dealing with occupational diseases.

Use of Dicta

Dicta in an opinion can be used not only to persuade Congress to act or to help establish a climate of opinion in which Congress can act, but can also be used to try to guide the action which Congress will take.[16] In writing for the Court, or for a minority, in a case holding a federal statute unconstitutional or interpreting it to deny its effective application to the problem at hand, a Justice can point out another way in which the same general purpose could be accomplished.

In 1922 *Hill* v. *Wallace* invalidated the Future Trading Act of 1921, a congressional effort to curb speculation in grain futures through the imposition of a tax of 20 cents per bushel on contracts for future delivery. Speaking through Chief Justice Taft, the Court found that such a use of the taxing power was an invasion of the reserved authority of the states. Taft, however, told his brother the morning the decision was announced that he was convinced that Congress could regulate such practices.[17] And he inserted in his opinion for the Court a sketch of how a new statute might be cast: "It follows that sales for future delivery to the Board of Trade are not in and of themselves interstate commerce. They can not come within the regulatory power of Congress as such, unless they are regarded by Congress, from the evidence before it, as directly interfering with interstate commerce so as to be an obstruction or a burden thereon. . . . But the form and limitations of the act before us form no such basis . . . for federal jurisdiction and the exercise of the power to protect interstate commerce."

Congress responded by passing four months later a new statute, this one expressly declaring that speculation in grain futures was adversely affecting interstate commerce. When this second statute was challenged, the Court, again speaking through Taft, sustained the exercise of congressional power, pointing out: "The Grain Futures Act which is now before us differs from the Future Trading Act [of 1921] in having the very features the absence of which we held in somewhat carefully framed language of the foregoing quotations prevented our sustaining the Future Trading Act. . . . [T]he [1922] Act only purports to regulate interstate commerce and sales of grain for future delivery . . . because it finds that by manipulation they have become a constantly recurring burden and obstruction to that commerce."[18]

The Chief Justice was proud of his work in these two cases. As he told his son:[19]

> Today I decide one of the most important cases that I have had to dispose of. . . . I decided the stockyards case [*Stafford* v. *Wallace*] last year, and now this comes up this year, and I think I have carved out a view of interstate commerce which is useful for the purpose of bringing within Congressional control the real centers of our interstate and foreign commerce. How valuable in results the control by Congress may be we can not guarantee—that is not our business—but we shall have put the power where in substance and real effect under the Constitution it ought to be.

PERSONAL CONTACT

In addition to or instead of using opinions and public speeches to nudge Congress, a Justice may talk directly—and privately—to legislators. A number of Justices have been senators, and most members of the Court have had long experience in practical politics and have accumulated uncollected IOU's. A telephone call, a conversation at a dinner party, a simple and straightforward request may recall old debts and induce a member of Congress to push for legislation. In return, the Justice, if he still has influence with other politicians, may be of further assistance to the member of Congress. Taft, for example, tried (although unsuccessfully) to get Senator McKinley of Illinois renominated in 1926, and in 1924 the Chief Justice used his contacts to assist in a minor way Coolidge's nomination and election.[20]

In the same fashion, a Justice may utilize his influence within the executive department to push for congressional legislation. Taft worked closely with the Department of Justice in trying to reform the judicial system[21] and even drafted that portion of Coolidge's 1923 message to Congress which dealt with the judiciary.[22] Much more subtly, Harlan Fiske Stone encouraged Secretary of Labor Frances Perkins in her work for social security legislation. "I had said to him," Miss

Perkins has written, "that I had great hope of developing a social insurance system for the country, but that I was deeply uncertain of the method since, as I said laughingly, 'Your Court tells us what the Constitution permits.' Stone had whispered, 'The taxing power of the Federal Government, my dear; the taxing power is sufficient for everything you want and need.' "[23]

A Justice may also work with interest groups such as bar associations, using them as levers to move Congress. As Taft confided to a friend before leaving to attend the 1923 American Bar Association meetings:[24]

> I deem this one of the most important extra curriculum things that I have to do as Chief Justice. I want, so far as I can, to organize the bench and the Bar into a united group in this country dedicated to the cause of improvements in the judicial process and in the defense of the constitutional provisions for the maintenance, through the judiciary, of the guaranties of the Constitution. There is no reason why the Bar should not exert a tremendous influence through the country. Its organization is necessary to bring about such a result.

Taft did more than merely talk about the importance of the bar. He attended ABA meetings as long as he was able, and when his health restricted his travels he encouraged other Justices to go in his place.* He also maintained constant touch with Thomas Shelton, one of the southern lawyers who dominated the ABA's policy-making, and discussed with him matters of legislation and judicial appointments. In addition, the Chief Justice tried on several occasions to act as a power behind the scenes in ABA politicking and to choose the association's president.

A Justice may also try to build up rapport with individual congressmen. In his efforts to secure passage of the Circuit Court of Appeals Act of 1891, Chief Justice Fuller carefully cultivated members of the Senate Judiciary Committee.[25] Taft, of course, was always extremely sensitive to personal relations. In 1923 when Frank Brandegee became chairman of the Judiciary Committee, the Chief Justice wrote him: "I am glad you have come to the head of the Judiciary Committee, and I hope that you will find it possible to give much time and energy to helping the administration of justice in the Federal Courts. I think a

---

* He even went in 1927 to ABA meetings at Buffalo, although he knew that his health was so poor that he could not afford the expenditure of energy.

great deal can be done there, and that the people will be very grateful if you can initiate it and carry it through. I would like to talk with you on the general subject when I reach Washington."[26]

At the same time, Taft wooed and won over his old enemy from 1912, Senator Albert B. Cummins of Iowa. After the Chief Justice put his charms to work, Cummins, a ranking member and later chairman of the Judiciary Committee, not only did not oppose Taft's legislative proposals but actually sponsored and doggedly fought for them. After Cummins' death, when George Norris became chairman of the committee, Taft swallowed his bitter contempt for the Progressive leader and went out of his way to establish and maintain cordial relations with him.

The Chief Justice was also solicitous of Hatton Summers, a Democrat on the House Judiciary Committee, and was soon writing him as "My dear friend." In June, 1926, Taft invited Summers to visit him at Murray Bay, Canada, and later that summer the Chief Justice wrote to congratulate Summers on his renomination: "I am greatly tickled that you were nominated by such a thumping majority. It shows that the Fifth District in Texas knows a good man when it sees him, and has the sense to understand that if it wishes to exercise real influence, it must take a man of high character and ability and then keep him where he is. . . . I am delighted that you are coming back."[27]

The following year, when Summers went on a European tour, Taft gave him letters of introduction to a number of foreign dignitaries as well as American ambassadors. Later, during Hoover's administration, the Chief Justice tried to help Summers get appointed to the Wickersham Committee. "He has whispered to me," the Chief Justice confided to the Attorney General,[28] "that he would like to be on that commission, and for the reasons that I advanced to Mr. Wickersham, I think that if it can be done, it would be a great help to the commission to have his influence and his activities in the matter. His standing in the House is such that it would at once give real Democratic support and sympathy for the workings of the commission. I am quite sure that Justice Van Devanter will agree."*

A Justice may take the very bold step of trying to select the personnel

---

* Taft was unsuccessful. He explained to Summers: "My dear friend: I am quite sure that the Administration will not select any member of Congress or any official for that commission. I think that this is a mistake. . . ." Taft to Summers, May 20, 1929, William Howard Taft Papers, Library of Congress.

of the judiciary committees of Congress, though this would seem to be a dangerous, even a foolhardy step. Taft, however, felt he should make such an effort during his first year on the Court. Writing to Henry Cabot Lodge, Senate Majority Leader, the Chief Justice said:*[29]

> I wish to urge that if it is possible, George Pepper be put on the Judiciary Committe of the Senate. It seems too bad that two of the leading lawyers of the Senate should not be on that Committee, to wit, Frank Kellogg and George Pepper. . . . I am writing to Frank Brandegee [chairman of the Republican Committee on Committees] about it, too, with the hope that between you, you could arrange something so that these two men could be at the source of legislation.

Lodge was courteous, though very discouraging in his reply. Brandegee, on the other hand, delivered a condescending lecture on Senate protocol in selecting committees.[30] Taft replied to Brandegee that he had not intended "to put so much trouble upon you. . . . I realize the difficulty there is, and that usually the men who are least fitted for the Judiciary Committee are the ones who seek it the most. If they cannot get a reputation as lawyers in any other way, they think this will help them."†[31]

LOBBYING

The seriousness of his need for a new statute and favorable conditions of personal access to a number of influential legislators might combine

---

* It should be noted that in 1922 Senators Borah, Norris and Walsh—later also Selden Spencer and Thaddeus Caraway—were on the Judiciary Committee. With some risk of understatement, it may be said that Taft detested all of these men.

† In 1927 Taft complained to Thomas Shelton: "The truth of the matter is that the Republicans seem to dodge the [Senate] Judiciary Committee, and the Progressives are stronger in that committee than on any other one. The real Republicans seem to be dodgers of any responsibility. It is quite evident that Brother Norris is very confident, if only he can get a good lawyer on the committee, that he can moderate everything to his desire, but in hunting a good lawyer they will have to go outside the Senate." Taft to Shelton, Dec. 14, 1927, Taft Papers.

Taft was not the first, and probably not the last, Justice to complain of the quality of personnel on the judiciary committee. In 1872 Justice Miller wrote that it was "the damnedest nuisance the Congress presents. Every man on it thinks himself the embodiment of constitutional wisdom and statesmanship, and each is jealous of the others." Charles Fairman, *Mr. Justice Miller and the Supreme Court 1862–1890* (Cambridge, Mass.: Harvard University Press, 1939), p. 404.

to make it feasible for a policy-oriented Justice to engage in a systematic lobbying campaign. The history of the Court is spotted with instances which range from merely drafting a bill, as Story did in 1816, to stalking the halls of Congress buttonholing individual congressmen as well as wining and dining them to obtain their votes.

During Reconstruction, several Justices, including Chase, Miller, and Field,* pressed congressmen hard for a bill to create an office of circuit judge and thus give the Justices some relief from circuit riding. The final statute, the Judiciary Act of 1869, was in part drafted by Field and Miller.[32] In 1866 Chase suggested to some of his friends that Congress might curb Andrew Johnson's appointing power by providing that no vacancies on the High Bench should be filled if the total number of Justices should exceed seven.[33]

In the winter of 1870–71 Chase helped prepare a bill to raise judicial salaries and liberalize retirement benefits. Since the Chief Justice was still recovering from the effects of a stroke, the burden of drafting the measure and lobbying for it fell on Richard C. Parsons, marshal of the Supreme Court.[34] The resulting statute did improve salaries, but not as much as Chase had hoped it would. The following year found Miller again drafting and pushing a bill to secure further relief from circuit riding and to reduce the kinds of cases which the Supreme Court had to take on appeal. The Judiciary Act of 1875 carried out some of Miller's proposals, but it was not until after his death that the act of 1891 established an intermediate federal appellate court to take much of the burden off the High Bench.[35]

In 1893, Chief Justice Fuller sent to the Senate, at the request of the chairman of the Judiciary Committee, a draft of another jurisdictional proposal,[36] and the Judiciary Acts of 1915, 1916, and 1925 were written by members of the Court.[37] Congress has now to a great extent institutionalized judicial participation in the legislative process where court matters are concerned by: (1) allowing the Justices to prescribe, with only a minimum of congressional supervision, rules of procedure for federal constitutional tribunals; and (2) establishing the Judicial Conference of the United States and enjoining it to recommend needed statutory changes to Congress.

While one would suspect that a Justice's lobbying would be most effective where judicial matters were concerned, not all members of the Court have restricted themselves to pressing only for bills of special

---

* Chase also asked Davis and Swayne to pressure their friends in Congress.

concern to the court system. Chase was extremely worried about the development of Reconstruction policy and, the Attorney General noted, the Chief Justice "leaves the Court daily to visit the Senate."[38] Chase's burning desire for Negro suffrage and a tough line toward the southern states involved him in the drafting of the Fourteenth Amendment. Eventually one of his suggestions was embodied almost verbatim as section 2 of the amendment and the essence of another in section 4.[39]

In 1881, Justice Field gave further evidence of his deep interest in the problem of Chinese on the West Coast by lobbying vigorously for Senate approval of a treaty with China to limit immigration. According to his biographer, the Justice went around Washington "looking up Senators, and for days he made it a point to be always on hand to explain away doubts and settle questions of international law."[40] In this century Stone took an interest in several pieces of legislation; and, as one would expect, Taft found it difficult to keep his hands off any important question of public policy.

Perhaps a detailed case study of one phase of Taft's lobbying for a judiciary act would provide a clear picture of the range of possible tactics open to a Justice. When he became Chief Justice, Taft saw that the federal court system was in need of a drastic overhaul if it was to perform its functions as the protector of property rights and as the linchpin of conservative government. The Supreme Court's docket was so jammed with cases, and the district courts were so hopelessly swamped with litigation, that Taft's dream of government by the judiciary was a practical impossibility.

In the Chief Justice's view three basic reforms were necessary to remedy the situation: (1) an increase in the number of trial judges and the establishment of a centralized system of judicial assignment and administration; (2) a simplified set of rules for trial procedure, with the Supreme Court rather than Congress having primary responsibility for formulating and modifying these rules; and (3) a severe curtailment of the mandatory jurisdiction of the Supreme Court with a consequent increase of its discretionary jurisdiction via the writ of certiorari.[41] With these three objectives clearly before him, Taft set out to get the appropriate legislation through Congress.

Since I have published elsewhere[42] a lengthy narrative of Taft's participation in the drafting and enactment of the bill to increase the number of federal judges and to establish a judicial conference, the bill which later became the Judiciary Act of 1922, and since his tactics

137

in striving for the two other objectives were very similar,* only an account of Taft's work to streamline Supreme Court jurisdiction will be given here.

Within a few weeks after he was appointed to the Court, Taft was consulting and corresponding with the Attorney General, laying the groundwork for his program. Shortly thereafter, in August, 1921, even before he had yet presided over a meeting of the Court, the Chief Justice began to beat the bushes for professional support for his three point scheme. Addressing the judicial section of the American Bar Association, he gave the first of a series of speeches stressing the dire need for his reform proposals and urging lawyers to assist in obtaining the necessary legislation.[43]

As soon as the Justices assembled in Washington for the October 1921 term of the Court, Taft appointed a committee composed of Justices† Day,‡ Van Devanter, and McReynolds to draft a new juris-

---

* The Judiciary Act of 1934, 48 Stat. 1064, which finally gave the Court authority to prescribe a full set of rules of procedure for all federal constitutional courts represented the culmination of Taft's lobbying for simplified procedure. His activity for this bill—which he drafted in part—differed from the others only in that he relied more heavily on lobbying by representatives of the American Bar Association and that he was unable to persuade Congress to act during his lifetime.

† In his memorandum of May 11, 1927 (now in the Taft Papers), designed to refresh the Chief Justice's memory so that he could reply to a query from Professor Frankfurter, who was then preparing with James M. Landis *The Business of the Supreme Court,* Van Devanter emphasized that the Justices had begun work on the bill at the invitation of Senator Albert Cummins of the Senate Judiciary Committee. (See also Van Devanter's testimony before the Senate Judiciary Committee, below, p. 143.) In Floor debate, however, Senator Cummins said only: "I introduced this bill at the suggestion of the members of the Supreme Court." 66 *Cong. Rec.* 2754. While I cannot document my belief, I think that either (1) Taft maneuvered Cummins into tendering the invitation; or (2) Taft interpreted some general comments which Cummins had made as a specific invitation and so informed his colleagues. I believe that with or without an invitation, Taft would have pressed for such legislation. My belief is reinforced by Van Devanter's repeated reminder to Taft of the ethical problems posed by judicial involvement in the legislative process. Taft, however, did say to Van Devanter in 1927 that the Justices "acted on the suggestion of the Senate Judiciary Committee that we prepare a bill. . . ." Taft to Van Devanter, Feb. 21, 1927, Taft Papers.

‡ Day retired shortly after joining the committee. He had been in poor health during most of the 1921 term and it is improbable that he had played

138

dictional bill. The committee members asked Taft to join them, and, it may be surmised, he was easily persuaded. In 1922, when Sutherland came to the Court, Taft put the ex-senator to work by also assigning him to the committee, even though the drafting had been largely completed.

On December 4, 1921, Taft alerted Solicitor General James Beck to the fact that the judges' committee was at work on a bill and asked for comments on a rough draft of the proposal. Beck, however, wanted to follow the suggestion of the ABA's Committee on Jurisprudence and Law Reform[44] to increase the size of the Court to eleven Justices, with nine sitting at any one time and two writing opinions.[45] Taft was somewhat taken aback by the suggestion and quickly talked the matter over with Beck. After this conversation, the Chief Justice tried to prevent any possible misunderstanding by sending the Solicitor General a letter pressing the Court's plan. "I hope you will examine with some care the bill that we are taking a good deal of time to prepare. . . . We are all convinced that the only way to help the situation is to enable us to reduce our jurisdiction by cutting off more writs of error and by the extension of the writ of certiorari."[46]

Taft's protests apparently stopped Beck's plans, and the Justices proceeded with their own project. Later in December, the Chief Justice laid some additional public relations groundwork. Speaking to the Chicago Bar Association, he asserted that existing statutes governing Supreme Court jurisdiction posed two dangers to an efficient judicial system. First, they were so complex and scattered that they were now "almost a trap to catch the unwary."[47] Second, they were forcing the Justices to take more cases, many of them trivial, than they could possibly intelligently decide. What was needed, Taft said, was a codification of jurisdictional regulations and a drastic curbing of the Court's mandatory jurisdiction. The Chief Justice then told his audience that "some of us" were drafting a bill to accomplish these purposes. "Congress," he noted, "has shown itself in the past quite willing to follow suggestions with reference to such changes in [the Court's] jurisdiction as may enable it to keep up with its work, and I hope that we shall find Congress in the same attitude of mind when this bill is perfected and introduced."[48]

---

a major role in the drafting. Van Devanter was undoubtedly the chief architect of the bill.

On February 17, 1922, the Chief Justice sent a copy of the completed Judges' Bill to Senator Cummins and to Representative Joseph Walsh of Massachusetts. The two legislators immediately introduced the measure,[49] and the next day Taft made a formal speech to the New York County Lawyers' Association extolling the merits of the plan.[50] In taking up and passing the proposal to increase the number of district judges, Congress was giving as much attention to the judiciary as it cared to devote, and little was done in that session on the Court's jurisdictional proposal other than desultory hearings by the House Judiciary Committee.

The Chief Justice was irked at this inaction, and he put the blame on the personal spite of the Progressives. "Of course," he told an old friend, "Norris and Borah and Johnson and La Follette are all against it [the Judges' Bill], as they are against everything I like, partly because we do not agree on anything, and partly because they like to defeat a measure of which I am a sponsor. However, I am so used to being beaten in elections and in measures which I favor that I try not to allow it to enter much into my happiness or lack of it."[51]

Taft appeared at the House hearings in March, 1922, and formally presented his views. Since this overt lobbying failed to achieve a catalytic effect, he turned to more covert methods. In early April he went over to the House and talked to several influential legislators. When he returned to his home on Wyoming Avenue, he wrote letters to the Speaker of the House and the chairman of the Rules Committee, enclosing copies of his statement before the Judiciary Committee. "This is the bill," the Chief Justice said, "of which I spoke to you this morning, and in the passage of which I solicit your assistance."[52]

Still nothing happened. Taft waited a decent interval, and then in June, after consulting with his friend Representative Walsh,[53] applied more pressure. Assuming that Walsh would be able to get the bill out of the Judiciary Committee, the Chief Justice looked ahead to the next legislative hurdle. He wrote to House Majority Leader Frank W. Mondell: "The Court is very anxious to have the bill, which it has prepared with great care, given a rule, so that it may be considered in the House. . . . May I count on you?"[54] Taft told the chairman of the Rules Committee that Walsh would call on him to discuss the Judges' Bill. "I hope that your committee will think it wise to give the rule."[55] The Chief Justice also again contacted Speaker Gillett: "I want to enlist your aid in securing a rule for the bill defining the jurisdiction of the Supreme Court. . . . If it gets through the House, I shall make an effort to get it up in the Senate."[56]

Despite this additional prodding, the House took no action. Indeed, the Judiciary Committee did not even report the measure. Taft then carried his fight to the public. In August, 1922, he spoke to the ABA's annual meeting,[57] explaining the necessity of reform, criticizing alternative suggestions, and praising the advantages of the plan set forth in the Judges' Bill. In this address the Chief Justice once more candidly acknowledged that a committee of the Justices had drafted the bill, and he used this admission to emphasize the fact that the Justices thought a crisis in judicial administration was approaching.

The ABA, which had earlier endorsed legislation to abolish the Writ of Error,[58] now also recommended that its Committee on Jurisprudence and Law Reform—a committee which included among its members Henry W. Taft, the Chief Justice's brother—should work to secure passage of the Judges' Bill.[59] But this boost came too late in the session to have any effect on Congress, and the short fall session was too hurried for further action. Taft, however, was not discouraged. After all, in September the additional judges-judicial conference bill had become law and his new jurisdictional proposal was still very much alive. In February, 1923, he told his brother that he doubted if "the present Congress will do anything with the bills* I had introduced, but I mean to help it up, because that is the way to get things through Congress."[60]

In December, 1923, Taft inveigled Coolidge into letting him draft for inclusion in the President's State of the Union message a plea for Congress to enact the Judges' Bill.† To counter this victory came a danger signal from within the Court. Justice Brandeis had begun to express doubts about the prospects of comprehensive reform and suggested instead several minor bills to take care of "odds and ends."[61] The Chief Justice—who suspected that Brandeis' doubts were not all

* Also S. 2061 to give the Supreme Court increased authority to formulate rules of procedure for lower federal courts.

† On Nov. 15, 1923, Daugherty wrote Taft: "The Memorandum you sent to the President was fine. I will talk to him about it. I must see you in the next day or two." Coolidge's message to Congress is printed at 65 *Cong. Rec.* 98. The Chief Justice told his son: "I wrote a part of his [Coolidge's] Message— that is I wrote a passage to be embodied in his Message, which he cut down some, but in effect he has put in all of my recommendations." Taft to Robert A. Taft, Dec. 2, 1923, Taft Papers.

intellectual—urged his colleague to wait. "It is quite possible that we should come to the piecemeal bills of which you speak, but I don't want to adopt that policy until the House is organized and we know who the Judiciary Committees are, and until I have talked with the Chairmen of both of them. The President in his message is going to recommend legislation in respect to the Supreme Court. I drafted something for his compression, and I am informed it is going to appear in the message. So let's wait and see."[62]

Once again the wheels of Congress began to grind, and the Senate Judiciary Committee scheduled hearings for early February, 1924. Taft confided to his younger son that he was relying on Senator Cummins to get the bill through. "I am not sure what Frank Brandegee [chairman of the Judiciary Committee] will do, but I think he is ambitious to be useful and that we can count on his service."[63] Cummins' first piece of advice to the Chief Justice was that he send other members of the Court to testify at the hearings rather than come himself. ". . . some of my old enemies on the committee," Taft mused, "rather resent my being prominent in pressing legislation. . . . I am delighted to escape the friction of that kind of contact, and in incompassing legislation I can not afford to ignore the irrelevant reasons of the small minded."*[64]

Taft asked Van Devanter, McReynolds, and Sutherland to represent the Court at the Senate hearings. Each had been a member of the Judges' Bill committee, but the Chief Justice had other reasons for making the selection—reasons which no doubt he had also considered in putting each man on the drafting committee: "McReynolds has been a Democrat and knows many of the Senators. Sutherland has been a Senator, and Van Devanter is one of the most forcible of our Court and most learned on questions of jurisdiction."[65] In requesting his colleagues to appear, Taft took the further liberty of sketching the shape their testimony might take—though with the diplomatic concession: "You will know better than I what to dwell on, but I make these suggestions because of my talk with Senator Cummins."[66]

* In late January, Thomas Shelton spoke to Cummins and urged that Taft appear at the hearings. Taft immediately wrote to Shelton to give him the reasons why he should not testify and also wrote to Cummins to assure him that Shelton had spoken without authorization. Taft to Shelton and Taft to Cummins, Jan. 31, 1924, Taft Papers.

The hearings took place on February 2, 1924, with Van Devanter carrying the brunt of the Court testimony. The Justice gave a full explanation of the jurisdictional changes which the Judges' Bill would effect and pressed the same two lines of argument which the Chief Justice had advanced in his speeches: the need for codification of the scattered statutes and the even greater need for the Court to be able to reject the piddling claims which were so frequently brought before it as a matter of right. At the beginning of his testimony Van Devanter emphasized that the Justices had reluctantly entered the legislative arena:[67]

> Mr. Chairman, this bill is one which has received the consideration of the several members of the Supreme Court; not that they would wish to step into the legislative field or that they would presume to suggest a course of legislation, but they were asked by some members of the Judiciary Committee of the Senate and the House to present their observations and to outline something that would better meet the existing situation than the present statutes. It is only in this way that they have taken the matter up.

Later Van Devanter gave a bit more information on the background of the plan:[68]

> The bill was prepared just as it is here by members of the Supreme Court, all participating at one time or another. A committee was appointed to consider the subject, in response to requests from some members of the Judiciary Committees of the Senate and the House. After this committee of the Supreme Court had gone over the subject they reported it to all the members of the Court, in conference, and the matter was gone over several times and the draft revised until it came to represent the composite judgment of the members of the court as to what would operate well for litigants and at the same time enable the court to discharge in an appropriate way the functions which rightly belong to it.

McReynolds, Sutherland, and Shelton followed Van Devanter but were able to add little to his testimony on the Judges' Bill. After the hearings Thomas Shelton of the ABA wrote Taft a full account of the proceedings, saying that Van Devanter had been "most impressive."[69] Shelton also enclosed the results of a straw poll of the committee: six

143

senators were in favor of the bill, four opposed, and six uncommitted, two of whom had been opposed to it in 1923.*

The Judiciary Committee filed a favorable report on April 8, 1924,[70] but once more the bill bogged down. In November, Taft again prodded his friends in Congress with pleas to support the legislation.[71] The Chief Justice also had some suggested changes to make in the bill itself, and he forwarded these to Senator Cummins[72] and to Representative George S. Graham, chairman of the House Judiciary Committee.[73] Meanwhile, Taft made preparations for the coming House hearings. He sent Graham seventeen copies of the Senate remarks of Van Devanter, McReynolds, and Sutherland so that the House committee would have advance notice of the kind of testimony which would be offered; and, as in previous years, Taft was looking beyond the committee stage to the problems of getting a rule.

Just at this time, Brandeis began to express fresh doubts about the bill. He was particularly worried about what the Chief Justice might say at the coming hearings. Despite his personal misgivings, which he described as "grave," Brandeis said that he would remain silent and that he thought it would be proper for Taft to say that "the Court approves the bill—without stating whether or not individual members approve it. For, in relation to proposed legislation directly affecting the Court, the Chief Justice, when supported by a clear majority, should be permitted to speak for it as a unit; and differences of view among its members should not be made a matter of public discussion."[74]

Taft thought that Brandeis' doubts were due to his close friendship with Senator Thomas Walsh of Montana, who was leading the opposition to the Judges' Bill. The Chief Justice commented to his older son that Brandeis "tries hard to be a good fellow but he misses it every little while."[75] Taft, however, soon had reason to be grateful for Brandeis' willingness to suppress his opposition. At the hearings, Representative Michener asked the direct question:[76]

*	*For*	*Against*	*Uncommitted*
	Brandegee	Caraway	Borah
	Cummins	Shields	Norris
	Colt	Walsh	Stanley
	Ernst	Reed	Sterling
	Overman		Ashurst
	Spencer		Shortridge

144

Mr. MICHENER. Is it the judgment of each individual member of the Supreme Court that this legislation should be enacted?

Chief Justice TAFT. Well, I am told by all the members that I can say that the court is for the bill. There may be one member—I do not think there are more—who is doubtful about it, or, I should say, doubtful as to its efficacy; but he said to me that I could say the whole court were in favor of the bill. The only question that he has is as to how far this will be effective to accomplish all that we hope for.

Justice VAN DEVANTER. I want to say that some have thought it ought to go farther than it does. . . .

After almost four years of relative indifference to the Judges' Bill, Congress suddenly began to move swiftly. The House Judiciary Committee favorably reported the measure on January 6, 1925;[77] and on February 2, the House by voice vote passed the measure, almost without discussion.[78] There was considerable debate in the Senate, but Taft took two additional steps to insure passage. First, he sent a series of letters to Senator Royal Copeland (letters which Copeland printed in the *Congressional Record*) in which the Chief Justice tried to refute some of the more serious objections to the reform proposal. More important, Taft agreed to a compromise with Senator Walsh whereby two minor, clarifying amendments were added to the bill.[79] (Interestingly enough, Cummins told the Senate that the changes had the approval of the Justices and Walsh.[80]) Thereupon Walsh not only ceased his opposition, but defended the bill in the last stages of debate and actually voted for it.[81] When the final vote was taken on February 3, the measure passed by a thumping majority of 76–1.[82]

Needless to say, Taft was delighted, though he regretted the time he had had to take from his Court work to lobby. He told his sons: "We got our Supreme Court bill through this week, and we are greatly rejoiced. We mollified Walsh and by a slight concession [actually two] secured his assistance. . . . I have had to give up three full days this week to do it. . . . Brandeis was reluctant, but we ran over him. He evidently sympathized with Walsh."[83]

II THE PRESIDENCY

As in his relations with Congress, a Justice might find that in some circumstances he needs presidential action to execute his policies or to defend the Court or its policy choices against attacks from other political officials or against hostile public opinion. While the same general strategic alternatives are available to a Justice as in obtaining legislative action, there are some important variations due to the peculiar nature of the executive branch of government.

PLACING THE COURT IN JEOPARDY

If extraordinary presidential assistance were needed to carry out a judicially ordained policy, a Justice might simply allow the Court to plunge ahead where he calculated that the President would be forced to come to the judiciary's assistance. The first factor which might impel the Chief Executive to come to the Court's aid would be a coincidence of interest, either in regard to the particular policy involved or a more general value. The most common situation in which extraordinary executive aid would be needed would be one in which state officials would be resisting execution of a Court decision. Here the President and his aides, regardless of their views on the desirability of the particular policy involved, might perceive an overriding interest in preserving national supremacy. A second factor which would strongly motivate a President to help the Court would be his feeling—or that of his advisers—that he had a moral obligation to rescue the Court. A third factor would be a fear that a significant portion of the electorate would believe such an obligation existed.

While the concentration of both power and responsibility in the executive branch makes this in many ways a less risky strategy than in dealing with Congress, it can still be a dangerous one. A Justice must be sure of the real—as opposed to the merely publicly announced— policy preferences of the President and of the aides on whom the President is most likely to rely for advice. Obviously, if the Justice's policy coincides with that of the President, he is much more likely to come to the Court's assistance than if their goals are mutually incompatible.

The Justice must also have accurate information about the President's conception of his office as well as about the intricacies of any particular political situation. A President like Eisenhower, who time and again repeated the simplistic notion that it was his duty to enforce the law as interpreted by the Court regardless of his personal beliefs,[84] would be more apt to think he was duty-bound to assist the judiciary than would a President whose concept, like that of either

Roosevelt, of his office was much more complex and sophisticated. Similarly, a Kennedy, heavily dependent on the Negro vote, might find it politically expedient to use federal troops to crush state defiance of civil-rights decisions, while an Andrew Jackson,[85] deeply concerned to prevent the spread of a subversive doctrine like nullification, might be willing to pay a price in judicial humiliation to attain what to him were more important goals.

PERSUASION

As always persuasion would be an important element in any strategic plan. It may take the form of an intellectual or emotional appeal. It may be directed specifically at the executive department, at particular interest groups, or at public opinion generally in the hope that pressure will be exerted against the administration. It may be contained in a Court opinion, a public speech, a message relayed through mutual confidants, or in private correspondence or conversation. The Justice may help persuade the President, directly or indirectly, to adopt a new policy, or by legitimating an existing policy allow the Chief Executive —or provide an opportunity for presidential advisers, other officials, or interest-group leaders to pressure the President—to push for more aggressive versions of existing programs.

While a busy President probably has little time to read Supreme Court opinions or off-the-bench speeches of the Justices, many executive officials certainly do, and as a group they are probably no less open-minded than congressmen and only slightly less sensitive to currents in public opinion, though they are usually concerned with different kinds of currents.

As has already been indicated, where a Justice is intimate with the Chief Executive or trusted presidential advisers, he may press his arguments in a less formal fashion than in official opinions or public addresses. A number of Justices have had special advantages in being in a position to advise Presidents. Despite the Court's refusal to give George Washington an advisory opinion, John Jay offered the President the benefit of his wisdom on a variety of political problems[86] and, of course, served as Minister to England while still Chief Justice. For a short period, Chief Justice Ellsworth also served as John Adams' Minister to France, and for a briefer period John Marshall was Adams' Secretary of State *and* Chief Justice of the United States. President Monroe felt close enough to Justice William Johnson to ask for—and

147

to receive[87]—an advisory opinion on the constitutionality of congressional proposals to make internal improvements in the states. Andrew Jackson, according to Carl B. Swisher,[88] continued to consult with Taney after appointing him Chief Justice; and Justice Catron, after seeking the President-elect's aid in switching Justice Grier's vote in the Dred Scott case, helped Buchanan draft his comments on the slavery problem for his inaugural address.[89] Several of Lincoln's appointees remained on sufficiently intimate terms with the President to offer him advice[90]—much of it apparently unwanted and unheeded— and Chase was a frequent adviser to Andrew Johnson during the early days of his administration.[91] Theodore Roosevelt consulted with Moody,[92] his former Attorney General; and when the President urged Taft to accept an appointment to the Court, he implied that he was anxious to have Taft in Washington where he could be at hand to discuss political problems.[93] Vinson's friendship with Truman continued to be very warm after 1946, and according to newspaper reports the President frequently conferred with the Chief Justice on political problems.[94]

We have considerable documentation on the important advisory roles which Brandeis, Stone, and Taft played while on the bench. Brandeis was, according to Arthur Link, the "chief architect of the New Freedom. . . . The man whose opinions on economic questions [Wilson] respected above all others. . . ."[95] After his appointment to the bench Brandeis continued to advise the President, sometimes directly, sometimes through Josephus Daniels.[96] "I need Brandeis everywhere," Wilson remarked, "but I must leave him somewhere."[97] During the war Brandeis recommended Herbert Hoover's appointment as food administrator and McAdoo's appointment as director of the railroads. To Colonel House, Brandeis outlined a sweeping plan to end the crisis in munitions production, which, as he said, was "imperiling success abroad and also the ascendency of the Democratic Party upon which we must rely for the attainment of our ideals at home."[98] He also gave Hoover detailed instructions on how to handle the Russian question at the Paris peace conference, and the Justice spent part of the summers of 1918 and 1919 in London and Paris on Zionist missions, conferring with American and foreign diplomats. As Mrs. Brandeis commented in a letter to her sister, describing a visit from the President to the Brandeis home to discuss transportation problems: "Here surely was the scholar, the student at his work. And

148

yet it is as a practical man of affairs, a statesman, that Louis's advice is so much sought."[99]

Although probably not as influential with Hoover's administration as Brandeis had been with Wilson's, Stone maintained close contact with the White House from 1929 to 1933. Because of his long friendship with the Justice, the President-elect was in frequent touch with Stone during the transition period from November 1928 to March 1929, asking his suggestions about appointments and trying to get him to leave the Court and join the administration. During much of Hoover's presidency, Stone was a member of "Medicine Ball Cabinet," a group which met on the White House lawn and exercised together before breakfast. As the Justice once said, he and the President sometimes used these meetings to discuss public affairs.[100]

Again it was Taft who left the clearest records of his attempts to influence the executive. Not only did the Chief Justice keep up a barrage of notes to Harding, Coolidge, and their Attorneys General, but he was also a frequent visitor to the White House, constantly offering suggestions. His letters refer to such diverse matters as America's joining the World Court and the League of Nations, selection of an ambassador to Germany, appointment of a Secretary of the Navy, choice of a Governor General of the Philippines, enforcement of prohibition, not to mention judicial matters and personnel for the Department of Justice. On one occasion, Taft wrote Secretary of the Treasury Andrew Mellon urging him to recommend that the President veto six different pieces of legislation which Congress seemed likely to pass: (1) a tax reduction bill; (2) a proposal for immediate payment of World War I bonuses; (3) a bonus bill for Spanish-American War veterans; (4) increased appropriations for the army and navy (unnecessary, Taft said, because there was no chance of war with Japan); (5) an increase in the salaries of postal employees; (6) the McNary-Haugen bill—"wrong in economic principle, and a wasteful outlay that could do no good to anybody."[101]

As the Chief Justice told his son, "I cannot keep my mind out of politics, especially when I have no responsibility about it."[102] Taft's advice to Coolidge, when the new President was first worriedly assuming unfamiliar duties, could, with only a small touch of humor, be described as the classic example of a successful advisory opinion on general policy. Coolidge asked Taft what course he should follow in the White House. "I told him," the Chief Justice recounted a short time later, "that I thought the public were glad to have him in the White House doing nothing."[103]

INFLUENCE WITH LESSER OFFICIALS

While it helps if a Justice is an old friend of the President, the two need not have known each other intimately or even at all if the Chief Executive understands, sympathizes with, and respects the Justice's point of view. Personal contact can be begun or, if it is already established, supplemented through the use of emissaries. One effective way of insuring access to people close to the President—and therefore to the President himself—would be for the Justice to have his friends appointed (or to make friends with) presidential advisers. It may happen that without any effort on the Justice's part the President might appoint a friend—or friends—of the Justice. Where the Justice and the President are of the same party and political generation, the chances of such an occurrence are quite good, given the pre-Court political experience of most Justices. Of course, a Justice who was already in a position to influence the President—as, for example, Stone was with Hoover—would be much more likely to have a voice in naming subordinate executive officials.

In its most extreme form, this approach would require a Justice to try to surround the President with people who thought as the Justice did, so that the advice the Chief Executive would be most likely to trust would largely conform to the policies which the Justice wanted followed. Rexford Tugwell has claimed that Brandeis, working especially through Felix Frankfurter and Morris Ernst, tried to influence Franklin D. Roosevelt in precisely this fashion and in fact succeeded in honeycombing the executive department with friends and disciples.[104]

Tugwell's acceptance of mammoth business corporations as a fact of life which demanded equally large governmental operations ran directly counter to Brandeis' "curse of bigness" philosophy, and it may be that the bitterness of their disagreement has colored Tugwell's interpretation of the events of the first New Deal.* It is true, however, that

---

* Tugwell has supplied little documentary evidence for his assertion, but his general reasoning is supported, as he knew, by some of the material in the Franklin D. Roosevelt Papers at Hyde Park. The President received a number of letters from Norman Hapgood, an old friend of Brandeis and editor of *Collier's* when that magazine first published *The Curse of Bigness*, relaying comments about contemporary problems from "our friend from Cape Cod." Copies of these letters were sent to Brandeis and are now in the Brandeis

a very large share of the staffing of New Deal agencies was accomplished through Frankfurter and that these "Happy Hotdogs" included such influential presidential aides as Thomas Corcoran and Benjamin Cohen. Arthur Schlesinger, Jr., accepts it as true that Brandeis frequently pressed his theories of decentralized economic and political power on his followers in the administration and that at one point he even urged his followers to get out of Washington and back to the states, where he thought any true reform movement had to grow and flourish.[105] It is also true that Brandeis' cures for the Depression—vigorous antitrust action, fair trade laws, and government spending on public works programs—eventually triumphed in the second New Deal.

It might be prudent for a Justice to operate on a more modest scale and try to locate (or, again, make friends with) one or two people close to the President. Moreover, the White House is not the only place in the federal government where executive policy is formulated. A policy-oriented Justice may feel it only slightly less important to influence appointments of officials at cabinet rank and below, lest men unsympathetic to his goals be in these positions where they could frustrate his policy aims. Thus Taft tried to help Coolidge select an Attorney General and a Solicitor General;[106] and after his failure to get what he considered a good Attorney General for Coolidge, Taft was all the more insistent in naming Hoover's chief legal adviser.[107] Fear of what could happen even at the local level may also explain Taft's interest in the selection of U.S. Attorneys.

A Justice might also want to use appointing influence to reward men who have supported his policies or independently pursued similar goals, or he may wish to punish those who have opposed his views. Chase interceded with both Johnson and Grant for his friends,[108] and Field advised Cleveland on many appointments. Field explained to a confidant that he was using his influence to keep patronage away from men whom he described as of "communistic or agrarian views, thinking only those should hold office who believe in order and law and property and the great institutions of society upon which progress and

---

Papers at Louisville, Kentucky, but no notation was made on them as sent to the President indicating that Brandeis was also receiving copies. There are similar letters in the Roosevelt papers, though not so many, from J. L. Davis and from Brandeis' nephew, Louis B. Wehle. Josephus Daniels also reminded Roosevelt of Wilson's habit of obtaining Brandeis' advice on difficult problems and suggested that the President could profitably follow the same course.

civilization depend."[109] In fact, Field was more concerned with punishing enemies and rewarding friends who had affected his efforts to run for the presidency.

Taft's efforts to persuade Hoover to choose William Mitchell as his Attorney General provides an interesting example of the range of possible tactics in influencing executive appointments. Since he blamed Coolidge's Attorney General William Sargent for many "bad" appointments to the lower courts, Taft was particularly anxious that Hoover should be advised on judicial matters by a right-thinking man. The Chief Justice was concerned lest the post be given to William Donovan, a lawyer for whom he professed little professional respect ("a short horse," Taft called him), and a man, no doubt, with whom Taft did not expect to be able to work closely. For a few weeks after the 1928 election, the Chief Justice tried to drum up support for George Wickersham, but by late November he had decided that the current Solicitor General, William Mitchell, would be the best of the available candidates. Mitchell, like his old friend and former law partner, Pierce Butler, was a nominal Democrat; but Taft had such great faith in their fundamental conservatism that he strongly supported Butler's appointment to the Court and Mitchell's selection as Solicitor General.*

Soon after deciding on Mitchell, Taft asked his son, Robert, to try to talk to Hoover about the appointment.[110] Stepping up his campaign, the Chief Justice wrote Robert McDougal of Chicago that Mitchell was "a wonderful man" whose appointment as Attorney General would be Hoover's "greatest opportunity."[111] To Henry Chandler, owner of the *Los Angeles Times,* Taft coyly confided that he had an important suggestion for the new President's cabinet which he would like to make to Chandler, providing he could relay it to Hoover.[112] Chandler replied that he would be happy to pass the name on to the President-elect.[113]

---

* For Taft's intervention on behalf of Pierce Butler, see my "In His Own Image," 1961 *Supreme Court Review,* pp. 159–93, and the forthcoming book by David Danelski, *A Supreme Court Justice Is Appointed* (New York: Random House, 1964). Taft was also active on behalf of Mitchell: Taft to Attorney General Sargent, April 21, 1925; Taft to Horace Taft, March 22, 1925; Taft to Judge Arthur Denison, March 22, 1925, Taft Papers. One might surmise from the close relationship between Mitchell and Butler that Butler was influential in moving Taft to intervene so actively where Mitchell's interests were involved.

On Christmas Eve, the Chief Justice wrote Chandler a long letter extolling Mitchell's ability. "The Court has such confidence in him that it reads his briefs first in order to know what there is in the case." Taft admitted his obvious personal enthusiasm but claimed that in this regard "I represent the feeling of the entire Court. . . ."* In closing the Chief Justice added: "Now I mean myself to go to speak with Mr. Hoover, but what I would like to do is to stimulate you, who will advise Mr. Hoover, to inquire into the very exceptional qualities of Mr. Mitchell." A week later Chandler answered that he would do what he could to help.[114]

Meanwhile, Taft had also written George Wickersham and asked if he could not "do something to get to Hoover this conception?" Wickersham replied that he would do all he could, but doubted that Hoover even knew Mitchell. It seemed to Wickersham that Donovan was still the most likely choice.[115]

During much of this period Hoover was out of the country on a good will tour of Latin America; but, the Chief Justice knew, the President-elect had been in frequent contact with Justice Stone about appointments, and Taft was hoping that he, too, might get in on the consultations. He was finally able to do so on January 11, 1929. Two days later, the Chief Justice wrote his daughter a succinct account of the visit:[116]

> I went over to see Hoover Friday night to advise him about his Attorney General, but I am afraid he was not disposed to take, with the confidence that I think he ought, my recommendation. He has some rather grandiose views . . . and unless he changes his view he will find himself with a very poor Attorney General, with nothing like the capacity of the man he is looking for.

* Whether Taft could in fact speak for the Court can, of course, never be proved, but Justice Stone's opinion of Mitchell was very similar to that of the Chief Justice. On March 22, 1928, Stone wrote to John Foster Dulles: "I would say, all in all, no man who appears in our Court makes as satisfactory arguments as does he, or aids the Court so much. He is a prodigious worker and has done great things in the Solicitor General's office. . . . He has a striking quality of intellectual integrity and straightforwardness which has won the confidence of the Court to a remarkable degree." Harlan Fiske Stone Papers, Library of Congress.

Judge Thomas D. Thacher said that he acted as an intermediary between Taft and Hoover and that he felt free to report to the President-elect that the Court was unanimous in "urging" Mitchell's appointment as Attorney General. Thacher file, Oral History Project, Columbia University.

Taft's gloom was deepened later in the week when he received a letter from Chandler stating that he had now concluded that Mitchell did not have a chance. Nevertheless, Chandler promised to try "through a very close friend and influential individual to have your suggestion urgently supported. . . ."[117]

The Chief Justice believed that Mitchell's main competitor was not Donovan but Justice Stone.* Stone, however, had no intention of leaving the Court for a cabinet post, and in late February Taft's hopes for Mitchell were boosted when he heard that Brandeis and Senator Borah were supporting the Solicitor General and that many of the people who had been backing Stone were coming over to Mitchell as it became clear that Stone would not leave the bench.

Fortunately for Taft—and Mitchell—Hoover had known the Solicitor General for some years in Washington and had a high professional opinion of his work; and after his first two choices had turned down the job, the President offered the post to Mitchell.† The Chief Justice was delighted and hopeful that the problems of lower court appointments could be greatly lessened. As he explained to Charles P. Taft, II: "Congress has created a good many new Judges, and I am glad of it, if we can be sure that they will be good Judges. I think they are going to be in the hands of an Attorney General who will insist on having good ones and will find Hoover behind him in making the same contention."[118]

* Stone was being pushed to join Hoover's cabinet, but apparently as Secretary of State rather than as Attorney General. See Alpheus T. Mason, *Harlan Fiske Stone: Pillar of the Law* (New York: Viking Press, 1956), pp. 267–70.

† On January 21, 1963, Mr. Hoover wrote me: "My memory of secondary events thirty-five years gone by is not too certain. I can assure you only of the following considerations in that matter:

"1. I had offered The Attorney Generalship to two qualified men who had refused.

"2. The Chief Justice was carrying on a considerable campaign on behalf of Mr. Mitchell.

"3. Similar campaigns were in progress for other persons. Too often the persons recommended had less legal and character qualifications than the appointment required.

"4. I had known Mr. Mitchell for some years in the usual Washington contacts, and had great respect for him. He had a distinguished record as Solicitor General.

"5. The Chief Justice's views no doubt had weight in this selection, but certainly, the appointment was far from due solely to his recommendations."

When the President and the Justice are from different parties or mutual esteem is lacking, the Justice will have to rely on more formal means of persuasion than direct personal contact, though he still might be able to influence congressmen, state officials, interest-group leaders, or public opinion generally to pressure the Chief Executive. Even when there is a party difference, all lines of communication need not be cut. It is more probable, for instance, that Taft, when President, would have consulted with Chief Justice White, a Democrat, than would have Wilson; more likely that Kennedy would have identified with Earl Warren's policy choices than would Eisenhower. Furthermore, friendships can transcend party lines. In the early days of the New Deal, Stone was able to work through Felix Frankfurter to help keep J. Edgar Hoover in his job as director of the Federal Bureau of Investigation and Erwin N. Griswold in the Solicitor General's office.[119] Lack of mutual respect, policy disagreements, interests in different problems, or the simple fact of not knowing each other personally are often more serious factors in preventing communication than are party differences.

6 The Political Checks: Preventing or Minimizing Hostile Action

A Justice may well find himself in a situation in which his policy goals have been impaired by congressional or presidential action, or in a situation in which his objectives would be threatened by programs currently being considered seriously in the legislative or executive branches of government. To cope with either eventuality, a Justice would have open to him a broad range of strategic or at least tactical alternatives. Since his policy would typically be both controversial and vulnerable to hostile political action, he would have to devote careful attention to formulating these parts of his strategic plan.

I CONGRESS

MINIMIZING DAMAGE

The obvious strategy open to a Justice in confronting a statute which threatens his policy objectives is the simple and direct one of attempting to sweep it into constitutional oblivion by declaring it invalid—assuming again, as in all of the discussion in this chapter, that he could muster a majority of the Court behind him. In some instances a Justice might be certain that such a direct course was necessary and prudent; in other circumstances he would have grave doubts about the appropriateness or effectiveness of its use. First, while a Justice who met the definition of "policy oriented" offered in chapter i would be firmly convinced of the wisdom and constitutional validity of his own policy preferences, he might not be able to persuade himself—much less his colleagues—that *any* competing policy would be unconstitutional as well as unwise. Even where he had doubts about the validity of congressional action, he would be restrained in nullifying the statute by his concept of his proper role in a democratic system of government.

Second, at the same time as he is trying to minimize the effect of one congressional statute, a Justice may be trying to persuade congressmen to pass a new statute related to his policy. Depending upon specific political circumstances, it may or may not be helpful to his efforts to get a new law for the Court to invalidate an older statute. Third, as chapter ii pointed out, the effect of a declaration of unconstitutionality is in large part psychological. Since frequent use can depreciate its value in focusing public attention and disapprobation, a prudent Justice would invoke it sparingly, saving it to protect the Court itself or to strike down a statute which posed the gravest kind of threat to the means most vital to the attainment of his policy goal.

Fourth, there is always the danger of constitutional decisions generating a counterattack, either against the particular policy which was defended from congressional opposition or against the Court itself. The objective of judicial strategy is to achieve a policy goal, not simply to win a battle with Congress. If this objective can be accomplished without a time- and prestige-consuming fight, then the alternative which allows peaceful attainment is certainly the most rational course. Given the importance and controversial nature of many issues, a major conflict with Congress may sometimes be unavoidable; but, any battle, if it must be fought at all, should be fought at the time and under the political conditions most favorable to the cause of the Justice, not merely whenever an individual litigant chooses to challenge the validity of a statute.

The ideal combination of strategy and tactics in relying on constitutional interpretation would be the kind that Marshall so artfully applied in *Marbury* v. *Madison, Cohens* v. *Virginia,* and *Little* v. *Barreme.* In the first of these cases he managed both to condemn as immoral Jefferson's refusal to give Marbury his commission and at the same time to establish the doctrine of judicial review. In the second case he was able to reaffirm in the most unequivocal and eloquent language the supremacy of federal over state authority. Most important in strategic and tactical terms, in neither case did Marshall issue an order that could be flouted or disobeyed. In *Little* he made explicit what had been implicit in *Marbury,* that is, that the Supreme Court

157

could invalidate presidential as well as congressional action. While the Court did issue an order here, it was an order overturning an act of President John Adams not of Thomas Jefferson. To have defended executive authority against judicial power, Jefferson would also have had to uphold the aggressively anti-French policy of his Federalist predecessor, a most embarrassing situation, to say the very least.

Fortunately for most Justices, since few if any of them have been gifted with Marshall's nimble genius, a number of alternatives to constitutional interpretation are open. A Justice can also try to convince legislative and executive officials of the necessity of repealing an objectionable statute or combine such efforts at persuasion with a campaign of public education on behalf of repeal. Separate from, or as a part of, an educational campaign, a Justice may decide to strike indirectly at the statute's policy either through interpretation or through strict application of procedural technicalities. Alternately, he may decide to delay, to avoid for the time being any decision on the merits. At worst he might have to reconcile himself to living with a hostile congressional statute, and to be content to ameliorate some of its effects while modifying or shifting his own policy goals.

The most effective strategy in any particular circumstances would be determined by the same sorts of factors that shape other strategic choices. A Justice would have to weigh: the state of the Court's prestige and professional reputation; the nature of his own and the statute's policy and the seriousness of the statute's impairment of his own policy; the status of public opinion in general and the relative strengths and skills of the groups most apt to press for threatening or supportive action; the size of his majority on the Court and the degree of commitment to his policy by his colleagues on the bench; the degree of congressional commitment to the statute's policy; the attitude of the President and other executive officials toward the statute as well as the state of their current relations with Congress; his own access to, and personal influence with, members of Congress, executive officials, and interest-group leaders, as well as the relative skill and power in Congress of these men; and the Court's control over its own bureaucracy. In assessing apparent opportunities and threatening situations, he would also have to keep in mind his own talents and weaknesses.

No matter what combination of strategic approaches the Justice might conclude was the most promising, some elements would be present in any operational plan. The threat of a constitutional decision would be constantly in the background, and persuasion would be a continuing part of any scheme since every opinion, every speech, every effort to exercise personal influence is, in effect, an attempt to convince intellectually or emotionally.

Where the Justice's campaign to educate legislators and the public about the merits of his policy was still in progress, or where he believed that one or both audiences were hostile or as yet unreceptive to his ideas, he might think it more promising to avoid a direct decision on the effects of a statute on his policy. He might persuade his associates to deny certiorari in cases which presented such questions or, where four Justices felt it necessary to hear these cases, to decide them on the narrowest of technical, procedural grounds.

As an essentially Fabian strategy, delay involves a gamble—which may or may not pay off—that the future will be better rather than worse for the Justice's policy. Mere avoidance is the more passive of the two alternatives to this strategic approach, and reliance on technical rulings the more aggressive since its systematic application might hamstring enforcement of a congressional policy almost as effectively as a direct attack. Moreover, a Justice might use dicta in his opinions in such cases to indicate doubts about the validity or wisdom of the substantive policy.

Resort to dicta for this purpose would have to be preceded by a careful appraisal of the political situation. On the one hand, widely-publicized remarks may warn and help unite the foes of the Justice's policy to attack the Court if not to press more strenuously for their policy objectives. On the other hand, an opinion, even its dicta, can be an effective educational vehicle as well as a subtle means of reminding congressmen, as in the Passport cases of 1958,[1] that the shotgun of judicial review is still loaded. One might even view such action as a form of tacit bargaining. In essence, the Court would be threatening to invalidate efforts to extend or rigorously apply a particular policy, while at the same time offering to withhold its edict of nullification for the time being if other officials also abstain from pressing for their objectives.

When a Justice felt that his policy was receiving support that was sufficiently strong to squelch likely attempts to get Congress to attack the Court or to strengthen the statute to which he was opposed, he might resort to statutory interpretation to hold that Congress had never really meant to adopt a policy contrary to his own.* Judging from the Court's handling of the Interstate Commerce Act during the last ten years of the nineteenth century,[2] or the Clayton and Federal Trade Commission acts during the 1920's,[3] or the Warren Court's decisions on a whole set of statutes regarding internal security,[4] it is apparently not very difficult for members of the Court to read their own policy preferences into what seems to many other men to be a contrary congressional policy choice.† In any event, this strategy would be particularly effective where the statute had been passed some time earlier and had lost its political support over the years,[5] and the Justice did not

* Statutory interpretation of this kind can also be part of an educational campaign, an attempt to say to congressmen: What you have seemed to have done raises such grave constitutional doubts that we will assume you have not meant your words to be taken literally. Reconsider the consequences of what it is you are trying to accomplish. See C. Herman Pritchett, *The Political Offender and the Warren Court* (Boston: Boston University Press, 1958).

† Perhaps scholars have been too severe in criticizing judges for consistently finding their own value preferences in the vague wording of constitutional or statutory phrases. Often judges may not perceive that they have a choice between competing values. According to Hadley Cantril: "Our perception depends in large part on the assumptions we bring to any particular occasion. It is, as Dewey and Bentley long ago pointed out, not a 'reaction to' stimuli in the environment but may be more accurately described as a 'transaction with' an environment. . . . It would seem, then, that a person sees what is 'significant,' with significant defined in terms of his relationship to what he is looking at." "Perception and Interpersonal Relations," 114 *Am. J. of Psychiatry* 119, 119–21 (1957).

Cantril bolstered his conclusion that values condition perception by citing the results of experiments which psychologists have used to demonstrate the concept of "binocular resolution." In these experiments, a subject (people with certain kinds of eye problems are screened out) is asked to look through a stereoscope and report what he sees. He is actually looking at a pair of words or symbols, one of which reinforces his value preferences and one of which goes counter to or is alien or indifferent to them. The subject, however, usually sees only the reinforcing word or symbol. For example, when presented with paired Jewish and Catholic symbols, Jews tend to see only the Jewish symbols and Catholics the Catholic ones. When paired symbols which are both indifferent to the subject's value orientation are shown him, he tends to see both symbols or a mixture of the two. My colleague Glenn Paige, who first told me about binocular resolution, and I have used this kind of experiment independently of each other and have obtained comparable results.

One would expect—and hope—that a judge's intellectual discipline would minimize any tendency to see only what he wants to see. While my own work with the binocular problem is too unscientific to be reliable, it indicates,

feel the situation justified using judicial review to resolve the issue. This might also be a promising strategy where the Justice disapproved of the means which Congress had employed to attain an objective but was indifferent to, or actually in favor of, the objective itself.

Where statutory interpretation and procedural rulings were not technically feasible or would be ineffective, and where the immediate future promised political circumstances no more favorable than the present, a Justice would have to weigh the alternatives of employing a bold strategy centered on judicial review or of accommodating himself to the congressional policy for the short run and hoping for long-run changes, meanwhile allocating his resources to achieving the goals of secondary policy preferences.

Some issues might be so fundamental to the Justice's value system that the latter alternative could not be considered, no matter what the cost of the first. When the issue was of less fundamental importance but still of great significance, the Justice would find the bolder strategy more attractive as one or more of the following sets of conditions more strongly obtained: (*a*) where the Court's prestige and reputation were high and public opinion supported or was indifferent to the Justice's policy; (*b*) the executive department approved of the Justice's policy on its merits or would try to block efforts to curb the Court or reinstate the congressional policy for other political motives; (*c*) there was a minority in Congress which would protect the Court and its policy against counterattack either because of respect for the Court, agreement with the particular policy, the political expediency of opposition to the majority, or because of the personal influence of the Justice; or, (*d*) there was actually a majority in Congress favoring repeal or major modification of the statute but unable to act because of minority vetoes.

Preventing Hostile Action

When Congress is seriously considering passage of a bill which would make achievement of the Justice's policy goals more difficult, it would

---

however, that on some important issues each of us can perceive only one image —that is, we cannot see a choice.

There is a good bibliography on binocular resolution in Leonard A. Lo Sciuto and Eugene L. Hartley, "Religious Affiliation and Open-Mindedness in Binocular Resolution," 17 *Perceptual and Motor Skills* 427 (1963).

be of major interest to him to block this projected action. The only strategy really open would be persuasion on the merits, though as in convincing Congress to adopt a statute a wide variety of tactics is open, including intellectual and emotional appeals, threats, and bargaining.

Intellectual and emotional appeals can be aimed directly at legislators as well as at creating a general climate of opinion in the country as a whole. As in other tactical fields, these appeals can be contained in opinions, in speeches, in the Justice's own writings or those of his friends, or in private conversations with government officials or interest-group leaders. Appeals to congressmen may be more effective if they are backed with hints of what the Court might do if Congress does pass the bill in question. More than once the Justices have indicated in the dicta of their opinions the fate they contemplated for statutes which Congress had not yet enacted.[6] Such hints may also be thrown out in private conversations. As Taft told his brother in 1925 when confronted with the possibility that Congress would pass a statute of which he disapproved, "I am going to take time by the forelock to prime Senator David Reed of Pennsylvania on the probable unconstitutionality of such a law."[7] One might surmise that in his many conversations with senators and representatives the Chief Justice did not miss many opportunities to convey his prediction of what the Court would do to certain other bills.[8]

Probably the neatest example of judicial intervention in the legislative process to kill a bill was Hughes's three-phase attack against President Roosevelt's Court-packing proposal of 1937.* Phase 1 consisted of the Chief Justice's famous letter to Senator Burton Wheeler, which destroyed point by point the President's claims that his plan would promote more efficient judicial administration. The letter also contained a warning against any attempt to require the Court to sit in divisions. "The Constitution," Hughes noted, "does not appear to authorize two or more Supreme Courts or two or more parts of a Supreme Court functioning in effect as separate courts."[9] Phase 2 opened the following week when Roberts and to a lesser extent Hughes himself altered their constitutional views and began to vote to sustain the kind

---

* Cf. Hughes's testimony with Van Devanter and Brandeis against Hugo Black's bill to provide for a direct appeal to the Supreme Court from any district court decision enjoining the enforcement of an act of Congress. U.S. Senate, Committee on the Judiciary, *Hearings on S. 2176*, 74/1 (1935).

of social legislation that the Court had held unconstitutional in the previous term, making the President's charge that the Justices were obstructing national progress seem outdated if not false.[10] Phase 3 consisted in the Chief Justice's co-operation with Borah, Van Devanter, and Wheeler in timing the announcement of Van Devanter's retirement[11]—and the creation of a vacancy on the bench—to coincide with the Senate Judiciary Committee's recommendation that the President's bill "do not pass."[12]

Where Hughes acted with dramatic decisiveness which in one series of rapid blows crippled the opposition, Taft operated in a more drawn-out fashion, wearing down his opponents through repeated sallies. Yet for all his lack of drama, Taft was still effective in attaining his objectives. Two case studies of his maneuverings supply a detailed picture of what a policy-oriented Justice might do to deter congressional action.

The Caraway Bill.—One of the pet ideas of Senator Thaddeus H. Caraway of Arkansas was a plan to bar federal judges from commenting to jurors on the credibility of witnesses in civil or criminal trials. This bill, which Caraway in the Senate and Representative McKeown, also of Arkansas, in the House introduced at several sessions of Congress during the 1920's, infuriated Taft. He described the measure as "vicious"[13] and "inconceivable,"[14] and dismissed Caraway as "one of these small barrelled criminal lawyers and ambulance chasers who have gotten into the Senate."[15] The Chief Justice explained the fact that the bill received strong support on Capitol Hill as "evidence of the supineness, the lack of real interest and patriotism of the entire body of the Republican party as represented in both Houses of Congress. . . ."*[16]

Working in close co-operation with Thomas Shelton of the American Bar Association, the Chief Justice exerted a great deal of time and energy to defeat this legislation. He approached Speaker of the House

---

* There may have been a personal reason for Taft's rather vindictive evaluation. It was Caraway who revealed the fact that during the Taft administration Harry Daugherty had earned a large fee for securing—under conditions which smacked strongly of fraud—a presidential pardon for a wealthy client, Charles W. Morse. The incident reflected not on Taft's integrity but on his judgment or rather on the judgment of the staff of George Wickersham, Taft's Attorney General; in any event, Caraway's use of the information probably did nothing to endear him to the Chief Justice. Henry Pringle, *The Life and Times of William Howard Taft* (New York: Farrar & Rinehart, 1939), II, 627–37.

Nicholas Longworth, and Representatives Snell and Graham, chairmen of the Rules and Judiciary committees and got them to block the bill on several different occasions.

Staking out another line of defense, Taft visited Attorney General Stone and argued against the bill. The Chief Justice also called on the President several times, and in 1924 personally presented Coolidge with a twelve-page memorandum developing his reasons for opposing the bill.[17] This memorandum, probably the most detailed advisory opinion on record, contained two complementary arguments. The first consisted of a lengthy discussion of judicial procedure, concluding that Caraway's plan went against the best in traditional British and American practice and would thereby "lower the standard of the administration of justice . . . and only add to the present unsatisfactory condition of the prosecution of crime in this country." "Fortunately," the Chief Justice continued in the second line of reasoning,

> the right of the [federal] Judge to exercise this power of summing up to a jury upon the facts is conferred upon him by the Constitution of the United States and cannot be taken away by legislation. . . . It was an essential element of the jury trial in English Courts when the Declaration of Independence was signed and our Constitution was framed and adopted, and when the Seventh Amendment became part of it. That being true, Congress may not impair the institution by attempting to restrain Federal Judges from the discretion to exercise the power vested in them by fundamental law.

Taft later sent a copy of this memorandum to his brother Henry, who was a partner in practice on Wall Street and a member, and from 1925 to 1928 chairman, of the ABA's Committee on Jurisprudence and Law Reform. Henry did not act on his brother's suggestion that he personally contact several key senators, but he said he had "freely"[18] used the memorandum in preparing the committee's report to the ABA opposing the Caraway Bill.[19]

In 1926 when Caraway again pressed his bill, the Chief Justice made no serious attempt to influence his friends in the Senate. His opinion of the upper chamber had never been favorable; and he concluded that since the judiciary group in the Senate was "a very poor committee, consisting mostly of radicals and progressives," there was not much hope there or for successful floor action either.[20] Instead he concentrated his efforts on the House and executive department relying on Longworth, Snell, and Graham to delay the bill, and hoping that he had convinced Coolidge to veto the measure if it did get through the House.

This time the bill did not even come up for a vote in the Senate, but in 1928 Caraway made another major effort and got the bill through the Senate for the second time. Taft's friend David Reed was apologetic in reporting to the Chief Justice his failure to stop the bill,* but promised to see the House leaders and continue the fight there.[21] The Chief Justice thanked the senator for his help. "Of course," he went on, "all we can do is to bring the matter to the attention of the House and to the President. . . . I think it might be helpful if you will call the attention of the President to the untoward results that will follow the passage of the bill."[22] Taft then consulted with Nicholas Longworth[23]— the two men were on a "Dear Nick" and "Dear Bill" basis.† The Speaker reported that he was watching the parliamentary situation closely and thought that with the help of Snell and Graham he could keep the measure from coming to a vote on the floor.[24] Longworth made good on his pledge and the bill died quietly.

Norris Bill.—The Chief Justice was also active in defeating Senator Norris' proposal to curtail federal jurisdiction. As an outspoken Progressive, Norris had been a sharp critic of the conservative ideology of federal judges. In 1922, he had proposed turning all federal trial business over to state courts,[25] and in 1927 he came up with a bill only slightly less drastic.[26] In April, 1927, shortly after he became chairman of the Judiciary Committee, the senator asked for an appointment with the Chief Justice to discuss with him and a representative of the Department of Justice the problem of over-crowded federal dockets.[27] Apparently Norris and Taft did confer a few days later about Norris' jurisdictional plan. The senator proposed that Congress should abolish federal trial jurisdiction in civil suits except for cases brought by the United States. The Chief Justice's reaction was negative. He called the plan "the most radical bill in respect to the organization of our Government and its three branches that has been introduced in either House of Congress in more than a century."[28]

Congress was not in session when Norris and the Chief Justice had

* In fact, Caraway had whipped him badly in debate. 69 *Cong. Rec.* 4965.

† Most of Taft's old friends called him "Will," but some people, even occasionally one of his brothers, addressed him as "Bill." His boyhood nickname had been "Lub."

their conference, but at the next session, Norris formally introduced his bill.[29] The Judiciary Committee held no hearings—Norris said none were necessary since all the members of the committee were lawyers and the bill was strictly a legal issue[30]—but favorably reported the measure on March 27, 1928,[31] six weeks after it had been introduced.

Taft quickly swung into action. Believing that Norris was trying to sneak the measure through Congress, the Chief decided that publicity would be the best way to fight the proposal. He immediately wrote to George Wickersham about this "great attack on the administration of justice," and suggested that Wickersham "in a deft way bring the attention of the New York press to the radical nature of this bill."[32] Taft also offered the thought that the "American Bar Association might well act on this subject. . . ." Although the Chief Justice mentioned that the proposal would make the Supreme Court's work more difficult, the principal argument that he used with Wickersham, who was now Henry Taft's partner in a Wall Street firm, was that "eastern capital" would be reluctant to invest money in western states if subject to the delays and disadvantages which non-residents frequently faced in law suits in state courts. The result, Taft predicted, would be a raise in interest rates to cover the extra cost.*

The Chief Justice also wrote to Casper Yost, editor of the *St. Louis Globe–Democrat,* and explained that this "vicious" bill would raise interest rates and so "strike the worst blow against the farmers that could be imagined. . . ." Taft had yet another string to his bow. He pointed out to Yost: "I should think that our Negro fellow citizens would think that the passage of this bill would weaken almost fatally their means of protecting themselves under the Federal Constitution. . . . I think a great deal could be done to rouse the Negroes on this legislation." Putting on a helpless air which was totally contrary to the facts, the Chief Justice came to the point of his letter: "Of course I am so situated that I cannot take a political part, but you can, and I invoke your influence in maintaining the protective power which citizens may secure from the Federal Judiciary in defense of their rights."[33]

On the same day he wrote Yost, Taft suggested to his brother Henry that he go to the editors of the *New York Times* and the *New York*

* Taft had made the same point in 1922 in opposing suggestions for removing from federal courts jurisdiction to hear cases based solely on diversity of citizenship. "Possible and Needed Reforms in Administration of Justice in Federal Courts," 8 *A.B.A.J.* 601, 604 (1922).

Herald Tribune and persuade them to oppose the measure. (Although he was in touch with his friend Senator Deneen, the Chief Justice still had no faith in the Senate—"A most bolshevik body,"[34] with no strength at all in the Judiciary Committee.) Taft had a subtle plan to kill the bill. 1928 was a Presidential election year and he thought that, if the Negroes were aroused, the Norris proposal could become campaign "dynamite." Accordingly, he asked Henry Taft to see Charles D. Hilles, chairman of the finance committee of the Republican National Committee, and try to get a plank opposing the bill in the national platform. The Chief Justice also told Henry that one of the principal reasons he wanted the *Times* and the *Tribune* briefed was to scare the Democrats away. To further his plan the Chief Justice sent Newton Baker a copy of the bill and the Senate Committee report. "It is," Taft wrote, "the most radical bill affecting the usefulness and efficacy of the Federal Judiciary that I remember ever to be suggested."[35]

A few days later Taft again contacted his brother and suggested that he get in touch with John W. Davis and Charles Evans Hughes and organize opposition among leaders of the New York Bar.[36] Henry obliged by bringing together Hughes, Davis, and representatives from the New York State Bar Association, the Association of the Bar of the City of New York, and the New York County Lawyers Association, but the results were disappointing. Henry felt that he had been the only one of the group who had done any work preparing for the conference. Moreover, the Chief Justice's broad strategy was too subtle for the members of the conference, and they preferred to try to persuade individual senators to oppose the bill.[37]

Thomas Shelton of the ABA had also been talking with senators, including Norris, and was reporting back to the Chief Justice. Henry Taft, as chairman of the ABA's Committee on Jurisprudence and Law Reform, wrote a long letter to the Senate, outlining in detail the committee's objection to the bill.[38] Two months later, Henry reported the committee's reaction to the Norris bill to the ABA's annual meeting and obtained the association's endorsement to oppose the legislation. Paraphrasing his brother, Henry had called the proposal "the boldest and most radical attack upon the federal courts that has been made in recent years."[39]

In the face of increasing opposition from both bar groups and senators—and perhaps also moved by Taft's efforts to stir up party leaders—Norris backed down. In May he asked for unanimous consent from the

Senate to modify his bill so that it would eliminate only federal jurisdiction over civil suits in cases where no question of federal law was involved but the parties were citizens of different states.[40] Even this reduction in aims was not enough to insure passage, and Norris did not try to force a vote on his bill.*

II THE PRESIDENCY

A Justice might also see achievement of his policy goals threatened by actual or projected executive action, and to minimize or prevent these dangers he has much the same choice among strategic alternatives as in coping with legislative opposition. Where the executive department is considering endorsement of a policy inimical to that of the Justice, he could try to block such a move by use of formal means of persuasion in Court opinions or public speeches or by the more informal means of personal influence. He might back up each or both of these methods of persuasion by hints that the contemplated executive policy was unauthorized by Congress or the Constitution.

Similarly, in minimizing the damage done to his policy by action already taken by the President, a Justice may rely on persuasion to move the President or his advisers to see the error of their ways. In other circumstances the Justice might plan to strike directly at the opposing policy by actually declaring it unconstitutional or contrary to or unauthorized by congressional policy. Alternatively, he might follow a course of harassment—interpreting executive orders to hold that the President had not in fact approved a policy contrary to the Justice's, or basing the Court's decisions on procedural rather than substantive grounds but still reversing lower court rulings favorable to the hostile executive policy. This approach can be particularly effective if it is coupled with a veiled threat of use of the judicial veto. For example, in *Greene* v. *McElroy* (1959) the Court explained at length that confrontation of accusers was a fundamental rule of fairness, required by the Constitution even in loyalty-security proceedings. The Court only

* Defeat of the Norris measure gave the Chief Justice no real comfort. He looked with fear at the years ahead. This was the kind of legislation, he said, which the country could expect if the Democrats won the 1928 presidential election. "I haven't a bit of doubt that we could induce Coolidge to veto the Norris Bill, but I'm not so sure we could do so with respect to Smith, although I doubt if he would consent to so radical a measure." Taft to Henry Taft, July 11, 1928, William Howard Taft Papers, Library of Congress.

held, however, that in setting up the Industrial Security Program neither Congress nor the President had authorized government officials to deny an "accused" the right to confront a hostile witness. The Eisenhower administration quickly amended the Industrial Security Program regulations to broaden the right of confrontation,[41] and shortly thereafter the Atomic Energy Commission made similar modifications in its loyalty-security procedures.

As a variation on this last approach, the Justice may calculate that it would be most prudent to follow a temporizing course and avoid for the time being any decisions involving the contrary policy. In extreme situations he might find it necessary to accommodate his policy goals to those of the President and to concentrate on attaining secondary objectives.

As in other phases of his planning a Justice would most probably find it desirable to pursue a strategy composed of two or more of these elements. His actual choice would depend on the same sorts of factors as his choice in other aspects of his planning: the prestige and reputation of the Court; the size of his majority on the Court and the intensity of the other Justices' commitment to the policies involved; the intensity of the commitment to the executive policy by the President and other important officials; the likely impact of the executive policy on his own; the Justice's access to and personal influence with the President or his more trusted advisers; the status of the climate of opinion in the general political environment and the comparative strength of probable efforts by interest groups at threatening or supportive action; the status of congressional opinion, the access and personal influence of the Justice with legislators, and the political strength of those lawmakers who would sympathize with or could be persuaded to assist the Justice's policy or at least oppose the President's; the likelihood that the President would encounter bureaucratic resistance in his own department; and the probable reaction of lower court judges. Once again in considering courses of action the Justice would have to weigh carefully the strengths and weaknesses of his own personality.

Again the implementing tactics would be similar to those available to cope with legislative checks—judicial review, interpretations of statutes or executive orders, denials of certiorari, dismissals of appeals, and capitalization on procedural errors. Persuasion might be attempted through formal opinions, public speeches, or informal personal contact and may be aimed directly at executive officials or at broader segments of the public in an effort to create a climate of opinion favorable to the Justice's policy and unfavorable to the President's.

Some Justices, like Taft, have undoubtedly been quite successful in their efforts to exploit their personal influence with Presidents. Others have not fared so well. Justices Swayne and Davis tried but failed to persuade Lincoln to ameliorate the administration's policy of arbitrary arrest, confinement, and trial of civilians by military authorities.[42] On one occasion, Davis even attempted to convince Lincoln that to win the war he had to withdraw the Emancipation Proclamation.[43] Chase took full advantage of his acquaintance with Johnson. In the spring of 1866 he called on the President and, as the Chief Justice confided to a friend, "urged him to issue a proclamation, submitting at the same time a draft of one, declaring, in unequivocal terms, that martial law was abrogated and the writ of *habeas corpus* restored in all cases of which the courts of the United States had jurisdiction. . . . But this was not done."[44] Despite this and other rebuffs Chase freely offered advice to the President and other executive officials, including army officers, on a range of topics from Negro suffrage to relieving military commanders to the best way of handling the national debt.*[45]

Moreover, just as in trying to secure executive assistance, a Justice may utilize any influence which has come to him through the appointment to executive office of friends or persons sympathetic to his policy aims. Tugwell has claimed that Brandeis constantly stirred up his followers to fight the co-operative philosophy of the first New Deal. Indeed, Tugwell has placed the blame for the failure of the first New Deal squarely on Brandeis' political maneuvering. In 1958, Tugwell described the methods which the Justice used to move F. D. R. away from the early policies of his administration:[64]

> The first of these means was his disciples; the second was the threat of unconstitutionality. The first apostle in the Brandeis hierarchy was Frankfurter, although Morris Ernst was an earnest aspirant. Through Frankfurter, mostly, the staffing of New Deal agencies was controlled

* See also the letter that Chief Justice Taney sent to Chase, when the latter was Secretary of the Treasury, offering the opinion that the Civil War income tax was unconstitutional as applied to the salaries of federal judges. The Court had this letter placed in its official records, and the majority cited it and reprinted it as an appendix to the decision invalidating the income tax in *Pollock v. Farmers' Loan & Trust Co.* (1895). I am indebted to Professor Alpheus T. Mason for this reference.

and dissenters were got rid of. And because Brandeis was, after Holmes's death, the most influential member of the court among intellectuals and liberals—and with Roosevelt—a word from him was very nearly a command. And this was much more true after the adverse decisions on the collectivist measures of the Hundred Days. In these Brandeis joined with reactionaries to make a majority. . . . Roosevelt was partly intimidated and partly antagonized by the Brandeis tactics. The blandishments of Frankfurter, the alternatives offered by Corcoran and Cohen, and the threat of judicial disapproval if they were not agreed to were sufficient. The process by which it happened is unlikely to be revealed in any detail, but the results are plain enough.

III SPECIAL CASES OF CONFLICT

A Justice may face two other, more specialized kinds of situations in which Congress or the executive is considering action inimical to his policy goals. The first would occur when, because of the strength, skill, and organization of opposition to his policy, either within and/or outside of the other departments of government, the Justice anticipates that at this time a certain decision or the announcement of a policy in an opinion would stir a political reaction which would gravely threaten that policy and probably judicial power itself. Second, because of previous decisions or policy pronouncements, such a dangerous reaction may already be under way in the political processes, and additional cases bearing on this issue may be coming up through the judicial process. A Justice's choices would be in some respects similar to but in other respects different from those in confronting general legislative or executive opposition to his policy.

Anticipating Political Reaction

Accurate prediction of a political reaction is hardly an easy task. It involves weighing of intangibles on a scale calibrated to the unknown quantities of the future. Yet this is the sort of problem which decision-makers in other government positions must regularly handle. Thus it is also the kind of problem which most Justices, considering their wide range of political experience before coming to the bench, have also frequently handled. A Justice can get the facts on which he bases his estimate of the situation from newspaper reports, leaks, and analyses, from professional or scholarly journals, from the *Congressional Record,*

from committee hearings and reports, from presidential press conferences, from statements by cabinet members or bureau chiefs, and, of
course, from the celebrated Washington grapevine. If need be, he can,
as Taft sometimes did, simply ask old friends in government for information about their colleagues and for their judgments on the chances
of particular bills being passed or policies being endorsed. Ultimately,
a Justice has to sift through these pieces of intelligence and arrive at
his own conclusion based on his own experience. If nothing else, he
can draw some comfort from knowing that the opposition will also
have to predict on the basis of incomplete information and will probably be even more hampered by lack of time in making difficult assess-
ments. Like other public officials and interest-group leaders, a Justice
will sometimes make mistakes in his perception of events and his interpretation of their implications.

Where a Justice has reason to foresee a political reaction which will
be dangerous to his policy or to the Court if a case is decided a certain
way or if the opinion announces a particular policy, he still might
decide to pursue a "damn the torpedoes" strategy and forge ahead.
He might do so because he judges that the immediate importance of
the decision or the policy announcement is so immense that even
martyrdom would be an acceptable price. Or, where the issue was still
important but not absolutely vital to his value system, he might conclude that the strength of general and specific societal supports to the
Court, when added to the specific supports the policy would accrue
on its own merits, would make the risk of open conflict worth taking,
especially since the Justice could use his personal influence to try to
prevent hostile congressional or presidential action. The status of the
prestige and reputation of the Court would be among the most crucial
factors in this assessment, as would the size of his majority on the
Court. It is far more difficult to invoke the sacred mysteries of the cult
of the robe for 5–4 rulings than for those which are unanimous or
nearly so.

Where the Justice is less sure about the support that will be forthcoming, he might decide to avoid for a time decisions on this issue or
to restrict them to narrow, procedural points. At the same time he may
engage in an educational campaign to influence elected politicians and
their constituents. Or, the Justice might estimate that while a full-
blown statement of his policy would provoke a damaging reaction, he
might succeed in establishing at least some of his policy. Where he

was concerned about the degree of his associates' commitment to his policy, this compromise approach would appear especially prudent.

Last, when he could not avoid a decision on the merits, the Justice might reckon that the opposition was so strong that in the long run it would do more harm than good to his policy and to the Court to make the sort of ruling he really wanted or even to write a compromise opinion. Under these conditions, he might conclude that the only sensible course was to preserve judicial power and switch his interests and resources to achieving his secondary policy goals. He might do so, of course, without giving up the hope that the fight would be continued more successfully in another forum or that the future would work great changes in political outlooks.

MEETING ATTACKS IN PROGRESS

To cope with the second special situation, in which reaction against previous decisions is mounting and new cases involving the controversial issue are coming before the Court, the Justice can choose among the same sorts of strategic alternatives as in anticipating political action. Again the Justice would have to estimate his own support within the judicial system as well as within the political environment as a whole, the strength of the opposition, and the nature and objective of the attack. A constitutional amendment, while very difficult to obtain, can do permanent damage to a policy or to the Court itself, while a statute, though stinging, may represent only a temporary defeat. Although more difficult to bring off, an assault against judicial power can be far more perilous than an attack against a particular facet of public policy.

Weighing these and the other strategic factors discussed in this and previous chapters, a Justice may again decide: (1) to push ahead aggressively with his policy; (2) to continue to apply as much of his policy as he has in the past but to make a point of refusing to extend its application; (3) to avoid further decisions on the merits of the issue; (4) to compromise by executing a tactical withdrawal; or, (5) in the face of overwhelming opposition to conduct a massive retreat. At the same time as he is pursuing any one of these alternatives a Justice may also be exploiting his personal influence with legislators and executive officials to block the passage of a threatening bill or to head off projected presidential action.

In a sense alternatives (2), (3), (4), and even (5) might be viewed as examples of tacit bargaining. In exchange for the end of a political attack, the Justices offer to hold up or back down from policies which they have been pursuing. For whatever motivation, the Justices have relatively frequently stopped their advance or actually retreated when confronted with serious legislative resistance. John Marshall set the pattern[47] when, in the face of Jeffersonian attacks, he swallowed his own belief that the Judiciary Act of 1802 was unconstitutional, wrote an opinion sustaining its validity, and followed its provisions by resuming circuit-riding duties. Hughes, of course, led the Court in the most dramatic retreat in its history. More recently the Warren Court in the late 1950's executed a series of maneuvers which have been described either as tactical withdrawals or refusals to continue to advance.[48]

One of the reasons why the Court has backed down on occasion and why these attacks have rarely resulted in Court-curbing legislation or application of executive sanctions* and relatively seldom in policy-changing legislation or constitutional amendments may well be the advantage which both sides have seen in compromise over all-out conflict. The existence of independent and rival seats of power in the other branches of the federal government, in the lower courts, in the administrative bureaucracy, and state governments makes Court-congressional and Court-presidential relations—like those within the judicial system—more analogous to a mixed-motive than to a zero-sum game. There is conflict but also a need for at least some degree of co-operation to achieve almost any important policy goal. Furthermore, a massive struggle between any two of these three institutions could lead to the triumph of a policy which is opposed by both sets of contestants, as well as to the domination of policy-making in this and related fields by rival public officers.

A number of other factors might also move a Justice to compromise with congressional or presidential policy preferences, not the least of which may be gnawing doubts about the propriety of his opposing public policies which apparently have strong and seemingly permanent support in the population as a whole. On the other hand, a Justice's concept of his duty as a judge to vote as his conscience dictates in cases which come before him may push him the other way. Problems of

* Every President, it may be assumed, attempts to influence future decisions through his appointments to the Court.

conscience and political philosophy aside for the moment, purely as a matter of prudence a Justice has to beware of becoming or even of appearing timid, a course as dangerous in its own fashion as seeking battle simply for the joy or glory of winning a fight.

As in dealing with associates, a Justice cannot always be ready to compromise or back down if he wants to preserve his own and the Court's reputation and prestige. A prudent judge would not underestimate the risks to his policy, to the Court, or perhaps even to the American system of government which are involved in a major clash with Congress or the presidency; neither would he forget how much more difficult it is to pass a controversial bill—and get it approved by the President—or to secure comprehensive formulation and effective application of an executive policy than it is to defeat or sabotage such a measure. Nor would a prudent Justice underestimate the prestige of his tribunal and the general support it receives from the political community, and the importance of prestige and support to the survival of the Court's role in American politics.

A Justice who wishes to preserve judicial power—and thus to maximize the chances of achieving his policy goals—would not seek conflict for its own sake, but neither would he allow the Court to acquire a reputation for timidity. He would want the Justices to appear to be cautious, broad-minded, and reasonable men—but also brave, strong-willed, decisive, and both willing and able to use their sanctions on fundamental issues.

7 *Ethics and Strategy*

So far this book has been concerned with strategies oriented toward accomplishing the possible rather than merely verbally expressing a preference for the ideal. But achievement of desirable goals, even if attainable through impeccable law court procedures, cannot be the sole criterion of choice for judges who believe that an end does not justify any and all means. Some perfectly legal courses of action raise ethical questions, and it would be a fair assumption that the overwhelming majority of men who have sat on the High Bench would be no less opposed to unethical than to illegal conduct.

To say that the concept of judicial strategy poses difficult ethical issues is to indulge in gross understatement. "In actual life," Reinhold Niebuhr has pointed out, "no clear distinction between moral principles and strategy can be made."[1] But the fact that the distinction may be blurred—or that morality and strategy cannot be separated—makes imperative an investigation of the ethical implications of strategic choices.* And the problem cannot be resolved simply by reference to history, by citation to the actions of judges like Marshall, Miller, Taft, Hughes, or Stone. There is a strong presumption that the way these men acted is the proper way for judges to behave, but practice is not of itself a normative standard, though it may be an excellent means of discovering such standards.

The initial problem is semantic: the meaning of "ethical." To avoid as far as possible the pitfalls of word-chopping, "ethical" and "moral"

* This is the rationalization I use to try to escape a feeling of presumptuousness in discussing the ethics of men of the strength of character of Supreme Court Justices.

will be used here interchangeably to refer to the standards of official conduct which the office of Supreme Court Justice imposes upon the incumbent. The question, "Is the judge's action ethical?" I will take to mean: "Does the judge's action comport with his duty as imposed by the Constitution, relevant statutes, and, not least, his oath of office?"

Clear analysis of judicial ethics is hindered by a widespread tendency to think of Justices as acting only as arbiters of disputes between individual litigants. There are two roles here, and, as is typical of dual roles, their combination does present problems of proper conduct. The role of a judge as "the mouth of the law" and his role as "animate justice" may well make conflicting demands. The Canons of Judicial Ethics promulgated by the American Bar Association state quite explicitly that the demands of the first role take precedence over those of the second*—though it is doubtful that judicial practice on the point is uniform. While this conflict of roles causes thorny and intellectually interesting problems—the easy solution of the ABA's code of ethics notwithstanding—the really complicating factor is that judges, especially Supreme Court Justices, play a third role. As chapters i and ii stressed, these judges are inevitably policy-makers, and they have responsibilities in addition to those to the individual parties in a case. The ABA's canons deal hardly at all with this third role and the relationship between its demands and those of the other two roles.†

---

* Canon 20 provides: "A judge should be mindful that his duty is the application of general law to particular instances, that ours is a government of law and not of men, and that he violates his duty as a minister of justice under such a system if he seeks to do what he may personally consider substantial justice in a particular case and disregards the general law as he knows it to be binding on him. . . . He should administer his office with a due regard to the integrity of the system of the law itself, remembering that he is not a depository of arbitrary power, but a judge under the sanction of law."

† Particularly relevant are canons 19 and 23:

"19. . . . It is of high importance that judges constituting a court of last resort should use effort and self-restraint to promote solidarity of conclusion and the consequent influence of judicial decision. A judge should not yield to pride of opinion or value more highly his individual reputation than that of the court to which he should be loyal. Except in case of conscientious difference of opinion on fundamental principle, dissenting opinions should be discouraged in courts of last resort."

"23. A judge has exceptional opportunity to observe the operation of statutes, especially those relating to practice, and to ascertain whether they tend to impede the just disposition of controversies; and he may well contrib-

Moreover, these canons are themselves the subject of a conflict of interest. The bar association's code was drawn up by a committee headed by Chief Justice William Howard Taft. Since the rest of the committee and the ABA approved them, these canons represent more than the personal views of the Chief Justice. However, it would seem of doubtful propriety to allow Taft to be both actor and judge of the legitimacy of his own actions.

Absence of a neatly ordered set of widely accepted and objective standards does not mean that one cannot intelligently discuss the kinds of ethical problems raised in this book and offer, if not solutions, at least potentially fruitful avenues of approach to solutions. Rather than trying to meet all the ethical questions implicit here, this chapter will concentrate on two problems which are central to the analysis in earlier chapters and will try to examine the ethical implications relevant to the Justice's policy-making role as well as to those roles involved in settling disputes between litigants. The two areas are: (1) lobbying by a Justice to generate executive, legislative, or popular support for his policy goals; and (2) compromise in judicial decision-making.

I LOBBYING

The picture of a Justice of the United States Supreme Court stalking the halls of Congress ambushing senators to arrange support for or opposition to a proposed bill is as contrary to the public image of a judge as is a Justice's calling at the White House to advise the President on legislative or personnel matters. If a policy-oriented Justice considers that the practical advantages of such activity justify the practical risks involved, he must still consider whether he can ethically engage in the political process. One Justice could answer with a firm no. The Constitution, he might reason, has established a separation of powers. To him it has given a share of the authority to shape public policy, but only in deciding "cases." It has not authorized him to help draft legislation or advise executive officials or individual legislators. The framers specifically rejected giving the Justices a share of the veto power. This Justice may see himself as bearing responsibility for the efficient and wise running of government but only limited responsi-

---

ute to the public interest by advising those having authority to remedy defects of procedure, of the result of his observation and experience."

bility. Other officials also partake of that responsibility. If they fail, the voters can remove them and select better qualified men. If the Constitution cannot survive administration by occasionally inept as well as by skilled hands, it is not a fit instrument to frame the government of a great nation.

For another Justice the ethical question may be more complex. Seeing a man whom he knew to be a poor judge and suspected to be dishonest being touted for the Supreme Court, a Justice might well wonder whether his duty lay in silence or in speaking out to those who would listen and could control the nomination. A Justice might face the same quandary if he believes that proposed legislation would cripple judicial power and threaten values which he deemed basic, or if he thinks the ideology of a particular candidate for judicial office would endanger those fundamental values. Under such circumstances, a Justice would have cause to wonder whether he has the right to refuse, solely on ethical grounds, to use his personal influence. Intervention as neat as that of Hughes in 1937 obscures the ethical problems which are resplendent in such untidy maneuverings as Taft tried, but much the same problems were present in each situation.

Judicial intervention in the legislative or administrative process is an extraordinary step. There are no laws or written rules against it. Its ethical problems arise from the practical dangers of imperiling judicial independence and lowering respect for the individual judge in particular and judicial decisions in general. These are problems of prudence insofar as preservation of the Justice's influence on the Court and the power of the Court itself are concerned. These are also problems of ethics insofar as they affect the capacity of the Justice and the Court to fulfil the duty to protect the rights of the people by making law-court decisions—decisions which will be respected and obeyed.

Ethics, like prudence, would demand at least that the issue motivating the intervention be of such gravity and the danger—or need—so pressing as to outweigh the ill effects which might be caused either by a request for a *quid pro quo* or by publication in full detail of the Justice's extra-judicial activities. This judgment is not only highly subjective but also involves a predictive weighing of intangibles. There may be no *quid pro quo* asked. If one is asked it may be only very minor, such as an appearance at some ceremonial occasion or a lunch with a congressman's friends. On the other hand, the return favor may, as it did with Taft on at least two occasions, involve his participation

179

in a political nomination or election campaign. There may be no publicity about the lobbying; even if there is it may not necessarily hurt the Court. Whatever blows the prestige of the Supreme Court suffered during the 1930's, they were certainly not due to Chief Justice Hughes's successful attack on the Court-packing bill, and there is little evidence that Taft's lobbying hurt himself or the Court. Yet the publicity may be damaging. Even the false charge of collusion between Buchanan and Taney on the slavery issue[2] hurt the Court's prestige, and it would seem that this danger is greater today, when the expectation is widespread that Justices will stand aloof from politics.*

NON-JUDICIAL ISSUES

Issues which do not directly concern the judiciary raise other sorts of questions. Not only is a judge less likely to be effective, since he can usually speak with less expertise, but also the moral justification of personal influence is much more tenuous. The distinction between judicial and non-judicial issues is not so clear-cut as to constitute an objective measuring rod which all who run might read, but it may still be useful. Taft's intervention to "save" judicial power from what he honestly believed to be the evils of the Caraway and Norris bills or to further the administration of justice through the Judges' Bill raised problems very different from his intervention to defeat such measures as the McNary-Haugen bill or the bonus legislation. Taft himself realized the probable impropriety of his action in the latter situation. He wrote Andrew Mellon just three days after his original letter in

* Taft was concerned about the ethics of many of his political activities, and he wanted some sort of institutionalized means of advising Congress of the need for improvements in the federal court system. It was on this ground that he justified some of his lobbying for the 1922 Judiciary Act and its establishment of the Conference of Senior Circuit Judges. Taft, of course, never felt himself restricted to this device in dealing with Congress, but the Judicial Conference has become a legitimate institutional means by which federal judges can make their needs on legislation known. Since only the Chief Justice takes an official part in these Conferences, it might be worthwhile if Congress were to set up some formal machinery—beyond appearances at congressional hearings to discuss bills already under consideration—whereby Supreme Court Justices might offer their views on legislation for the peculiar problems of their tribunal. Such machinery could raise many ethical problems, but hardly any more than the formal procedure of inviting Justices to appear and testify at congressional hearings or the informal one of having Justices draft or comment privately on bills to public officials.

which he had requested that the Secretary of the Treasury persuade Coolidge to veto six different measures: "As I look back I think it was presumptuous of me to write such a letter to you, but I hope that you and the President will understand that the motive was good, however questionable the propriety."*3

SPEECHES

Public speeches and writings of the Justices involve related questions. Here as in most other areas of judicial activity there are no written rules, few principles, and varied practice. Some Justices, like Brandeis, have consistently refused to speak or write for public consumption except from the bench.† Others, like Brewer, Douglas, and Frankfurter, have spoken and written on a wide range of topics. It could not be claimed that the Justices have exchanged their right of free speech for their robes,[4] but their office does impose some limitations on the exercise of their rights. For instance, elementary judicial ethics would forbid discussion of pending cases or those likely to come to the Court.

In addition, two other situations can be immediately eliminated. First, even the most prudish Justice could not object on ethical grounds to such projects as a simple description of the mechanics of Court decision-making or explanations to the bar of means of improving appellate advocacy. At the other extreme, it would be exceedingly improper for a judge to participate in a campaign for nomination or election to public office, such as that in which Samuel Chase engaged for John Adams in 1800 or Learned Hand for Theodore Roosevelt in 1912, and those in which John McClean, Salmon Chase, and Stephen Field indulged for themselves. It would also be impossible to justify partisan political polemics delivered from the bench, such as those with which Samuel Chase harangued grand juries in the early years of the last century. No more than military commanders can judges ethically exercise their right to free speech so as to expound political

* How much the Chief Justice really repented his action is doubtful. On the same day that he apologized to Mellon, he told his brother Horace that he knew that Coolidge would veto the World War I bonus bill. "What I am trying to induce him to do is to veto a lot of other bills."

† Brandeis did appear with Hughes and Van Devanter before the Senate Judiciary Committee in 1935 to speak against Senator Black's bill, but even there Brandeis spoke only two sentences to the effect that he agreed with what his colleagues had said. See chap. vi, p. 162 n.

views to audiences which are compelled by law to attend and forbidden by law to rebut. A Justice who feels passionately about current issues of public controversy is always free to resign and campaign openly, as Justice Black offered to do in 1940[5] to assist Roosevelt's third-term efforts.*

Elimination of extreme situations still leaves unanswered ethical questions about the vast majority of judicial speeches and writings. Indeed, such questions are probably unanswerable except on the basis of a speech by speech or article by article analysis, and even then many, if not most, would probably have to be categorized as "doubtful." In a practical sense, public statements of the Justices *should* cause less intense problems than does lobbying. Speeches and writings are public and the Justice has—presumably—fully thought through the situation and has had to decide that his reputation and the prestige of the Court will not be hurt by what he is saying.

Ethical and prudential considerations again merge here: in whatever he says or writes a Justice should not identify himself or the Court with a political party or faction. General themes, such as Black's plea for respect for the Bill of Rights,[6] create less serious problems than would support of or opposition to very specific policy proposals which are being debated in the political process. A Justice might avoid some of the ethical problems by couching his argument in broad terms, as Frankfurter did in opposing suggestions to require prior judicial experience for Supreme Court appointees.[7]

It is manifest that off-the-bench statements of the Justices raise ethical problems. It is also obvious, as the leading student of such speeches and writings has concluded, that these can be both proper and useful means of appealing to the public conscience.[8]

II COMPROMISE AND ACCOMMODATION

Supreme Court Justices have as much independence in the sense of job security as any free society can safely give its rulers. With this protection, a Justice might reason that he can, indeed must, vote his conscience and speak his mind on all cases which come before him regardless of the reaction of his colleagues, other government officials,

---

* A desire to stir up public opinion in favor of American entrance into the League of Nations was one of the reasons Justice John Clarke gave for leaving the bench in 1922.

interest-group leaders, or the public at large. The Constitution, the Justice could say, gives him a share of authority to decide cases according to the law as he sees it. What other people do with their share of law-making and policy-making authority is their business.

For a Justice who reasons in this fashion, moral choice is clear and his conscience easy. Except for trivial incidentals, he cannot compromise, he cannot accommodate, he cannot delay or retreat. Certainly one can understand this point of view, and while admiring it still wonder whether a Justice could not in good, though less easy, conscience think in a very different fashion. A Justice who perceived that his power was limited might feel that he should establish a hierarchy of values he wanted promoted. Every decision, a policy-oriented Justice would believe, requires the expenditure of such scarce resources as energy, time, prestige, or good will. Indiscriminate use of these resources could leave him or the Court exhausted at crucial moments. Thus, the Justice might decide that, since he cannot do all the good he would like, he must allocate his resources to accomplish those ends which he thinks most important, knowing that this allocation may mean that other tasks will not be accomplished.

Where speaking out in favor of a given policy would be certain to antagonize his colleagues or to be voted down in conference or, if pushed through the Court, to provoke bureaucratic resistance, hostile congressional legislation, executive refusal to enforce, or public rejection, the Justice might well ask himself whether he has the moral right to try to persuade his colleagues to adopt such a policy or to vote for it himself, even though he believes the policy involved to be morally correct, constitutionally impeccable, and, if accepted, conducive to the interests of the nation. Under such circumstances, he might decide that it would be more moral to compromise and aim for a lesser but possibly attainable good.

A Justice faces the same problem in opposing a policy which is sure to triumph in the Court or in the other processes of government. He may find that his choice is whether to fight and lose all or to compromise and accept a lesser evil. To select a lesser evil is a hard task, but one which practical politicians frequently face and moral theologians respect. Thomas Aquinas stated that "a wise law giver should suffer lesser transgressions that the greater may be avoided."[9] As chapter iii pointed out, a Justice may reasonably decide that to refrain from a

183

searing dissenting opinion with an open plea to Congress to reverse a particular policy is a lesser evil, since such a dissent might so antagonize his colleagues on the bench as to cause him to lose influence over them in equally or more important decisions.

Indeed, a Justice might reverse the usual question and ask himself whether it would be moral for him to sacrifice making some immediate improvement for the sake of a future and greater gain. He could decide that he should make such a sacrifice if on the available evidence he believes that: (1) doing the smaller good now would materially weaken the chances for later accomplishment of the greater good; and (2) the ultimate advantage of the greater good would outweigh the disadvantages of waiting. In discounting the long-range goal, the Justice must keep in mind that he is dealing with human beings of limited life span. As Keynes is said to have remarked, "In the long run we're all dead."

COMPROMISE WITHIN THE COURT

The ethical problems confronting a judge are somewhat different when he considers compromise within the Court, within the judicial system, with other branches of government, and with opinions and prejudices held by significantly large or vocal segments of the public at large. It is perhaps easiest to justify accommodation within the Court. There are three general institutional procedures open to a multi-judge tribunal which follows the tradition of publishing a reasoned statement explaining the considerations which led to particular decisions: (1) the judges can agree to abide by majority rule and join in one opinion for the court with no expression of separate views; (2) the judges can write their opinions seriatim in each case; or (3) the judges can try, whenever possible, to frame one institutional opinion but also agree that individual judges have the right to file separate opinions.

The first rule is more compatible with the civil than the common law tradition and has no chance of widespread acceptance in federal courts. The second rule would go far toward eliminating the necessity for compromise within the Court, though it might not affect the expediency of other tactics in intra-Court relations. Jefferson, in an effort to destroy Marshall's influence on the other Justices, urged an end to the practice of the Court agreeing to opinions "huddled up in conclave."[10] The former President would have required each Justice to publish his own views, on the theory that "a regard for reputation, and the judgment of the world, may sometimes be felt where conscience is dormant, or indolence inexcitable."[11] Court foes through the years have repeated Jefferson's suggestion, but this reform has no chance of success. As a practical matter the volume of the business of the Court makes it a physical impossibility.

Since John Marshall,[12] the practice of the Court has been that of the third rule, carrying with it the necessity for compromise on many issues. "When you have to have at least five people to agree on something," one Supreme Court Justice has commented, "they can't have that comprehensive completeness of candor which is open to a single man, giving his own reasons untrammelled by what anybody else may do or not do if he put that out."[13] Knowing that he will have to operate largely within the tradition of the institutional opinion, it is difficult to see how a Justice who voluntarily accepts his commission can raise ethical objections against compromise with his colleagues as a general principle, though he may reasonably refuse to accommodate his views on specific issues.

INTER-COURT RELATIONS

Sensibility to the personalities and influence of inferior court judges is not of itself a matter of ethics. Compromise, however, again raises ethical problems. Accommodation in this area is more difficult. A Justice may know with considerable accuracy how his colleagues will react to given proposals, but he can seldom predict precisely the divisions within the judicial bureaucracy. It may be that the ethical problems are also more difficult, yet they are similar in kind to those created by being a member of a multi-judge tribunal.

Neither the framers of the Constitution nor a majority of Congress have seen fit to give the Justices formal authority to decide who shall be appointed, promoted, retained, or removed from lower court posts.* Neither the framers nor Congress have restricted jurisdiction over federal questions to federal courts, where the Justices' physical and psychological control over their bureaucracy would be greater. With their

---

* Article II, section 2 of the Constitution authorizes Congress to allow the courts to make appointments of "inferior Officers." Presumably this would permit Congress to have the Supreme Court appoint federal district and circuit judges. Congress, of course, has not and probably never will pass such legislation.

authority over lower court judges thus limited, the Justices cannot always be certain that they can count on their bureaucracy wholeheartedly to carry out their policies. A Justice must therefore ask himself if his conscience would really be clear if he persuaded his brethren to adopt (or did not try to dissuade them from adopting) a policy which would be frustrated by hostile lower court judges.

POLITICAL COMPROMISE

Compromise with the other branches of government or with public opinion creates the most difficult kinds of practical and ethical problems. Once more there is the practical problem of predicting not only how elected politicians will shape their policy preferences to the various kinds of pressure to which they are subject, but also of determining the nature both of the policy preferences and the pressures. The ethical dilemma is also more acute. The framers of the Constitution took great pains to make the Justices independent of political control, whether exercised by elected politicians or by segments of the electorate. For a Justice to weigh current political reactions or to anticipate future political reactions in his decision-making would seem to defeat the very purpose of judicial independence.

Unfortunately for members of the Court, their choice is not so clear. First, the Constitution does give them an extensive field of independence, but it does not make their power completely independent. As chapter ii showed in detail, each of the other branches of government has a number of means of frustrating any policy which the Court may endorse and even the option of attacking the very power of the Court itself. Confronted with the possibility of a successful blocking action or counterattack, a Justice may, here too, see himself forced to choose a lesser good than he really wants in preference to an evil or a lesser evil in preference to a greater evil. John Quincy Adams said that the Constitution itself was "a compromise extorted from the grinding necessities of a reluctant people."[14] Reluctant compromise—through tacit or open bargaining—with colleagues, or lower court judges or members of Congress or executive officials or prevalent public opinion may also be one of the "grinding necessities" of judicial life.

The judge, however, faces these grinding necessities in a different context than does a legislator. Judges do make policy, but they do so on the basis of specific cases. They lay down general rules and at the same time are obliged to apply those rules to particular litigants or to

186

order other judges to do so. It is relatively easier for a legislator to compromise on a piece of public policy which will *later* be promulgated and applied to *future* conduct of a faceless mass of humanity. While a judge also hopes to influence future conduct, he applies his decision—whether or not diluted by various kinds of accommodation—to past actions of particular persons whose lives, freedom, or property hang in the immediate balance.

Thus one might make a further distinction between kinds of compromise, that is whether it involves a general policy doctrine or the specific result in a given case or both. The discussion of bargaining in this book has been principally concerned with that involving general statements of policy, though it would be unrealistic to deny that such general statements also affect the individual case which provides the occasion for a policy pronouncement. Insofar as the question of having the Court publicly *announce* broad policy is involved, the ethical problems of a Justice would seem to be little different from those of any other holder of public office. No ethical rule binds him to insist on having all or nothing in every case that comes up. It was surely ethical for the Justices, during the 1930's and 1940's, when they might have feared that national opinion was not yet ready to sanction the end of Jim Crow, to limit their opinions rejecting segregation to the specific facts of each case, rather than boldly announcing that it was unconstitutional for a state under any circumstances to demand racial separation in the use of public facilities. So too, during a period when legislative witch-hunting was the mood of the day, it would not necessarily be unethical —which is not to say "wise"—for the Justices to reverse convictions for contempt of Congress on technical and procedural rather than on broad, substantive grounds. The Justice may be an opinion leader, but he is not a dictator; he may be a powerful government official, but he is not an autocrat.

Where the *result* of a decision is concerned, the Justice has a different set of choices. Despite frequent statements from the bench that the Court does not take cases in which the issues are of importance only to the particular litigants, once the Court does decide that a case fits its criteria for certiorari or appeal and takes that case, the Justices have an obligation not merely to lay down wise policy to cover all similar situations, but also to guard, to the extent they are able, the rights of the litigants. Protection of the legal rights of litigants is not the only concern of the Court, but it must be a major concern as long as this

187

institution functions as a court of law as well as a policy-making branch of the national government and not solely in the latter capacity.*

At this point one might make still another distinction to clarify the Justice's ethical choice. On the one hand are those cases in which government officials, state or federal, try to utilize the judicial process to achieve their own policy objectives. Usually this is attempted through a criminal prosecution. On the other hand are those cases in which a private litigant asks a court either to restrain other private parties or, more commonly in public law cases, government officials from infringing on his rights or to assess reparations for such injury.

In the first kind of case, one might submit, the Justice has little if any ethical leeway to compromise on decision with the political branches of government or with public opinion at large. Courts in our society, as Justice Black has said, *should* "stand as havens against any winds that blow."[15] If the degree of independence which the Constitution gives judges is designed to perform any function at all, it is to insure that judges will not allow government officials to use the judicial process to take a man's life, liberty, or property without due process of law. One might go so far as to say that a Justice would have no room whatever to compromise on the actual decision with government officials or public opinion where the case originated in a federal constitutional court since the Court has an added duty to oversee the administration of justice in this system. There might conceivably be some room for such compromise on cases originating in state courts or in military

* This doctrinal-result distinction would have similar implications for compromise with lower court judges as for compromise with political officials or public opinion. On the other hand, this distinction would seldom have meaning in intra-Court relations. If a Justice is in the minority on the result of a case, he has given up nothing belonging to the losing litigant if he switches his vote in exchange for some doctrinal concession. One of the few occasions when this dichotomy would raise major problems of ethics in compromise within the Court would be where a Justice would engage in logrolling in the sense of switching his vote in one case where it would change the outcome in exchange for another Justice's switching his vote in a second case. It is possible that the gravity of the two situations would be sufficiently different to make this appear a reasonable choice. I should add that in going through the various private papers of the Justices I found no absolutely convincing evidence of such exchanges, though it is probable that Justices have given in on cases where the switch would not affect the outcome in the hope that when in the majority themselves they might pick up a few votes because of good will.

tribunals since the Court has measurably less control over these agencies of government.

In such cases, there may be, however, wide latitude for compromise with political officials or public opinion on matters of announced doctrine. If, for example, a Justice believed on the basis of available information that a decision that the Smith Act was unconstitutional would probably provoke a constitutional amendment legitimating such statutes, he could ethically try to persuade his colleagues to justify reversal of a conviction obtained under this act on some technical point of law —and it is a rare case in which a skilled lawyer could not find some such grounds for reversal.*

While not technically a conviction and certainly not an instance of the government's using the courts to effect a policy, *Bridges* v. *Wixon* may still provide an illustration of the sort of reasoning suggested by this distinction. After efforts to deport Harry Bridges under existing law had failed, Congress in 1940 amended the statute with, according to the author of the amendment,† the explicit purpose of expelling the West Coast labor leader. After a new set of hearings, the special inspector for the Alien and Immigration Service found that Bridges' *past* membership in the Communist party and his connections with the Marine Workers Industrial Union made him subject to deportation under the amended statute. The Board of Immigration Appeals, however, went over the record and findings and came to the opposite conclusion. The Attorney General reviewed the case, agreed with the special inspector, and ordered Bridges deported. A federal district court and the Circuit Court of Appeals denied Bridges' application for a writ of habeas corpus, but the Supreme Court granted review.

---

* This is not a perfect solution since a retrial is possible. Certainly one would have nothing but condemnation for a trial judge who allowed a case to proceed to a conviction in an atmosphere dominated by mob violence or fear of lynch law, especially if that judge tried to turn the case into an instrument to advance his own political career.

† "It is my joy to announce that this bill will do, in a perfectly legal and constitutional manner, what the bill specifically aimed at the deportation of Harry Bridges seeks to accomplish. [Congress was also considering at the time a proposal instructing the Attorney General to deport Harry Bridges, but objections had been raised that naming Bridges specifically made the proposal a bill of attainder.] This bill changes the law so that the Department of Justice should now have little trouble in deporting Harry Bridges and all others of similar ilk." 86 *Cong. Rec.* 9031.

189

According to Justice Murphy's notes of the conference,[16] Chief Justice Stone opened the discussion by stating that the issues before the Court were narrow: Did Bridges come under the amended act? If he did, was there evidence to support the deportation decision of the Attorney General? Since Congress had absolute power to exclude or expel aliens for any reason whatever, Stone could not see that it was relevant that Bridges was being deported for membership in the Communist party. Several members of the Court expressed agreement with Stone; others disagreed, and the conference discussion soon became heated. The question was asked whether the Court would sustain deportation because of membership of the Democratic or Republican parties. One Justice said he seriously doubted that Bridges had had a fair hearing. Another expressed wonder that the special inspector, who had been a federal judge, could have allowed in evidence the sort of hearsay testimony used against Bridges. A third Justice commented that in amending the statute Congress had done nothing less than to pass an ex post facto law.

Even the Justices who thought the Court should affirm the lower court decision admitted distaste for the whole business. One of them baldly stated that the Attorney General had behaved like a "damn fool." Another conceded that Congress had done a shabby thing. However, these judges insisted that the issue was one of power, not of wisdom or morality. Congress had the authority to deport aliens for any reason, good or bad, wise or foolish.

As the discussion went on, it became clear that there was a majority to reverse. One of the minority Justices then warned that the implications of the case went far beyond Harry Bridges. The Justice feared that, if the Court were to restrict the constitutional power of Congress to expel aliens, Congress would limit further immigration if not completely shut it off. Thus grave injustices would be done to generations of potential immigrants. "I beg of your conscience," Murphy recorded this Justice as saying, "not to write into law something born out of a special situation." Another minority Justice emphasized the same point: "It was a rotten thing Congress did but I would be slow to subject others to greater injustices in [an] effort to save Bridges."

Whether or not because of the minority's pleas, the opinion of the Court did not rest on constitutional grounds. Rather, following a line similar to that taken by Justice Reed at conference, Douglas' opinion for the majority based the decision on procedural grounds; testimony had been admitted against Bridges which violated basic standards of fairness. Justice Murphy, in a separate and lone concurrence, branded the amended statute as unconstitutional on its face. Stone, joined by Roberts and Frankfurter, dissented.*

If the majority Justices in fact perceived that there was a danger that Congress might react strongly against a decision favorable to Bridges by limiting or restricting further immigration, they faced a cruel choice between doing justice to Bridges and injuring perhaps millions of future immigrants—a consideration which was much more apparent in the closing days of World War II than it would have been ten years later or earlier. Assuming what is not at all clear from the evidence, that the majority Justices decided to use procedural rather than constitutional grounds to justify their decision to head off a congressional reaction, it is difficult to see how one could doubt that they acted ethically.† They had done justice to Bridges and had done so without jeopardizing the chances of future immigrants to come to America. Moreover, the majority opinion—and even more so Murphy's concurrence—contained enough material on the background of the case to reveal to all who read it the shameful way in which certain public officials had behaved.

There are different ethical problems present in the second kind of situation: one in which a private citizen has asked a court to order public officials to commit or not to commit certain kinds of action. Here the Court deals, where federal officials are involved, with officers of an independent and coequal branch of government. State officials, of course, are not coequal in authority with federal officials, but they are relatively independent of federal judicial control; indeed, in the absence of co-operation from the executive department of the national government, they are almost completely independent where a local constituency disapproves intensely of a Court policy, such as desegregation. In this second kind of situation, a Justice would have great ethical leeway to compromise with government officials or public opinion

* Justice Jackson took no part in the decision, probably because he had been Attorney General during the initial stages of the proceedings. Murphy had been Attorney General during part of the earlier effort to deport Bridges.

† This is not to say that there was or was not real danger of congressional reprisal against immigration or to imply that, for whatever motives the majority may have had, collectively and individually, they chose the best or worst course.

191

either on the kind of policy to be announced or on the possible result of a case.* Here, where the Court is asked, in a sense, to operate outside the confines of the courtroom and to order or persuade an independent and/or coequal branch of government to conform its behavior to standards set by the judiciary, the Justice's function becomes, in ethical terms, almost indistinguishable from that of any other government official. His obligation is to get as much as he can for a deserving litigant, consistent with the needs of society and the realities of politics.

It was just this distinction that Justice Robert H. Jackson was trying to explain in his much misunderstood dissent[17] against the Court's decision in *Korematsu* v. *United States* to uphold the conviction of a Nisei for violating the army's West Coast evacuation order during World War II. Perhaps in answer to one Justice's comment that were he the military commander he would maintain the evacuation policy despite any Court decision that it was unconstitutional,[18] Jackson wrote: "I should hold that a civil court cannot be made to enforce an order which violates constitutional limitations even if it is a reasonable exercise of military authority. . . . I do not suggest that the courts should have attempted to interfere with the Army in carrying out its task. But I do not think they may be asked to execute a military expedient that has no place in law under the Constitution. I would reverse the judgment and discharge the petitioner."

These manifold distinctions among the kinds of compromise which can take place with political officials or public opinion provide a tentative and hopefully useful basis for analyzing problems of judicial ethics. However, like prudence, ethics cannot be reduced to a neat set of formulae. In *Bridges,* the Justices could arrive at the "correct" result by several different roads; in other cases they may have far fewer options. A failure to compromise on result in a criminal prosecution may cause even greater injury to the rights of persons not immediately involved in that case and so create an ethical dilemma as cruel as that presented by *Bridges.* In 1954, for instance, shortly after the School Segregation cases, an Alabama miscegenation prosecution confronted the Court with this sort of problem. A state court had convicted and sentenced a Negro woman to the penitentiary for the crime of marrying a white man, and her lawyer petitioned the Supreme Court for

---

* As Holmes commented in speaking for the Court, "In determining whether a court of equity can take jurisdiction, one of the first questions is what it can do to enforce any order that it may make." *Giles* v. *Harris* (1903).

192

review. The Justices denied certiorari.[19] Although the reasons behind a denial of certiorari are seldom announced, some speculation is possible. First, from the rationale of the race cases immediately before and after this miscegenation controversy, it is clear that had the Court made a ruling squarely on the constitutional issue, it would have had to invalidate the Alabama statute forbidding mixed marriages or repudiate either explicitly or implicitly much of the doctrine of the School cases. Second, it is even more clear that racial intermarriage—"mongrelization"—has been the great bête noire of white southern society and one of the chief reasons behind the resistance to school integration.

On the basis of these two factors, the Justices had to decide whether a ruling against the constitutionality of miscegenation laws, coming so close on the heels of the School cases, would have further aroused the already resentful southern whites to the point where even token school integration would be practically impossible. Allowing an innocent woman to go to the penitentiary is a high price to pay for making school integration easier. On the other hand, jeopardizing the fate of integration and the rights of countless hundreds of thousands of Negro children is also a high price to pay for freeing one woman.* The Court's intricate maneuvering to avoid the miscegenation issue in another case, *Naim* v. *Naim*, indicates the Justices' awareness of the volatile nature of the problem, as does the remark which one Justice is supposed to have made after leaving the *Naim* v. *Naim* conference: "One bombshell at a time is enough."

Another dilemma may present itself when the Justice knows that refusal to compromise on the result in a criminal prosecution may seriously endanger not merely a particular policy but the effectiveness of the Court itself. The classic example is *Ex parte McCardle* in 1868. A majority of the Justices believed, so Justice Field told a confidant and so it would appear from the decision in *Ex parte Milligan* two years earlier, that Reconstruction carried out through military government was unconstitutional.[20] Yet in the face of Radical threats, the

---

* The Justices' moral choice may have been made easier by the fact that in the nineteenth century the Court had upheld the constitutionality of miscegenation laws, and under the doctrine that one disobeys the law at his or her own peril the Justices could have concluded that the woman had run a risk which she would have to accept. See particularly *Pace* v. *Alabama* (1883) and Note, "Constitutionality of Anti-Miscegenation Statutes," 58 *Yale L.J.* 472 (1949).

Justices, as Gideon Welles said, "caved in"[21] and delayed action until Congress had removed the Supreme Court's jurisdiction. Biting criticism has been heaped on the Justices over the years for this refusal to meet the Radicals head-on in constitutional combat. But had the Court decided against the constitutionality of military Reconstruction, there can be little doubt that Radical leaders would have launched an attack against the very foundations of judicial power. Indeed, the House had just passed a bill requiring a two-thirds majority of the Court to invalidate a federal statute, and some Radicals were proposing abolishing the Court.

Knowing that the Court's popular prestige in the North had not yet recovered from *Dred Scott* and realizing that Andrew Johnson would be unable to give them real help, the Justices would have shown little acumen if they had not recognized that the odds heavily favored the success of any such assault. "[T]he Republican majority in Congress and among the Northern people," James Ford Rhodes has written, "was determined to have its way and would no more be stopped by legal principles and technicalities than it had been by the President's vetoes."[22] The Justices thus had to consider whether they could in conscience order McCardle freed (not knowing whether the military authorities would obey the order) at the cost of a grave risk to the principle of judicial review itself and perhaps even the destruction of a system of separation of power.*

Whatever doubts one might have about the courage or the ethics of *McCardle,* its prudence is not open to question. The Court emerged from this conflict somewhat battered but with its power basically intact. Although the Justices had submitted to temporary legislative domination, by maintaining their power potential they had helped insure that this domination would be short-lived. The Justices turned what threatened to be a battle of annihilation into a stinging and humiliating but still not disastrous defeat.

* Chase's ability to preside over Johnson's impeachment trial was, of course, an important factor in maintaining the system of separation of powers. David Hughes in his study of Chase concludes that the Court's evasive tactics in the McCardle case were the result of the Chief Justice's planning. "Salmon P. Chase: Chief Justice" (Ph.D. diss., Princeton University, 1963), chap. v. Although Hughes does not say so, it is plausible that Chase perhaps thought he stood a better chance of defeating the Radicals in the impeachment trial and thus preferred to fight in the arena where the odds were in his favor. Certainly Chase's manner of presiding over the trial hurt the Radicals.

194

In situations like *McCardle,* a Justice might apply the principle which theologians call "toleration of evil," a doctrine which holds that a man is not under a moral obligation to fight what is beyond his power to influence or overcome. "Choice," Aquinas said, "is only of possible things."[23] Martyrdom may be a moral necessity for an individual, and under the very same conditions be a wanton luxury for a public official since in sacrificing himself he may be giving up the rights of others as well as risking his power to protect the rights of yet other citizens.

But even in confronting issues as difficult as those of *McCardle* or the miscegenation cases, the Justices have a third alternative to martyrdom or to knuckling under and falsely acknowledging that another branch of government possesses a certain authority. They may also do nothing, utilizing one or more of their technical, law-court instruments to avoid passing on the merits of any aspect of the controversy. And in fact this is precisely the course the Justices chose in the miscegenation cases and to only a slightly lesser extent in *McCardle.**

Adoption of this "passive"[24] alternative is hardly the sort of choice a Justice would make if he were free to act as he would prefer, but it may be the best choice available under particular circumstances. To declare unconstitutional an act which impinges on basic values knowing that this decision would not prevail may be more than an exercise in futility. It may not only severely damage the Court as an institution but may also result in the permanent validation, through other means of legitimation, of the infringement. Thus, such a decision involves considerations of both ethics and prudence. On the other hand, it would be a violation of his oath of office and a betrayal of his public trust for a Justice who believed in judicial review to cause or try to cause the Court to uphold an act which he was convinced contravened, beyond any reasonable doubt, the letter and spirit of the Constitution. Facing this sort of conundrum, a Justice could intelligently conclude that avoiding the dangerous question was both the most prudent and ethical course.

Again, in his *Korematsu* dissent, Justice Jackson was groping for a generalized explanation of this aspect of limited choice:

* In *McCardle* the Justices did rule a year after ordering reargument that Congress could revoke the Court's jurisdiction even where a case was *pendente lite*—without, however, intimating any view on the constitutionality of military Reconstruction.

195

It would be impractical and dangerous idealism to expect or insist that each specific military command in an area of probable operations will conform to conventional tests of constitutionality. . . . But if we cannot confine military expedients by the Constitution, neither would I distort the Constitution to approve all that the military may deem expedient.

Coming to the core of his argument, he stated:

Much is said of the danger to liberty from the Army program for deporting and detaining these citizens of Japanese extraction. But a judicial construction of the due process clause that will sustain this order is a far more subtle blow to liberty than the promulgation of the order itself. A military order, however unconstitutional, is not apt to last longer than the military emergency. . . . But once a judicial opinion rationalizes such an order to show that it conforms to the Constitution, or rather rationalizes the Constitution to show that the Constitution sanctions such an order, the Court for all time has validated the principle of racial discrimination in criminal procedure and of transplanting American citizens. The principle then lies about like a loaded weapon ready for the hand of any authority that can bring forward a plausible claim of an urgent need. . . . A military commander may overstep the bounds of constitutionality, and it is an incident. But if we review and approve, that passing incident becomes the doctrine of the Constitution. There it has a generative power of its own, and all that it creates will be in its own image.

IMPERFECT INFORMATION

Reference has been made in this and earlier chapters to the problem of incomplete information. A Justice not only has to weigh imponderables, but he must do so on a predictive basis. As George Graham has observed, "The role of the prophets has not been easy, and a thoughtful person does not now envy the justices of the supreme bench."[25]

Imperfect knowledge also means that it may be both practically prudent (the opposition also has to operate on imperfect knowledge) and ethically correct for a Justice to run the risk of injuring or even destroying judicial power in order to protect other values. Ethics, like prudence, requires only that a Justice should be sure that the good to be gained makes the risk worthwhile, careful in his timing, and as certain as possible that the decision will not stir up such reaction as to do more harm than good to the values he is trying to protect. It would be

196

a strange form of morality that forbade a Justice to gamble on the side of good—again as long as the risk were calculated rather than heedless or reckless.

THE CHOICE OF MARTYRDOM

Even a Justice who believed in the complex sort of ethics analyzed here might decide that in a given situation the only moral, and perhaps practical, course for him to follow would be one which appeared very likely to lead to official or public repudiation of the Court, loss of his own influence with his colleagues, impeachment, or the destruction of judicial power itself. To a goal-oriented judge, judicial power after all should logically be a means, sometimes an indispensable means, but nevertheless only a means, to another end.

If a value at the apex of the Justice's hierarchy of values were threatened, he might reasonably conclude that his only real alternative was martyrdom. His justification for such a course could be that the value was so important that a free society—and therefore the Court as an instrument of free government—could not exist without this value and that without an immediate statement from the Court the value would be lost. He might also believe that the Court's sacrifice might act as a catalyst to restore the lost value. There is a vast difference between a Justice accommodating his views to those of other officials when there is an agreed framework within which public authority should be exercised, even though there may be honest disagreement as to whether a specific act falls inside or outside the framework, and a Justice compromising with an ideology fundamentally divergent from his own.

8 Judicial Decision-making and Judicial Strategy

The major purpose of this book has been to suggest, through an inquiry into the capability of a Justice to influence public policy, an approach to the study of the Supreme Court. This approach, though not without difficulties, can with further refinement contribute toward a theoretical understanding of judicial behavior and the process of judicial decision-making. Thus the empirical evidence which has been offered to support the analysis has been less concerned with *patterns* of behavior than with illustrations, many of them perhaps episodic, of what kinds of planning and execution are open to a policy-oriented Justice.* Despite this over-all purpose, there have really been two threads running through this book—a close examination of the opera-

* I prefer to be guilty of understatement rather than overstatement, but I must make two qualifications. First, in my examination of the papers of the Justices, I found recurrent and rather consistent patterns of negotiation and bargaining within the Court. The patterns, however, do differ somewhat from period to period. I think that the Justices of the Taft Court were more apt to bargain over votes—as distinguished from separate opinions—than were the Justices on the Stone or Vinson Courts. Though marked, the differences were of degree, not kind. Among the factors which account for these differences are: (1) a change in Court mores regarding dissents, from strong disapproval to only mild disapproval or even general indifference; (2) the varied orientations, personalities, and values of the Justices and Chief Justices in the twenties and forties; (3) the radical lightening of the Court's work load, a lightening which provided increased opportunity for, and temptation to, write separate opinions.

The second qualification is that, God forbid, I could write a book of equal or greater length using the same frame of reference as in this one, but repeating less than a half-dozen of the illustrations used here.

tional concept of judicial strategy as well as a suggestion for a broader research design. The first part of this final chapter will, therefore, be a discussion of the implications of capability analysis for the study of judicial decision-making; the second part will consist of a further exploration of some general problems of judicial strategy.

I THE STUDY OF JUDICIAL DECISION-MAKING

Chapter i posed two questions as essential to theorizing about judicial decision-making: (1) What range of choice is actually open to a Justice? (2) How can possible choices be expressed? Chapters ii through vi, it would not be immodest to claim, have shown that the range of choice open to a policy-oriented Justice is very different from that usually pictured by "conventional wisdom." The complex political system within which he must function compels a Justice who wishes to act rationally in terms of achieving his policy goals to weigh a number of factors in addition to the specific legal issues in individual cases. In so doing, this political system restricts in many ways the courses of action open to a policy-oriented Justice. At the same time, careful assessment by a Justice of his available resources and of how they might be most efficiently used can greatly expand that range of choice in other directions. Similarly, these chapters have indicated that there exists a wide variety of means by which a Justice may express his preferences, a variety far beyond merely voting and writing opinions. Possibilities of negotiation, bargaining, and lobbying, to mention only the most obvious means, can increase the range of available choice as well as multiply the number of ways in which these choices can be expressed.*

* If the reader can stand another "for instance," Taft's action in *Craig* v. *Hecht* (1923) provides a further illustration of the range of choice open to a Justice. In that case Craig, the Comptroller of New York City, published a letter severely criticizing a decision of a federal district judge. Despite the fact that the litigation to which Craig referred had already been decided—thereby making it difficult to claim that the letter had interfered with the administration of justice—the judge held Craig in contempt and sentenced him to 60 days in prison. Instead of appealing, Craig sought and obtained habeas corpus from another federal judge. On appeal, the Circuit Court of Appeals reversed the release order, and a majority of the U.S. Supreme Court agreed that Craig had sought the wrong remedy; he should have appealed, not asked for habeas corpus. Taft wrote a concurring opinion voicing some concern over the proper balance between protection of administration of justice and

None of this presentation in any fashion detracts from the value of either the traditional or the more recent "behavioral" research methods. What it does assert is that, if we are to have the sort of empirical base needed to formulate and test hypotheses and later general theories, we must have information beyond voting and opinion analyses. Additional evidence of the kind utilized here can be found in quantity only in private papers or in confidential interviews. These are not easily come by, when they are extant they are incomplete, and they are and will continue to be subject to a considerable time lag as long as Justices insist on preserving the secrecy of intra-Court relations during their own lifetimes. Thus primary reliance for almost all data on contemporary judicial behavior, and for much past judicial behavior, will always have to be placed on other research techniques.

On the other hand, there need be no time lag in hypothesizing on

---

protection of free speech. He concluded, however, that Craig's seeking the wrong remedy had left the courts helpless to aid him.

The Chief Justice himself was not helpless. Within a week after the case was decided he talked to Coolidge about the possibility of pardoning Craig and then quickly wrote the President two letters. In the first, Taft offered the opinion (complete with citations to dicta in a previous Supreme Court opinion and to several opinions of the Attorney General) that the President had constitutional authority to pardon in cases of criminal contempt—a point of constitutional law which the Court was not officially to decide until two years later, when the Chief Justice wrote the opinion in *Ex Parte Grossman* (1925). The second letter urged Coolidge to give the pardon because of the severity of the sentence, because no appellate court had had or could have the opportunity to review the case on its merits, and because Craig's absence from his post for two months would injure the public business of New York City. Taft to Coolidge, Nov. 27, 1923, Nov. 29, 1923, William Howard Taft Papers, Library of Congress. In early December, Coolidge remitted the jail sentence, and a rhubarb ensued as to whether or not this remission constituted a full pardon.

As usual, the Chief Justice was thinking in larger terms than a particular piece of litigation. The arbitrary action of the judge in the Craig affair had aroused the indignation of labor and the Progressives, and Taft wished to head off their efforts to curb the contempt power. As he told his son: "I have been advising the President with respect to that [the Craig case]. This will be the basis for an attack on injunctions and on process of contempt and so on. How far it may be effective I do not know. It is a popular thing to denounce judicial action, and they may get a majority in both Houses for a measure of change in this regard. I think Coolidge should be induced to veto anything that would be really dangerous." Taft to Robert A. Taft, Dec. 2, 1923, Taft Papers.

the basis of capability analysis. Even where papers or interviews are not available the results of traditional and behavioral research can be combined to provide fruitful—and testable—hypotheses about how Justices will behave or have behaved, based on how they *can* act.*
These hypotheses—and again, later broader theories—can be used to predict the behavior of Justices and tested against actual experience. Apparent errors can be noted and the reasons for them could be more thoroughly investigated when private papers become available.†

Such a scheme may be utopian, as may be the premise that it is possible to obtain useful, testable generalizations about judicial decision-making or, in a broader context, about the role of the judiciary in the American system of government. But if this goal is attainable, it cannot be reached until we have fully faced up to the fact that judges, if they so desire, can systematically pursue policy objectives in ways which, though not identical with, are certainly analogous to, those open to other government officials. Moreover, until we know how a Justice *can* operate, it is not possible to conclude how he *should* operate—as long, that is, as we accept the dictum that choice is only of possible things— to achieve those ends which we think good.

It goes without saying that capability analysis, alone or in combination with more familiar approaches, will not provide all-encompassing

* One might, for example, formulate a specific and very obvious hypothesis about Brandeis. Scalogram analysis shows that during Taft's chief justiceship, and especially during the early years of that period, Brandeis often voted against the claims of labor and for the claims of business. One might infer from these data that Brandeis was neutral in his attitude toward labor-business-government relations, or that if not neutral he was at least able to keep his attitude from affecting his votes. Available biographical information on Brandeis does not support either of these conclusions. There are other possible explanations, of course. Capability analysis would suggest that Brandeis, as a passionate progressive, may have been bargaining—tacitly and/or openly —with his colleagues, frequently joining a conservative majority in exchange for or in hope of softening the effect of adverse decisions on his economic policy goals. Letters in the Woodrow Wilson Papers from Justice Clarke to Wilson, referred to above, p. 56 n., support this hypothesis, as does the general theme of Alexander Bickel's book, *The Unpublished Opinions of Mr. Justice Brandeis* (Cambridge, Mass.: Belknap Press of Harvard University Press, 1957). When restrictions on access to the Brandeis Papers have been removed, this hypothesis can be more fully tested.

† I am making an assumption which may be unwarranted—that the publication of this kind of study will not cause future judges to destroy their papers.

answers to every problem in the study of judicial decision-making. Undoubtedly, as research progresses, questions of fundamental importance will arise and demand new—at least in terms of application to public law—modes of analysis and original investigatory techniques. One important question which will inevitably come up when patterns of actual behavior are compared with possible courses of action open to a Justice is the kind of role which a Justice sees himself as playing vis-à-vis his colleagues, judges of other courts, other government officials, the public, and the constitutional system. To meet these sorts of problems, role analysis—hardly new in social science but rarely used in the study of judicial behavior[1]—will have to be exploited to yield concepts and categories which can be fruitfully employed where there are available only vague clues rather than detailed responses to questionnaires or interviews.

Most important, capability analysis has nothing to do with the decision as to which goals are best in a moral or philosophical sense. At most it helps indicate what goals are possible, not which ones are desirable. In short, capability analysis offers only a promise of aiding understanding of apparently disjointed empirical phenomena not of marching ineluctably to the discovery of the immediate public interest or to ultimate truth.

II JUDICIAL STRATEGY: AN OVERVIEW

In discussing strategies to minimize specific checks on a Justice's power, previous chapters have made frequent allusion to the problem of integrating any particular facet of planning into a comprehensive scheme to direct action. Essentially this involves the formulation of "grand strategy," a task analogous to but more complex than ordering tactical maneuvers to conform to the guidelines of a given strategy. Such a broad plan may help keep the Justice from becoming so immersed in strategy and tactics for their own sakes that he loses sight of his objective, the accomplishment of a policy goal.

An additional and essential purpose of grand strategy would be to provide the Justice with a rational basis for deciding on the allocation of time, energy, and other resources to the separate tasks of minimizing each of the various checks on his power. Just as he probably will not find himself in a position to accomplish every objective he thinks desirable, so even in pursuing a more limited goal or set of goals a Justice would probably only dissipate his energies were he to try to carry out simultaneously and with equal vigor feasible strategies to minimize all of the checks on his power. He would thus have to co-ordinate his work so that in executing a strategic plan against one obstacle he would not be crippling his attempts to cope with other difficulties. Second, he would also have to establish priorities. He would have to decide which forces posed the gravest threat or gave the strongest promise of success and to concentrate his efforts there.

Moreover, the formulation of a grand strategy, by compelling the Justice to take an overview of his current situation in the political system, allows him a firmer basis for choosing between a direct or indirect approach or to decide which facets of his over-all scheme should follow one approach or the other. In the judicial process, the direct approach consists of one swift blow or a series of blows aimed at the immediate attainment of an objective; the indirect approach consists in less rapid, less open, and less obviously goal-oriented maneuvering.

The distinction between the two approaches was personified in the behavior of Black and Stone toward the Court's role as guardian of laissez faire. Black wanted to overrule suddenly a half-century of precedents and to substitute for them fresh constitutional principles.[2] Stone, on the other hand, preferred to move slowly and circumspectly. When in the minority he would often suppress his real views and silently join the majority, saving his dissents for what he considered to be the most important constitutional cases. On the Taft Court, in the twenties, he developed the practice, when assigned the task of writing the opinion of the Court, of refraining from writing a new doctrine in bold, broad strokes—a doctrine which would probably be abruptly rejected and, if expressed at all, be relegated to a dissent. Instead he planted seeds of new concepts in the dicta of his writing. He operated, as one of his clerks recalled, "like a squirrel storing nuts to be pulled out at some later time. And there was mischief as well as godliness in his delight when his ruse was undetected and the chestnuts safely stored away."[3] Indirection became a habit, and even in later years when there was a liberal majority on the Court, Stone still preferred a gradual undercutting of old, erroneous rules to sudden change.[4] His tactical goal was for lawyers, judges, and government officials to ask impatiently not why the Justices had made new policy, but when they would do so.

The tradition-oriented nature of the judicial process usually makes the indirect, incremental approach, despite its disadvantages of slowness and lack of doctrinal neatness, the more promising one. The common law's inherent conservatism, its reverence for adherence to *stare decisis,* stability, and predictability would normally mean that a policy made in a piecemeal manner would be better able to win support within the Court and the judicial bureaucracy and to maximize the Court's prestige outside the judicial system. When the Court reverses itself or makes new law out of whole cloth—reveals its policy-making role for all to see—the holy rite of judges consulting a higher law loses some of its mysterious power.

There is a further reason favoring the slower, indirect approach. Facts, as Brandeis said, are stubborn; and behavior patterns are stubborn facts. The analysis in this book has frequently called attention to the potential reaction of government officials and to a lesser extent interest-group leaders. These people represent, however imperfectly in terms of their own claims or in terms of democratic aspirations, fractions of the population as a whole. In weighing alternatives the Justice must always ask himself whether or how the public, at least the affected public, will live with his policy. As all government officials are reminded from time to time, public opinion, no matter how difficult to define or predict, can be a real political force.

A Justice is under less compulsion—moral, legal, or practical—than elected officials to follow public opinion. Still, he cannot cavalierly toss off popular objections to his policy preferences and proceed freely to remake his society. Whether or not he should have, he does not have the power to do so. Even a unanimous Court in the 1850's could not have brought off a solution to the problem of slavery in the territories by cloaking the rights of slaveholders under the protection of the Fifth Amendment, or to the economic problems of the 1930's by finding that the Constitution required reliance on Adam Smith's Invisible Hand rather than on F. D. R.'s New Deal, or to the race problems of the 1950's by demanding that white America make instantly operational the kind of casteless society explicit in democratic theory and implicit in the Fourteenth Amendment.

History, so Robert McCloskey claims, shows that "the Court's greatest successes have been achieved when it has operated near the margins rather than in the center of political controversy, when it has nudged and gently tugged the nation, instead of trying to rule it. . . . The Court ruled more in each case when it tried to rule less, and that paradox is one of the clearest morals to be drawn from this history."[5]

It may be a general rule that the more radical the change from tradition or from prevailing policies the Justice wishes to bring about, the more he will find himself compelled to resort to indirection; still, the direct approach can by no means be written off. Pushing for more than one expects or even wants is a typical strategy in any situation in which bargaining is likely to occur. In addition, where the Justice's policy goal does not require a drastic change in doctrine, a direct approach may be both the easiest and most efficient method of proceeding.

Where the opposition or uncommitted actors may be questioning the determination of the individual Justice or of the Court, a direct approach may even be absolutely necessary. As previous chapters have emphasized, a prudent Justice would neither want to create the impression with his colleagues that he will always or usually accommodate his views to theirs, nor would he want other government officials or the public at large to believe that the Court is unwilling to assert itself or is constantly ready to back down in the face of real opposition. Prestige is not the same as popularity any more than statesmanship is the same as expediency. "The court that raises its hand against the mob may be temporarily unpopular," Justice Douglas has said, "but it soon wins the confidence of the nation. The court that fails to stand before the mob is not worthy of the great tradition."[6]

A direct approach may also be indicated where the Justice desires a radical policy change and such a change is supported by the political environment. Had he been so minded, for instance, Hughes might well have led the Court during the 1934 and 1935 terms to repudiate its protection of business interests and to have assisted moving the nation closer toward a governmentally controlled economy.

While Taft's desired course for the Court involved no radical break with tradition, it did constitute a change from the immediate past of constitutional adjudication.* Nevertheless, Taft could urge his brethren to join him in striking directly and boldly at state or federal legislation which interfered with what he conceived to be property rights. He could do this because—in part due to his own efforts—a majority of the Justices thought pretty much as he did on socio-economic issues. He could also do so because of his influence outside the Court. In some

---

* The change, of course, had begun prior to Taft's coming to the Court. See especially, *Adams* v. *Tanner* (1917), *Stettler* v. *O'Hara* (1917), and *Hammer* v. *Dagenhart* (1918).

measure this influence was due to his having been President, but only in some measure. Taft had foes as well as friends on Capitol Hill and, as no one knew more intimately than he, the advice of an ex-President is not always welcome in the White House.* Perhaps more important than his having been Chief Executive was the fact that Republican stalwarts at every level and in every branch of government knew that Taft believed in and would fight for much the same conservative goals as they themselves were advocating.

Ideologically at least, the Taft Court majority was an integral part of the political coalition that controlled the federal government during the 1920's. Despite the Chief's dire predictions in 1922 of a decade of conflict,[7] the Court was never in real political trouble during his tenure. The Progressives personally annoyed the Chief Justice and occasionally even harassed the Court, but the political notions of Harding, Coolidge, and Taft were cut from the same cloth, and their policy views fitted well the general mood of Congress and the country. With the benefit of hindsight, it is apparent that what the Progressives were waging was no more than guerrilla warfare. They were reminding, sometimes with a sting, the Justices—and conservatives generally— that there were limits to the consensus within which they operated; but La Follette and his group were not posing an immediate threat either to judicial power or to the policy preferences of a majority of the Justices. Despite occasional fits of temper and despair, Taft recognized that the power of the Progressives lay more in their ability to make blistering speeches or to block "desirable" legislation than in their capacity to bring off a legislative program. As the Chief Justice told his daughter, the Progressives "are not at all agreed on what they want, and each man is a candidate for the Presidency, so that when they come to constructive work instead of destructive, they will be divided into innocuous confusion."†[8] Only after the 1929 crash gave dramatic im-

---

* As Taft once wrote Harding: "I hope you will credit me with the IOU's of recommendations which I have refused to give, not because the applicants were unworthy, but because I did not propose to burden you, because I believe it is a rule of propriety that an ex-President shall avoid bombarding his successor. But once in a while a case comes along of which I venture to make an exception." Taft to Harding, April 19, 1921, Taft Papers.

† To his brother Horace, the Chief Justice noted: "Each [of the Progressives] is for himself—that is the canon of conduct of each. It is fortunate that it is so because it helps the conservatives who would keep things as they are, at least in their fundamental aspects." Dec. 28, 1922, Taft Papers.

petus to a long-term realignment within the electorate was the stage set for a complete overhaul of the prevailing policy of more and more business in government and less and less government in business.*

THE LIMITS OF JUDICIAL STRATEGY

In planning both grand strategy and particular strategies a Justice would undoubtedly perceive other choices and perhaps give different weights to factors which have been discussed in these chapters. Indeed, a Justice might conclude that his policy goals were not worth the price he would have to pay in time, energy, and, most important, in developing a coldly calculating outlook toward his colleagues and his environment. Certainly the Justice who was so policy-oriented as to try to put into effect the strategies outlined in this book would have to operate, as Arthur Schlesinger, Jr., said of Brandeis, "with the caustic intensity of a man who enlisted ruthlessness in the service of the moral and rational life."[9]

Even where a Justice chose to act as effectively as possible to achieve his policy goals, there are severe limits to what he could accomplish. By no legal means, of course, could he become a constitutional dictator. He may keep a majority of the Court together on some issues, and he may succeed in influencing executive and legislative officers or segments of public opinion so that the effectiveness of opposition to the Court's decisions will be reduced or positive co-operation induced. A Justice, however, cannot long dominate, though he may shrewdly and profitably negotiate—tacitly or openly—with an *unwilling* Court, Congress, President, or country. In bargaining situations, a Justice may gain something, but he cannot count on turning defeat into victory in the fashion of Talleyrand at Vienna.

When, as Taft did, he reflects the views of the political coalition then dominant in society, a Justice may be able to achieve all or most of his objectives; but he is capable of doing so in large part because his goals are widely shared not merely because he is astute. When he reflects, as Justices have so often, the views of a coalition dominant in the past, strategy offers him less tangible—though perhaps no less important—rewards. In this situation he must frequently be content with paring away some of what is obnoxious in new policies or even in postponing

* Taft was still Chief Justice until February 3, 1930, but his papers show that he had ceased to function intellectually by Christmas, 1929, if not shortly before that time.

the day when the old and cherished order collapses. When he represents views which have not yet triumphed in the political processes, a Justice may find his most profitable course is merely to lay the groundwork for later advances, to inform and educate his colleagues, other government officials, and the public at large.

To say all of this is not to assert that public policy is predetermined by the existing social milieu or to deny that dynamic national leadership can change that milieu. What is meant is only that a Justice of the Supreme Court is not often in a particularly favorable position to exert the dynamic sort of leadership which can mobilize effective reform or counterreform movements. On the other hand, although the general political environment may be beyond the power of a Justice to control, it is rarely beyond his power to influence. One may thus say of judicial strategy what Stanley Kelley has said of election campaigning: its object is to make marginal changes in result.[10] And that, as every student of politics—academic and practical—knows, is saying quite a bit.

PRUDENCE AND THE JUDICIAL VIRTUES

No combination of strategy and tactics can substitute for the other qualities which go to make a good judge. Personal integrity, wisdom, skilled craftsmanship, energy, intellectual acumen, and that elusive capacity called statesmanship are all very necessary. Nor can any mode of analysis prevent a Justice—or other decision-maker—from estimating falsely his own power or that of the opposition, or from misconstruing possible alternatives, or from arriving at a wrong moral or ethical judgment. No method can reduce the art of judgment, whether legal, political, or ethical, to an IBM punch-card system. Strategy is concerned with the systematic ordering and selecting of means conducive to the achievement of given ends; it helps little to determine what those ultimate ends should be.

In a confused world in which good is so often frustrated, bargained away, or even soundly defeated, it is comforting to look on the Supreme Court as one place where justice is done without regard to any factor other than the merits of a particular controversy as weighed on the scales of an impartial rule of law. The Court, however, plays not one but three different roles, and as chapter vii emphasized these roles sometimes make conflicting demands. The Supreme Court is a court of law operating within a malleable but recognizable set of rules; it is a tribunal dispensing justice between litigants; at the same time it is a coequal branch of the federal government with a responsibility for formulating national policy while deciding specific cases.

As every first year law student knows, established legal rules and justice in a specific case may point in different directions. The addition of a policy-making role may constitute nothing less than a cruel and unusual punishment to the Justices. In John P. Roche's phrase, the Court suffers from institutional schizophrenia, and this ambivalence inevitably affects expectations about the actions of the men who staff the Court as well as the behavior of the Justices themselves. Justices are expected to act like statesmen yet be aloof from all considerations of policy; at the same time they are selected through a blatantly political process, frequently for manifestly political purposes, and are asked to decide cases fraught with some of the most controversial of current public-policy issues.

The Justices are expected to operate on a much higher plane than elected officials, on a plane where compromise and devious stratagems have no place. To a great extent judges do operate on this higher plane, at least insofar as they deal with non-judicial officers. And to a greater extent than legislators or administrators, Justices must and do publish statements justifying their compromises in terms of fundamental principles of jurisprudence. But as rulers, judges who wish to see their policy choices become operative cannot always escape the necessity of negotiation or resort to devious stratagems. To paraphrase Pendleton Herring's remark about administrators, by giving judges the responsibilities of statesmen we have also imposed on them the burdens of politicians.[11] Judges operate in a different fashion than do other government officers: their capacity to influence policy is limited by different external forces and internal restraints; but they do share many of the tribulations, practical and ethical, common to elected officials and appointed administrators. No more than other policy-makers can judges ignore Max Weber's injunction that "in numerous instances the attainment of 'good' ends is bound to the fact that one must be willing to pay the price of using morally dubious means or at least dangerous ones— and facing the possibility or even the probability of evil ramifications. . . . [T]he early Christians knew full well the world is governed by demons and that he who lets himself in for politics, that is, for power and force as means, contracts with diabolical powers and for his action it is *not* true that good can only follow from good and evil only from evil, but that often the opposite is true. Anyone who fails to see this is, indeed, a political infant."[12]

In reflecting on the cardinal virtues of a judge, Lord Justice Denning has enumerated *"Patience* to hear what each side has to say; *Ability* to understand the real worth of the argument; *Wisdom* to discern where truth and justice lie; *Decision* to pronounce the result."[13] To this list one might add: *Prudence* to know how much truth and justice and wise policy can be achieved at any one time and how they may be most surely and effectively attained; *Courage* to pursue such a course even when it means risking some political dangers and enduring bitter criticism from contemporaries as well as from historians for refusing to risk other dangers. Strategy, of course, is concerned only with prudence. It does not affect courage, patience, wisdom, understanding, or decisiveness; but it can show how these can be most efficiently exercised.

Notes

PREFACE

1. Quoted in Alpheus T. Mason, *The Supreme Court from Taft to Warren* (Baton Rouge: Louisiana State University Press, 1958), p. 203.

2. Karl Llewellyn, *The Common Law Tradition: Deciding Appeals* (Boston: Little, Brown & Co., 1960), p. 324 n.

3. See Louis Gottschalk, *Understanding History: A Primer of Historical Method* (New York: A. A. Knopf, 1950); Louis Gottschalk, Clyde Kluckhohn, and Robert Angell, *The Use of Personal Documents in History, Anthropology and Sociology* (New York: Social Science Research Council, 1945).

4. See John Schmidhauser, "The Justices of the Supreme Court: A Collective Portrait," 3 *Midw. J. of Pol. Sci.* 1 (1959).

5. Compare the conclusions of Morton Kaplan, *System and Process in International Politics* (New York: John Wiley & Sons, Inc., 1957), chap. ix.

6. Thomas Schelling, *The Strategy of Conflict* (Cambridge, Mass.: Harvard University Press, 1960).

1. INTRODUCTION

1. J. W. Peltason, *Federal Courts in the Political Process* (New York: Random House, Inc., 1956), p. 3.

2. Alexander Bickel, *The Unpublished Opinions of Mr. Justice Brandeis* (Cambridge, Mass.: Belknap Press of Harvard University Press, 1957). It must also be said, however, that much of the data for such a study has long been available. Although their interests were very different from mine in this book, Alpheus T. Mason in his biography of Stone, *Harlan Fiske Stone: Pillar of the Law* (New York: Viking Press, 1956), and Charles Fairman in his biography of Miller, *Mr. Justice Miller and the Supreme Court 1862–1890* (Cam-

bridge, Mass.: Harvard University Press, 1939), published enough primary source material to begin the sort of study I have undertaken.

3. Cf. Klaus Knorr, *The War Potential of Nations* (Princeton: Princeton University Press, 1956).

4. This usage, I believe, conforms closely to that of Robert A. Dahl and Charles E. Lindblom, *Politics, Economics and Welfare* (New York: Harper & Bros., 1953), p. 38.

5. Andrew Tully, *Capitol Hill* (New York: Simon & Schuster, Inc., 1962), p. 75.

6. See below, p. 122 and p. 136. Justice William Johnson also once suggested to a friend that he should try to get Congress to vote on a bill to limit the Court's jurisdiction, but Johnson said he wanted this vote because he thought the Court would be vindicated by the result. See Donald G. Morgan, *Mr. Justice William Johnson: The First Dissenter* (Columbia: University of South Carolina Press, 1954), p. 184.

7. Theodore Sorensen, *Decision-Making in the White House* (New York: Columbia University Press, 1963), p. 7.

8. Harold D. Lasswell and Abraham Kaplan, *Power and Society* (New Haven: Yale University Press, 1950), p. 71.

9. Karl von Clausewitz, *On War*, trans. J. J. Graham (new and rev. ed.; London: K. Paul, Trench, Trübner & Co., Ltd., 1911), Book II, chap. i.

2. THE FRAMEWORK OF JUDICIAL POWER

1. The observation is that of William Grayson of the Virginia Ratifying Convention, quoted in Alpheus T. Mason, *The Supreme Court: Palladium of Freedom* (Ann Arbor: University of Michigan Press, 1962), p. 72.

2. Max Weber, *The Theory of Social and Economic Organization*, ed. Talcott Parsons (New York: Free Press of Glencoe, 1947), p. 328.

3. See, for example, William W. Crosskey, *Politics and the Constitution* (2 vols.; Chicago: University of Chicago Press, 1953).

4. Marbury v. Madison (1803).

5. Felix Frankfurter, *Law and Politics,* eds. E. F. Prichard and A. MacLeish (New York: Harcourt, Brace & Co., 1939), p. 30.

6. Henry F. Pringle, *Theodore Roosevelt: A Biography* (New York: Harcourt, Brace & Co., 1931), p. 259.

7. Justice Harlan's dissenting opinion in Standard Oil v. United States (1911) has a long list of such cases. Among the more important were: United States v. Trans-Missouri Freight Ass'n (1897), United States v. Joint Traffic Ass'n (1898), and Addystone Pipe Co. v. United States (1899).

8. Standard Oil v. United States (1911).

9. Compare United States v. E. C. Knight (1895) with Loewe v. Lawlor (1908).

10. Merle Fainsod, Lincoln Gordon, and Joseph Palamountain, *Government and the American Economy* (3d ed.; New York: W. W. Norton & Co., 1959), p. 603.

11. 21 *Cong. Rec.* 2460.

12. Walton Hamilton and Irene Till, *Anti-Trust in Action* (TNEC Monograph No. 16 [Washington, D.C.: Government Printing Office, 1940]), p. 11.

13. Cf. the comments of Walter Adams and H. Gray, *Monopoly in America* (New York: Macmillan Co., 1955); Mark Massel, *Competition and Monopoly* (Washington, D.C.: The Brookings Institution, 1962), chaps. i–ii; Clair Wilcox, *Public Policies toward Business* (rev. ed.; Homewood, Ill.: Richard Irwin, Inc., 1960), chap. xi; Fainsod, Gordon, and Palamountain, *op. cit.*, pp. 560 ff., 591–603; and the discussion in Standard Oil v. FTC (1951) and Automatic Canteen Co. v. FTC (1953).

14. McCulloch v. Maryland (1819).

15. Hamilton and Till, *op. cit.*, p. 7.

16. Max Lerner, *America as a Civilization* (New York: Simon & Schuster, Inc., 1957), p. 442.

17. Osborn v. Bank of the United States (1824).

18. Jackson, J., concurring in Youngstown Sheet & Tube Co. v. Sawyer (1952).

19. Quoted by James Reston in his column in the *New York Times,* May 31, 1961, p. 32, col. 3.

20. It was probably this role which Brandeis had in mind when he stated that "The most important thing we do is not doing." The Court's legitimizing function has been expounded by Robert A. Dahl, "Decision-Making in a Democracy: The Supreme Court as a National Policy-Maker," 6 *J. of Pub. L.* 279 (1957), and more fully developed by Charles L. Black, *The People and the Court* (New York: Macmillan Co., 1960), chap. iii.

21. Especially Massachusetts v. Mellon (1923).

22. For a general discussion see Walter F. Murphy and C. Herman Pritchett, *Courts, Judges, and Politics* (New York: Random House, 1961), chap. vi.

23. See below, chap. iv, pp. 109–10 for a discussion of the All Writs Act.

24. See, however, United States v. Shipp (1906).

25. This distinction is basically that of Richard Neustadt, *Presidential Power* (New York: John Wiley & Sons, Inc., 1960), chaps. iv–v.

26. V. O. Key, *Public Opinion and American Democracy* (New York: A. A. Knopf, 1961), p. 8.

27. B. N. Cardozo, *The Nature of the Judicial Process* (New Haven: Yale University Press, 1921), p. 168.

28. Owen J. Roberts, *The Court and the Constitution* (Cambridge, Mass.: Harvard University Press, 1951), p. 61.

29. For a general discussion and specific bibliography on the problems in this section, consult Murphy and Pritchett, *op. cit.*, chaps. vii, x.

30. See, however, Pierce v. Society of Sisters (1925) and Barrows v. Jackson (1953).

31. John P. Frank, "Political Questions," in Edmond Cahn (ed.), *The Supreme Court and Supreme Law* (Bloomington: Indiana University Press, 1954), p. 36.

32. For a development of this approach see Edward Levi, *An Introduction to Legal Reasoning* (Chicago: University of Chicago Press, 1948).

33. Holmes to Pollock, Jan. 24, 1918; Mark DeWolf Howe (ed.), *Holmes–Pollock Letters* (Cambridge, Mass.: Harvard University Press, 1942), II, 258.

34. For a more complete discussion, see my article, "Lower Court Checks on Supreme Court Power," 53 *Am. Pol. Sci. Rev.* 1017 (1959).

35. Robert A. Dahl and Charles E. Lindblom, *Politics, Economics, and Welfare* (New York: Harper & Bros., 1953), p. 342.

36. Graves v. New York ex rel. O'Keefe (1939).

37. In addition to the material in my article cited above, note 34, see Chief Justice Warren's listing in his dissenting opinion in Communist Party v. SACB (1961).

38. For example, the order of Judge Atwell in Borders v. Rippy (1957).

39. See the litigation summarized in the *per curiam* opinion in United States v. Haley (1962).

40. See the letter and testimony of U.S. District Judge Alexander Holtzoff before two subcommittees of the Senate Committee on the Judiciary, summarized at p. 1024 of my article cited above, note 34, and the testimony of Virginia Judge William Old before another subcommittee. U.S. Senate, Committee on the Judiciary, *Limitations on Appellate Jurisdiction of the Supreme Court, Hearings on S. 2646*, 85/2 (1958), pp. 167–73. There are also the famous 1958 recommendations of the Conference of State Chief Justices. For details see my *Congress and the Court* (Chicago: University of Chicago Press, 1962), chap. x. A copy of the report is conveniently reprinted as an appendix to C. Herman Pritchett's volume, *Congress versus the Supreme Court 1957–1960* (Minneapolis: University of Minnesota Press, 1961).

41. One might also prefer to list the Norris–La Guardia Act of 1932, although this statute primarily affected federal district courts.

42. Gerald I. Jordan, "The Impact of Crises upon Judicial Behavior" (paper presented at the 1960 meetings of the American Political Science Association).

43. Henry Pringle, *The Life and Times of William Howard Taft* (New York: Farrar & Rinehart, 1939), I, 267.

44. Administrators of Byrnes v. Administrators of Stewart (1812).

45. Much of this literature is cited and summarized in Karl Llewellyn, *The*

Common Law Tradition: Deciding Appeals (Boston: Little, Brown & Co., 1960), Part I. Next to Llewellyn, the most widely read of the Realists was probably Jerome Frank, especially his *Law and the Modern Mind* (New York: Brentano's, 1930).

46. Clement Vose, "Litigation as a Form of Pressure Group Activity," 319 *The Annals* 20 (1958). In NAACP v. Button (1963), the Supreme Court held that the right of an interest group to utilize the judicial process is protected by the First and Fourteenth Amendments.

47. Among the more notorious have been: Hylton v. United States (1796), Fletcher v. Peck (1810), Dred Scott v. Sandford (1857), Buck v. Bell (1927), and Carter v. Carter Coal Co. (1936).

48. Dissenting Justices frequently make this charge against the majority. In 1958, while at the Brookings Institution, I used the briefs and records on file at the Supreme Court Library to check out a number of such accusations. However, due to the fact that only rarely is a record of oral argument available (since Warren became Chief Justice the Court has taped all oral arguments, but these tapes are available only to the Justices), one can seldom be certain that a point was or was not raised, or a point raised in the briefs abandoned under pressure. In any event, among the cases in which such a charge has been made by minority Justices or responsible scholars are: Swift v. Tyson (1842), Scott v. Sandford (1857), West Coast Hotel v. Parrish (1937), Erie Railroad v. Tompkins (1938), Uveges v. Pennsylvania (1948), Terminiello v. Chicago (1949), Jencks v. United States (1957), and Sherman v. United States (1958).

49. See Kenneth C. Davis, *Administrative Law Treatise* (St. Paul, Minn.: West Publishing Co., 1958), III, 291: "The law of the Supreme Court [on standing] is both needlessly complex and needlessly artificial." Sec. 22.18, pp. 291–94 of Davis' work has a general critique of the standing rules. See the comments on this critique in Murphy and Pritchett, *Courts, Judges, and Politics,* p. 246.

50. The most famous was that in 1822 from Justice William Johnson on behalf of the Court to President Monroe. It is reprinted in Donald G. Morgan, *Justice William Johnson* (Columbia: University of South Carolina Press, 1954), pp. 123–24. For other instances, see below, chaps. v–vi. Professor David Danelski of Yale University has been systematically collecting these opinions and plans to publish them or selections from them.

51. Karl Llewellyn, *The Bramble Bush* (New York: Oceana Publications, 1951), p. 149.

52. Sir Henry Slesser, *The Art of Judgment* (London: Stevens & Sons, Ltd., 1962), p. 28.

53. See my article, "Civil Liberties and the Japanese-American Cases: A Study in the Uses of Stare Decisis," 11 *West. Pol. Q.* 3 (1958).

54. Monongahela Bridge Co. v. United States (1910).

55. Quoted in Alpheus T. Mason, *The Supreme Court from Taft to Warren* (Baton Rouge: Louisiana State University Press), p. vii.

56. See particularly John Dickinson, "Legal Rules: Their Function in the Process of Decision," 79 *U. Pa. L. Rev.* 833 (1931), and Karl Llewellyn, *The Common Law Tradition.*

57. Llewellyn, *The Common Law Tradition,* p. 201.

58. "An Approach to the Analysis of Political Systems," 9 *World Politics* 383 (1957). For similar and no less useful conceptual schema, see also Joseph Tanenhaus, "Supreme Court Attitudes toward Federal Administrative Agencies," 14 *Vand. L. Rev.* 473 (1961); Richard C. Snyder, "A Decision-Making Approach to the Study of Political Phenomena," in Roland Yound (ed.), *Approach to the Study of Politics* (Evanston, Ill.: Northwestern University Press, 1958); and Harold D. Lasswell, "The Decision Process," in Nelson W. Polsby, Robert A. Dentler, and Paul A. Smith (eds.), *Politics and Social Life* (Boston: Houghton Mifflin Co., 1963).

59. David Easton, *The Political System* (New York: A. A. Knopf, 1953), p. 129.

3. MARSHALLING THE COURT

1. The literature on influence is vast. Among the works which I have found most helpful are: Fritz Heider, *The Psychology of Interpersonal Relations* (New York: John Wiley & Sons, Inc., 1958); Sidney Verba, *Small Groups and Political Behavior: A Study of Leadership* (Princeton: Princeton University Press, 1961); Robert F. Bales, *Interaction Process Analysis* (Cambridge, Mass.: Addison-Wesley Press, 1950); George C. Homans, *The Human Group* (New York: Harcourt, Brace & World, 1950); Bernard Bass, *Leadership, Psychology, and Organizational Behavior* (New York: Harper & Bros., 1960); Paul Hare, E. F. Borgatta, and R. Bales (eds.), *Small Groups: Studies in Social Interaction* (New York: A. A. Knopf, 1955); and David Danelski, "The Influence of the Chief Justice in the Decisional Process of the Supreme Court" (paper delivered to the 1960 meeting of the American Political Science Association), a shorter version of this paper appears in Walter F. Murphy and C. Herman Pritchett, *Courts, Judges, and Politics* (New York: Random House, 1961), pp. 497–508.

2. Albert Pepitone, "Motivational Effects in Social Perception," 3 *Hum. Rels.* 57, 71–75 (1950).

3. Quoted in Donald Morgan, *Justice William Johnson* (Columbia: University of South Carolina Press, 1954), pp. 181–82.

4. Quoted in Eugene Gerhart, *America's Advocate: Robert H. Jackson* (Indianapolis: Bobbs-Merrill, Inc., 1958), p. 274.

5. William Howard Taft to Robert A. Taft, Jan. 25, 1925, and Oct. 23, 1927; William Howard Taft Papers, Library of Congress.

6. Taft to Robert A. Taft, Oct. 23, 1927, *ibid.*

7. Holmes made this remark to Felix Frankfurter. It is quoted in Alexander Bickel, *The Unpublished Opinions of Mr. Justice Brandeis* (Cambridge, Mass.: Belknap Press of Harvard University Press, 1957), p. 164.

8. Quoted in Alan Westin, *The Anatomy of a Constitutional Law Case* (New York: Macmillan Co., 1958), pp. 123–24.

9. Memorandum of Taft to the other Justices, May 12, 1922, Taft Papers. The memorandum was addressed to all members of the Court except John Clarke. Since the U.S. Reports do not note that Clarke did not participate, the omission was probably due to an oversight by the Chief Justice's secretary.

10. United Brotherhood of Carpenters v. United States (1947).

11. Black to members of the conference, May 2, 1945, Harlan Fiske Stone Papers, Library of Congress.

12. Box 4, West Virginia v. Barnette file, Frank Murphy Papers, Michigan Historical Collections, Ann Arbor, Mich. The Murphy Papers used in this book are arranged in boxes by terms of the Court, with each case having a separate file or set of files. The Taft Papers are arranged chronologically, with no topical order whatever. The Stone Papers are arranged in several different ways. Some correspondence is contained in files organized according to person; other correspondence and slip opinions are filed according to term; and some files are arranged by subject matter.

13. Frankfurter to Murphy, June 5, 1943, Box 4, Hirabayashi file, Murphy Papers.

14. Draft opinion, *ibid.*

15. June 10, 1943, *ibid.*

16. Bedford Cut Stone Co. v. Journeymen Stone Cutters (1927).

17. Taft to Stone, Jan. 26, 1927, the Stone and Taft Papers. For a full treatment of the incident, see Alpheus T. Mason, *Harlan Fiske Stone: Pillar of the Law* (New York: Viking Press, 1956), pp. 255–60.

18. The letter is dated only April 2, but Stone's reply is dated April 3, 1930, Stone Papers.

19. Box 4, Ex parte Quirin file, Murphy Papers. Although this memorandum was initialed and the style is unmistakable, I think the Justice who wrote it would prefer to remain anonymous.

20. Stone to Roger Nelson, Nov. 30, 1942, Stone Papers. Mason, *op. cit.,* chap. xxxix, presents a detailed account of the way the case was handled.

21. The reports were correct, but Stone had endorsed other candidates as well. See my "In His Own Image," *1961 Supreme Court Review* 159, 191 n. Charles C. Burlingham blamed Stone's failure to support only Hand as the reason for Roosevelt's appointment of Rutledge, C. C. Burlingham file, the

Oral History Project, Columbia University, p. 23. The truth is somewhat different or at least more complex. As will be mentioned later in the text, F. D. R. reacted against the heavy pressure to appoint Hand, pressure which the President told a friend he could trace back to a member of the Court.

22. Frankfurter to Rutledge, Nov. 6, 1942, Stone Papers.

23. Hughes to Frankfurter, Jan. 18, 1939, Charles Evans Hughes Papers, Library of Congress.

24. Frankfurter to Hughes, June 5, 1939, *ibid.*

25. Frankfurter to Hughes, February 24, 1940, *ibid.*

26. Yazoo & Miss. V. Rr. v. Clarksdale (1921); quoted in David Danelski, "The Chief Justice and the Supreme Court" (Ph.D. diss., University of Chicago, 1961), p. 179.

27. Lamar to Hughes, June 3, 1913, Hughes Papers.

28. Day to Mrs. Hughes, June 9, 1913, *ibid.* There is a similar letter of the same date in the Hughes Papers from Lurton to Mrs. Hughes.

29. Quoted in Merlo Pusey, *Charles Evans Hughes* (New York: Macmillan Co., 1951), II, 671.

30. Institutional Investors v. Chi., Milwaukee, St. Paul & Pac. Rr. (1943).

31. Feb. 20, 1943, Stone Papers.

32. The note is dated only "Friday." From its place in the Stone Papers, I judge the year to be 1940.

33. The Malcomb Baxter (1928), Stone Papers. The final decision was unanimous.

34. Broad River Power Co. v. South Carolina (1930), *ibid.*

35. Lamb v. Schmidt (1932), *ibid.*

36. Alaska Packers Ass'n v. Industrial Accident Comm'n (1935), *ibid.*

37. Quoted in Danelski, "The Influence of the Chief Justice in the Decisional Process," in Murphy and Pritchett, *Courts, Judges, and Politics*, p. 506.

38. Professor Glendon Schubert has been exploring the relevance of game theory to certiorari decisions. See his *Quantitative Analysis of Judicial Behavior* (New York: Free Press of Glencoe, 1959) and "Policy without Law: An Extension of the Certiorari Game," 14 *Stan. L. Rev.* 284 (1962).

39. Holmes, of course, once commented that "Judges are apt to be naif, simple-minded men"; and, he added, "they need something of Mephistopheles." "Law and the Court" (1913), reprinted in Max Lerner (ed.), *The Mind and Faith of Justice Holmes* (New York: Random House, Inc., 1943), p. 390.

40. Quoted in Mason, *Harlan Fiske Stone,* p. 254.

41. Few of Stone's early opinions escaped criticism from McReynolds, criticism of a kind which can best be described as "picky." In McReynolds' defense, however, it should be said that he believed—though he was not always able to translate his belief into practice—that a judicial opinion should say

no more than was absolutely necessary to decide a specific case. "When a judge fully appreciates that every unnecessary word in an opinion hurts it, he may be relied upon to write with good effect. But when vanity, or an itch to throw off new and striking phrases and shine in the books, troubles him, his outgivings are apt to be noxious." McReynolds to Judge Hollzer, Aug. 31, 1933, James C. McReynolds Papers, Alderman Library, University of Virginia. McReynolds felt (quite correctly) that Stone often put more into his opinions than the cases demanded. See below, p. 203.

42. See Joel Francis Paschal, *Mr. Justice Sutherland: A Man Against the State* (Princeton: Princeton University Press, 1951), pp. 115–16, for a discussion of the pleasant exchange of views which was always possible between Holmes and Sutherland and between Brandeis and Sutherland.

43. Clarke to Taft, undated memorandum, ca. 1922, Taft Papers.

44. The story is told in Willard L. King, *Melville Weston Fuller* (New York: Macmillan Co., 1950), pp. 185–86.

45. For an account sympathetic to Jackson, read Gerhart, *America's Advocate*, chap. xv; for an account sympathetic to Black, see John P. Frank, *Mr. Justice Black: The Man and His Opinions* (New York: A. A. Knopf, 1948), chap. vii.

46. Justice Jackson once remarked privately that the unpleasantness in personal relations within the Court during the forties made him seriously consider resigning.

47. Clarke to Taft, Sept. 12, 1922, Taft Papers.

48. Taft to Warren G. Harding, Sept. 5, 1922, *ibid.*

49. This memorandum is filed in the Stone Papers. I would suspect that, as with the Quirin memorandum cited in note 19, the Justice would prefer to remain anonymous. Moreover, unlike the Quirin memorandum, this one is not initialed, so it may not have been written by the purported author.

50. See generally, Robert A. Dahl and Charles Lindblom, *Politics, Economics, and Welfare* (New York: Harper & Bros., 1953), chap. xii.

51. The concept of tacit bargaining is ably developed in Thomas Schelling, *The Strategy of Conflict* (Cambridge, Mass.: Harvard University Press, 1960), chap. i.

52. Quoted in Bickel, *Unpublished Opinions of Mr. Justice Brandeis*, p. 18.

53. Quoted in Charles Fairman, *Mr. Justice Miller and the Supreme Court 1862–1890* (Cambridge, Mass.: Harvard University Press, 1939), p. 320.

54. Milkwagon Drivers Union v. Meadowmoor Dairies (1941).

55. Law clerk to Murphy, Feb. 2, 1941, Box 2, Meadowmoor Dairies file, Murphy Papers.

56. Frankfurter to Murphy, Feb. 7, 1941, *ibid.*

57. Jan. 20, 1941, Stone Papers.

58. Ogden v. Saunders (1827).

59. Bickel, *op. cit.,* p. 30.

60. B. N. Cardozo, "Law and Literature," 14 *Yale Rev.* 699, 715–16 (1925). Charles Evans Hughes made much the same comment in his book *The Supreme Court of the United States* (New York: Columbia University Press, 1928), p. 68.

61. Feb. 15, 1947, Box 8, Harris file, Murphy Papers.

62. The letter is published in Charles Fairman, "The Retirement of Federal Judges," 51 *Harv. L. Rev.* 397, 412–14 (1938).

63. Quoted in Morgan, *Justice William Johnson,* p. 182.

64. Feb. 4, 1935, Stone Papers.

65. See T. M. Newcomb, "The Prediction of Interpersonal Attraction," 11 *Am. Psychologist* 575 (1956); and Robert Lane, *Political Life: Why People Get Involved in Politics* (New York: Free Press of Glencoe, 1959), pp. 108–11.

66. Taft thought that Brandeis was supported by a "claque" of liberal professors who wrote for law reviews. Taft to W. L. Phelps, May 30, 1927, Taft Papers. More recently, other Justices have sometimes been alleged to have used their law-school connections to reward friends and punish enemies, or at least to carry on a fight from the conference room or the pages of the U.S. Reports to the pages of law reviews.

67. Home Building & Loan Ass'n v. Blaisdell (1934). Mason, *Harlan Fiske Stone,* pp. 360–65 has a full account of the intra-Court negotiations here.

68. Stone to Douglas, June 9, 1943, Stone Papers.

69. The following summary of the conference is from the notes which Murphy took. Box 2, Goldman file, Murphy Papers. While Murphy's conference notes are often quite extensive and sometimes use quotation marks, these documents must, of course, be used with great care. I have not quoted directly from them, except for a few phrases or an occasional sentence which seem likely to have struck the ear of a listener. I have used them as relatively accurate summaries where, as here, they are supported by other evidence. I should add here that I was fortunate in that Professor J. Woodford Howard of Duke University, an expert on Frank Murphy, was in Ann Arbor when I was going through the Murphy Papers. Without Professor Howard's help I would never have been able to decipher much of Murphy's scrawl.

70. The draft is filed in the Stone Papers.

71. Box 2, Goldman file, Murphy Papers.

72. Conference notes, *ibid.*

73. March 5, 1942, Stone Papers.

74. Frankfurter to Murphy, April 3, 1942, Goldman file, Murphy Papers.

75. This draft is in both the Stone and Murphy Papers.

76. So Jackson noted in his letter to Murphy of April 6, 1942; the original is in the Murphy Papers and a carbon in the Stone Papers.

77. *Ibid.*

78. Fairman, *Mr. Justice Miller and the Supreme Court 1862–1890*, pp. 349–68, 370–71, 381, 429.

79. King, *Melville Weston Fuller*, pp. 180–81.

80. *Ibid.*

81. For studies of Taft's activities in the appointing process and the criteria which he applied, see my "In His Own Image," *1961 Supreme Court Review* 159; and "Chief Justice Taft and the Lower Court Bureaucracy," 24 *J. of Pols.* 453 (1962). David Danelski, *A Supreme Court Justice Is Appointed* (New York: Random House, 1964), has an intricately detailed examination of the appointment of Pierce Butler.

82. Taft's old friend and former White House Press Secretary, Gus Karger, wrote Taft that Harding had told him this. Karger to Taft, May 25, 1921, Taft Papers.

83. Taft to Sutherland, July 2, 1921, George Sutherland Papers, Library of Congress.

84. Taft to Van Devanter, Oct. 27, 1922, Taft Papers.

85. Taft to Harding, Dec. 4, 1922, *ibid.*

86. Taft to Henry W. Taft, Jan. 6, 1923, *ibid.*

87. Taft to Harding, Dec. 4, 1922, *ibid.*

88. Taft to Henry W. Taft, Jan. 16, 1923, *ibid.*

89. Taft left a remarkable memorandum describing the background to and the actual discussion with McKenna about his resignation; see my "In His Own Image," *loc. cit.*

90. Taft to Robert A. Taft, July 2, 1925, Taft Papers.

91. See Mason, *Harlan Fiske Stone*, p. 184.

92. Taft to Horace Taft, June 8, 1928, Taft Papers.

93. Stone to G. Helman, May 29, 1939, Stone Papers.

94. Stone to B. Shein, Feb. 3, 1942, *ibid.* As other possibilities Stone also mentioned Newton D. Baker and Learned Hand. Stone to R. Hale, Feb. 15, 1932, *ibid.*

95. Stone to G. Helman, Nov. 30, 1939, *ibid.*

96. In 1939 Stone, disclaiming any altruism in offering to resign, said that he would not have been sorry to leave the Court because "I felt mine was a voice crying in the wilderness so far as the tendencies of the Court were concerned, and I had numerous opportunities to do worthwhile things." Stone to G. Helman, *ibid.* In 1929, less than three years before the Cardozo nomination, Stone faced no less opposition on the Court—indeed Hughes and Roberts were not as conservative as Taft and Sanford had been—but he turned down several opportunities to leave the bench for lucrative private practice as well as offers to become Secretary of State and head of the National Law Reform Committee. These persistent refusals do not appear to indicate an anxiousness to throw off the cares of the Court. On the other hand,

Stone had ambitions to become Chief Justice and his name had been frequently mentioned as Taft's successor. Hughes's appointment to the center chair may well have dampened Stone's enthusiasm for judicial work.

97. Feb. 15, 1932, *ibid.*

98. Pusey, *Charles Evans Hughes,* II, 650–51.

99. John Schmidhauser, "The Justices of the Supreme Court: A Collective Portrait," 3 *Midw. J. of Pol. Sci.* 1 (1959).

100. Taft, for instance, was asked several favors by politicians whose aid he had sought. See my "In His Own Image," *loc. cit.*

101. Fairman, *Mr. Justice Miller and the Supreme Court 1862–1890,* p. 171.

102. Glendon Schubert, *Quantitative Analysis,* pp. 246–47.

103. *The Secret Diaries of Harold L. Ickes* (New York: Simon & Schuster, Inc., 1954), II, 552.

104. See Danelski, "The Assignment of Court's Opinions by the Chief Justice" (paper presented to the 1960 meetings of the Midwest Conference of Political Scientists).

105. Charles Fairman, "John Marshall and the American Judicial Tradition," in W. Melville Jones (ed.), *Chief Justice John Marshall: A Reappraisal* (Ithaca: Cornell University Press, 1956), p. 94.

106. Draft of a tribute to Edward D. White, ca. May 1921, Taft Papers.

107. Pusey, *op. cit.,* II, 676.

108. King, *Melville Weston Fuller,* p. 290.

109. For an excellent discussion of the literature here see William H. Riker's bibliographical essay, "Voting and the Summation of Preferences," 55 *Am. Pol. Sci. Rev.* 900 (1961); Part II and the Appendix of Duncan Black's *The Theory of Committees and Elections* (Cambridge: Cambridge University Press, 1958) has an analysis of some of the earlier writings on this problem.

110. Black, *op. cit.,* p. 40. Actually Black is more specific than I have indicated. He says: "When the ordinary committee procedure is in use, the later any resolution enters the voting, the greater its chances of adoption." Timing is obviously important, but I think that Black's phrasing sets too rigid a rule.

111. For Hughes's manner of presiding over the Court, see Mason, *Harlan Fiske Stone,* pp. 788–90; Pusey, *op. cit.,* II, 672–78; Felix Frankfurter, "Chief Justices I Have Known," 39 *Va. L. Rev.* 883 (1953); Edwin McElwain, "The Business of the Supreme Court as Conducted by Chief Justice Hughes," 63 *Harv. L. Rev.* 5 (1949).

112. For Stone's concept of his role as Chief Justice, see Mason, *Harlan Fiske Stone,* chap. xlvii. Sociological research has documented the common-sense observation of most people who have had to do committee work: too much time spent in group discussion lowers satisfaction with the final decision. Similar research, however, contradicts the actual occurrence in the Stone Court—that is, several sociologists claim that free discussion increases group

coalescence, whereas the effect on the Stone Court was increased division and dissension. See the literature cited in Bass, *Leadership, Psychology, and Organizational Behavior,* pp. 131–32.

113. Albert J. Beveridge, *The Life of John Marshall* (Boston: Houghton Mifflin Co., 1916–19), IV, 480 ff., 512–14, 585; Charles G. Haines, *The Supreme Court in American Government and Politics, 1789–1835* (Berkeley: University of California Press, 1944), pp. 579 ff. Cf. William W. Crosskey, "Mr. Chief Justice Marshall," in Allison Dunham and Philip Kurland (eds.), *Mr. Justice* (Chicago: University of Chicago Press, 1956).

114. See Charles Hendel, *Charles Evans Hughes and the Supreme Court* (New York: King's Crown Press, 1951), p. 279. Pusey, *op. cit.,* II, 770–72, does not believe that Hughes did change. Pusey's reasoning and evidence, however, have been demolished by Alpheus Mason in "Charles Evans Hughes: An Appeal to the Bar of History," 6 *Vand. L. Rev.* 1 (1952). Cf. John P. Roche, *Courts and Rights* (New York: Random House, Inc., 1961), p. 94: "Like General Douglas MacArthur, Hughes never retreated—he firmly advanced to the rear. . . ."

4. MANAGING THE JUDICIAL BUREAUCRACY

1. Richard E. Neustadt, *Presidential Power* (New York: John Wiley & Sons, Inc., 1960), p. 19.

2. See, in particular: Morris Janowitz, *The Professional Soldier: A Social and Political Portrait* (New York: Free Press of Glencoe, 1960), p. 8 and Part II; Daniel Bell, *The End of Ideology* (new & rev. ed.; New York: Collier Books, 1961), p. 251; and generally the Hawthorne Studies, cited at pp. 48–49 of George Homans, *The Human Group* (New York: Harcourt, Brace & World, 1950).

3. *Washington Post & Times Herald* in an editorial of Aug. 31, 1963, made this suggestion in commenting on a speech by Justice Brennan asking for more intelligent newspaper reporting of Supreme Court decisions.

4. Toledo Newspaper Co. v. United States (1918).

5. See Fritz Heider, *The Psychology of Interpersonal Relations* (New York: John Wiley & Sons, Inc., 1958), pp. 120, 258; and Albert Pepitone, "Motivational Effects in Social Perception," 3 *Hum. Rels.* 57 (1950).

6. Nardone v. United States (1939).

7. "The Trials and Tribulations of an Intermediate Appellate Court," 44 *Corn. L. Q.* 1, 7–8 (1958).

8. See the literature cited in Bernard Bass, *Leadership, Psychology, and Organizational Behavior* (New York: Harper & Bros., 1960), p. 315.

9. In recent years the Court has followed a general policy of relying more heavily on Courts of Appeals to supervise federal district judges. See especially La Buy v. Howes Leather Co. (1957).

10. See Bell, *op. cit.*, pp. 262–63; Nancy C. Morse and E. Reimer, "The Experimental Change of a Major Organizational Variable," 52 *J. of Abn. & Soc. Psych.* 120 (1956); Homans, *op. cit.*, chap. iii; and the literature cited in Bass, *op. cit.*, chap. vii.

11. See, for example, the charge of Senator Shields of Tennessee, reported in 62 *Cong. Rec.* 4859.

12. This co-operation, it turned out, was not exactly to the Supreme Court's advantage. See my *Congress and the Court* (Chicago: University of Chicago Press, 1962), pp. 176–77, 194, 201, 206, 236. The ideological temper of the state chief justices or of Supreme Court Justices would have to change from that of the late 1950's for co-operation to be meaningful in affecting public policy in the direction most Supreme Court Justices would want.

13. Taft to the Chief Judge of the Kentucky Court of Appeals, Feb. 4, 1922, William Howard Taft Papers, Library of Congress.

14. Taft to each Senior Circuit Judge, Dec. 19, 1921, *ibid.*

15. Erich Fromm, "Individual and Social Origins of Neurosis," 9 *Am. Soc. Rev.* 380, 381 (1944).

16. Chase to Judge William Giles, April 1, 1867, Salmon P. Chase Papers, Library of Congress. (Part of the Chase Papers are at the Library of Congress, and part at the Pennsylvania Historical Society in Philadelphia.) Professor David F. Hughes of Centre College has allowed me to use his notes on the Chase Papers and the John Underwood Papers, Library of Congress. Where Hughes has quoted a relevant portion of a letter, I have cited his dissertation, "Salmon P. Chase: Chief Justice" (Ph.D. diss., Princeton University, 1963), rather than the manuscript source.

Giles was more in sympathy with Taney's views on the Civil War than with those of Chase. See Carl B. Swisher, *Roger B. Taney* (New York: Macmillan Co., 1935), pp. 557 ff.

17. David Hughes, *op. cit.*, pp. 304–6.

18. Taft described his efforts to persuade Congress and the President in a number of letters. Especially revealing are those to: Senator R. Ernst, Oct. 26, 1925; C. P. Taft, II, and R. A. Taft, March 15, 1926; Judge J. Buffington, March 18, 1926; Charles Evans Hughes, March 19, 1926; Chester Long, March 19, 1926. Van Devanter was also working on such legislation. Van Devanter to Taft, June 9, 1926. All of this correspondence can be found in the Taft Papers.

19. See my "Chief Justice Taft and the Lower Court Bureaucracy," 24 *J. of Pols.* 453, 454–55 (1962).

20. Offutt v. United States (1954).

21. *Washington Post & Times Herald*, Feb. 28, 1962.

22. Bailey v. Patterson (1962).

23. Leigh v. United States (1962).

24. Cooper v. Aaron (1958).

25. Judge Kimbrough Stone to Hughes, March 29, 1936; Hughes to K. Stone, June 2, 1936; K. Stone to Hughes, June 5, 1936, Charles Evans Hughes Papers, Library of Congress.

26. Swisher, *Roger B. Taney*, pp. 557–60.

27. Chase to Judge G. W. Brooks, March 20, 1866, quoted in David Hughes, *op. cit.*, p. 175. (In using the Chase Papers, I have cited Hughes's thesis where he has quoted the gist of a Chase letter; but here, as in several other places, I have used a more complete quotation from the letter—one Hughes has given me—than appears in the dissertation.)

28. See the statutory definition and provision, 14 Stat. 51.

29. Chase to Underwood, Nov. 18, 1868, Underwood Papers.

30. David Hughes, *op. cit.*, p. 277.

31. Fla. ex rel. Hawkins v. Board of Control (1957).

32. The various decisions and opinions in this case are reprinted in Walter F. Murphy and C. Herman Pritchett, *Courts, Judges, and Politics* (New York: Random House, 1961), pp. 606–18.

33. Ex parte Crane (1831).

34. Sec. 25; 1 Stat. 73, 86.

35. 14 Stat. 385, 387.

36. Henry W. Hart and Herbert Wechsler, *The Federal Courts and the Federal System* (Brooklyn: Foundation Press, 1953), p. 420.

37. Sec. 13; 1 Stat. 73, 81.

38. 28 U.S.C. 1651 (a).

39. Ex parte Fahey (1949).

40. Compare the decision in United States v. Peters (1809) with that in United States v. Haley (1962).

41. See, for example, In re Nevitt (1902).

42. Thomas Schelling, *The Strategy of Conflict* (Cambridge, Mass.: Harvard University Press, 1960).

43. For a detailed discussion of this doctrine, see Note, "Federal Judicial Power: A Study of Limitations—III," 2 *Race Rel. L. Rep.* 1215, 1222–31 (1957).

44. Los Angeles Brush Mfg. Co. v. James (1927).

45. Taft to Clarence Kelsey, July 21, 1921, Taft Papers.

46. Daugherty and the Chief Justice were old acquaintances, see Henry F. Pringle, *The Life and Times of William Howard Taft* (New York: Farrar & Rinehart, 1939), II, 626–37, 827, 833; William Allen White, *A Puritan in Babylon: The Story of Calvin Coolidge* (New York: Macmillan Co., 1939), p. 284.

47. ". . . it isn't true," Taft wrote to Edward Colston on Feb. 1, 1923, "that

the judicial appointments are submitted to me. I can only make my recommendations known by affirmative and unsolicited action." Taft Papers.

48. *Ibid.*

49. Taft to Colston, Feb. 21, 1923, and Taft to Charles P. Taft, II, March 4, 1923, *ibid.*

50. Oct. 19, 1923. William Allen White has some sidelights on Taft's relationship with Coolidge in general and specifically in regard to judicial appointments. *Op. cit.,* pp. 284–88, 348–49. White's observations must be read in light of Stone's denial that Taft had much influence with Coolidge. Stone to White, Feb. 23, 1939, Harlan Fiske Stone Papers, Library of Congress. In turn, Stone's downplaying of Taft's influence must be read in light of three facts: (1) Stone was writing some fifteen years after the event; (2) he was defending himself against Taft's claim that he had "rather forced" Coolidge to appoint Stone to the Court (Taft to R. A. Taft, July 2, 1925, Taft Papers, quoted in Pringle—which is how Stone saw the claim—*op. cit.,* II, 1043); (3) the Taft Papers contain a number of letters from Attorney General Stone to Chief Justice Taft asking advice about appointment matters.

51. Nov. 30, 1923, Taft Papers.

52. To Charles P. Taft, II, Feb. 14, 1926, *ibid.*

53. To Helen Taft Manning, Nov. 30, 1924, *ibid.*

54. Taft to Lowell, Jan. 3, 1922, *ibid.* Lowell had written Taft to solicit his help for Hitchcock on Jan. 1, 1922, *ibid.*

55. Taft to Casper Yost, Sept. 20, 1923, and Taft to Fred Murphy, Nov. 30, 1923, *ibid.*

56. Sept. 30, 1923, *ibid.*

57. Both letters were dated Oct. 28, 1923, *ibid.*

58. Oct. 30, 1923, *ibid.*

59. Nov. 2, 1923, *ibid.*

60. All these letters were dated Nov. 1, 1923, *ibid.*

61. Nov. 11, 1923, *ibid.* Hadley answered on Nov. 14, 1923, that he did not know all of the candidates but was able to speak highly of Grimm, Hill, and Hitchcock.

62. Nov. 21, 1923, *ibid.*

63. On Nov. 30, 1923 Coolidge thanked Taft for clippings on Garesche; the second Taft letter was dated Dec. 3, 1923, *ibid.*

64. Dec. 27, 1923, *ibid.* On Nov. 21, 1923, Yost had written to Taft: "Spencer, to speak frankly, is not to be trusted, and his insistence upon the appointment of Garesche is generally believed to be based upon his desire to control the patronage of the court after he returns to practice." *Ibid.*

65. Dec. 28, 1923, *ibid.*

66. Jan. 12, 1924, *ibid.*

67. Isaac M. Meekins to Taft, Nov. 24, 1924, *ibid.*

68. Dec. 2, 1924, *ibid.*
69. Charles D. Hilles to Taft, Dec. 2, 1924, *ibid.*
70. Meekins to Taft, Jan. 8, 1925, *ibid.*
71. Meekins to Taft, Dec. 3, 1924, *ibid.*
72. Grady to Taft, Dec. 1, 1924, and Burber to Taft, Dec. 2, 1924, *ibid.*
73. Taft to Burber, Dec. 2, 1924, and Taft to Grady, Dec. 3, 1924, *ibid.* Either the mails were much faster in the 1920's than in the 1960's or Taft's secretary predated letters.
74. Meekins telegram to Taft, Dec. 5, 1924, *ibid.*
75. Taft to Meekins, Dec. 5, 1924, *ibid.*
76. George Wickersham to Coolidge, Dec. 11, 1924, *ibid.*
77. Meekins to Taft, Jan. 8, 1925, thanks Taft for this phase of his assistance, *ibid.*
78. Chase to Robert A. Hill, March 1, 1867, Salmon P. Chase Papers, Library of Congress.

5. THE POLITICAL CHECKS: SECURING POSITIVE ACTION

1. Steele v. L. & N. Rr. (1944); Tunstall v. Brotherhood (1944); Graham v. Brotherhood (1949); Railroad Trainmen v. Howard (1952).
2. Standard Oil v. United States (1911).
3. Pennsylvania v. Nelson (1956).
4. The full legislative history is recounted in Harvey Mansfield, *A Short History of OPA* (Washington: Office of Price Administration, 1948), pp. 277–78. See also Edward S. Corwin, *Total War and the Constitution* (New York: A. A. Knopf, 1947), pp. 178–79.
5. Annotation, "Government's Privilege against Disclosure," 97 L. ed. 735, 739.
6. See my *Congress and the Court* (Chicago: University of Chicago Press, 1962), chap. vi, for a detailed description of the reaction to the Jencks decision and the resulting statute.
7. See Felix Frankfurter and James M. Landis, *The Business of the Supreme Court* (New York: Macmillan Co., 1928), p. 97.
8. Quoted in Edward S. Corwin, *John Marshall and the Constitution* (New Haven: Yale University Press, 1919), p. 124.
9. Alan F. Westin has brought together a large collection of such speeches and writings in his *An Autobiography of the Supreme Court* (New York: Macmillan Co., 1963). There is an extensive bibliography on pp. 35–47.
10. Albert J. Beveridge, *The Life of John Marshall* (Boston: Houghton Mifflin Co., 1916–19), IV, 318–23. Marshall's five volume biography of Washington, *The Life of George Washington* (Philadelphia: C. P. Wayne, 1804–7), was in large part a vehicle to explain and defend Marshall's Federalist principles of government.

11. Samuel F. Miller, *The Constitution of the United States* (Washington, D.C.: W. H. and O. H. Morrison, 1880).

12. Westin, *op. cit.,* p. 22.

13. David F. Hughes, "Salmon P. Chase: Chief Justice" (Ph.D. diss., Princeton University, 1963), esp. pp. 295–98. See also Henry Adams, *The Education of Henry Adams* (Boston: Houghton Mifflin Co., 1918), p. 250: ". . . the Chief Justice was very willing to win an ally in the press who would tell his story as he wished it to be read."

14. Alpheus T. Mason, *Harlan Fiske Stone: Pillar of the Law* (New York: Viking Press, 1956), pp. 302–3.

15. Urie v. Thompson (1949).

16. For an excellent survey of the effects of such "advisory" opinions, see E. F. Albertsworth, "Advisory Functions in Federal Supreme Court," 12 *Geo. L. J.* 643 (1935).

17. Taft to Horace Taft, May 15, 1922, William Howard Taft Papers, Library of Congress.

18. Chicago Board of Trade v. Olsen (1923).

19. To Robert A. Taft, April 16, 1923, Taft Papers.

20. See my "In His Own Image," 1961 *Supreme Court Review* 159, 192.

21. See my "Chief Justice Taft and the Lower Court Bureaucracy," 24 *J. of Pols.* 453, 455–59 (1962).

22. See below, p. 141.

23. Frances Perkins, *The Roosevelt I Knew* (New York: Viking Press, 1946), p. 268.

24. To Clarence Kelsey, Aug. 17, 1923, Taft Papers.

25. Willard King, *Melville Weston Fuller* (New York: Macmillan Co., 1950), p. 150.

26. Sept. 8, 1923, Taft Papers.

27. Aug. 4, 1926, *ibid.*

28. To William Mitchell, May 17, 1929, *ibid.*

29. Jan. 17, 1922, *ibid.*

30. Henry Cabot Lodge to Taft, Jan. 18, 1922; Frank Brandegee to Taft, Jan. 20, 1922, *ibid.*

31. Jan. 23, 1922, *ibid.*

32. Charles Fairman, *Mr. Justice Miller and the Supreme Court 1862–1890* (Cambridge, Mass.: Harvard University Press, 1939), p. 402; David Hughes, *op. cit.,* pp. 303 ff.

33. David Hughes, *op. cit.,* p. 306.

34. *Ibid.,* pp. 204–6.

35. Fairman, *op. cit.,* pp. 402–5.

36. 23 *Cong. Rec.* 3285–86. In 1890, the Justices sent the following letter to

the Senate Judiciary Committee (National Archives, Senate Judiciary Committee files, 51st Cong., File 51-A-F-16):

Washington, March 12th, 1890.

The Justices of the Supreme Court of the United States, having examined and considered the various Judiciary Bills transmitted to them by order of the Judiciary Committee of the Senate of February 17th, 1890, and pursuant to the courteous suggestion of the Committee that it would be agreeable to them to receive the views of the Justices in regard to those bills and the objects thereof, have directed to be communicated to the Committee their approval of the following features in those bills:

1. The establishment of a Court of Patent Appeals.

2. The restriction of appeals to the Supreme Court in patent cases to questions of law only.

3. The transfer to the Court of Patent Appeals of patent cases now pending in the Supreme Court.

4. The amendment of section 643 of the Revised Statutes so as to include other officers of the United States than revenue officers.

5. The establishment of a Court of Appeal in each circuit.

6. The appointment of two additional Circuit Judges in each circuit.

7. The Court of Appeal to be held by three judges, and may assign District Judges to sit in it as occasion may require.

8. The judgment of the Court of Appeal to be final on all questions of fact; and the facts to be specially found if requested by either party.

9. Cases in which jurisdiction is acquired by citizenship of the parties only, and no question arises under the Constitution, laws or treaties of the United States, not to be brought to the Supreme Court by appeal or writ of error, unless the Court of Appeal, or two judges thereof, certify that the question involved is of such novelty, difficulty or importance as to require a final decision by the Supreme Court. But any question shall be so certified, upon which there has been a different decision in another circuit.

10. No writ of error or appeal to lie to the Supreme Court from the Supreme Court of the District of Columbia, or from the courts of the Territories, except where the United States or some officer thereof acting under their authority is a party, or where the adjudication involves a question upon the construction of the Constitution, or upon the construction or validity of a treaty or statute of the United States.

11. The transfer to the Courts of Appeal of cases now on the general docket of the Supreme Court, not involving a question under the Constitution, laws or treaties of the United States.

Upon the question of restricting the jurisdiction of the Supreme Court or other courts of the United States in point of amount or value, and upon other details of the scheme of relief, the Justices have no wish to make any suggestions.

There is also a letter in the Archives from Justice Joseph Bradley to Senator G. F. Edmunds of June 5, 1890, to which the Justice attached a draft of a bill to exclude federal courts from participating in the distribution of the forfeited property of the Mormon Church. Sen. File 51-A-F15-F16.

37. Justice Van Devanter gave Taft the details of the drafting of the 1915 and 1916 statutes. Van Devanter to Taft, May 11, 1927, Taft Papers. For the 1925 Act, see below, pp. 137–45. According to Van Devanter, he himself drafted the 1915 law and McReynolds did most of the work on the 1916 statute, though Day and Van Devanter made some changes in McReynolds' draft.

38. So Gideon Welles said. *Diary of Gideon Welles* (Boston: Houghton Mifflin Co., 1911), II, 251. See generally David Hughes, *op. cit.*, chaps. iv–vi.

39. David Hughes, *op. cit.*, p. 302. Chase to Stephen J. Field, April 30, 1866, reprinted in J. W. Schuckers, *The Life and Public Services of Salmon Portland Chase* (New York: D. Appleton & Co., 1874), pp. 526–27. It should also be noted that Chase was opposed to what eventually became sections 1 and 5 of the Fourteenth Amendment.

40. Carl Brent Swisher, *Stephen J. Field: Craftsman of the Law* (Washington, D.C.: The Brookings Institution, 1930), p. 224. In 1872 Chase advised Secretary of State Hamilton Fish of the probable interpretation that the Court would give a proposed treaty, but with the warning that, although he had consulted with Justices Clifford and Nelson, their opinions might change were an actual case brought to the Court. David Hughes, *op. cit.*, p. 302.

41. Taft outlined his program in his speech to the American Bar Association, "Three Needed Steps of Progress," 8 *A.B.A.J.* 34 (1922).

42. See note 21, above.

43. W. H. Taft, "Adequate Machinery for Judicial Business," 7 *A.B.A.J.* 453 (1921).

44. 46 *A.B.A. Repts.* 390–92 (1921).

45. Beck to Taft, Dec. 16, 1921, Taft Papers.

46. Dec. 18, 1921, *ibid.* Whether or not this exchange had any effect on their relationship, Taft later expressed a very low opinion of Beck's abilities. Commenting in 1922 on the possibility that Harding might appoint Beck to the Supreme Court, Taft said: "The President could not make a weaker appointment." Taft to Van Devanter, Aug. 31, 1922, *ibid.* Ten days later the Chief Justice wrote Charles D. Hilles that Beck "is a lightweight, makes a fair Solicitor General, but has no stamina to justify his appointment to the Bench." Sept. 9, 1922, *ibid.*

47. W. H. Taft, "Three Needed Steps of Progress," *loc. cit.*, p. 35.

48. *Ibid.*, p. 36.

49. 62 *Cong. Rec.* 2686, 2737.

50. *New York Times,* Feb. 19, 1922, p. 18, col. 1, has a long report on the speech.

51. Taft to I. M. Ullman, April 6, 1922, Taft Papers.

52. Taft to Philip P. Campbell, April 8, 1922, Taft to Frederick Gillett, April 8, 1922, *ibid.*

53. Taft to Joseph Walsh, June 5, 1922, *ibid.*

54. June 5, 1922, *ibid.* Taft closed with an expression of hope that Mondell would be successful in his campaign for election to the Senate. He was not.

55. Taft to P. Campbell, June 5, 1922, *ibid.*

56. June 5, 1922, *ibid.*

57. W. H. Taft, "Possible and Needed Reforms in Administration of Justice in Federal Courts," 8 *A.B.A.J.* 601 (1922).

58. 46 *A.B.A. Repts.* 396 (1921).

59. 47 *ibid.* 72, 362 (1922). The ABA included a stipulation that the committee also continue to work to abolish the writ of error.

60. Taft to Horace Taft, Feb. 1, 1923, Taft Papers.

61. Louis D. Brandeis to Taft, ca. Dec., 1923, *ibid.*

62. Taft to Brandeis, Dec. 3, 1923, *ibid.*

63. Taft to Charles P. Taft, II, Jan. 27, 1924, *ibid.*

64. *Ibid.*

65. Taft to Thomas Shelton, Jan. 31, 1924, *ibid.*

66. Taft to Van Devanter, Jan. 29, 1924, *ibid.*

67. U.S. Senate, Committee on the Judiciary, *Hearings on S. 2060 and S. 2061,* 68/1, Feb. 2, 1924, p. 25.

68. *Ibid.,* p. 27.

69. February 4, 1924, Taft Papers.

70. Sen. Rept. 362, 68/1; 65 *Cong. Rec.* 5831.

71. Taft wrote at least to the following senators: Reed, Nov. 19, 1924; Bayard, Nov. 21, 1924; Stanley, Dec. 5, 1924; Copeland, Dec. 9, 1924; and Cummins, Dec. 17, 1924, Taft Papers. It is possible, indeed likely, that he wrote to others as well, since he told Charles P. Taft, II, on Dec. 14, 1924, that "I have been writing to a lot of Democrats to interest them in the Supreme Court bill. . . ." Of those listed above, Bayard, Copeland, and Stanley were Democrats, but three are hardly "a lot." Taft usually relied heavily on his secretary to type his correspondence, but he frequently wrote his brothers in longhand (apparently most of these letters were sent to the Taft Papers after the Chief Justice's death), and occasionally wrote others this way as well. I have come across such notes in the Sutherland, Stone, and Coolidge Papers, and Professor David Danelski has also done so in the John Clarke Papers.

72. Dec. 17, 1924, Taft Papers.

73. *Ibid.*

74. Nov. 30, 1924, *ibid.*

75. Taft to Robert A. Taft, Dec. 17, 1924, *ibid.*

76. U.S. House of Representatives, Committee on the Judiciary, *Hearings on H.R. 8206,* 68/2, Dec. 18, 1924, p. 29.

77. H. Rept. 1075; 66 *Cong. Rec.* 1359.

78. 66 *Cong. Rec.* 2880.

79. *Ibid.,* p. 2919.

80. *Ibid.*

81. *Ibid.,* pp. 2923, 2925–26.

82. *Ibid.,* p. 2928.

83. Taft to Charles P. Taft, II, Feb. 8, 1925; there is a similar letter of the same date in the Taft Papers to Robert A. Taft.

84. See, for example, his remarks at the press conference of February 25, 1959. *Public Papers of the Presidents of the United States: Dwight D. Eisenhower—1959* (Washington, D.C.: Government Printing Office, 1960), pp. 214–15.

85. For a thorough investigation of Jackson's relations with the Marshall Court, see Richard P. Longaker, "Andrew Jackson and the Judiciary," 71 *Pol. Sci. Q.* 341 (1956).

86. David Danelski, "The Chief Justice and the Supreme Court" (Ph.D. diss., University of Chicago, 1961), p. 8.

87. Donald G. Morgan, *Justice William Johnson* (Columbia: University of South Carolina Press, 1954), pp. 123–24.

88. Carl B. Swisher, *Roger B. Taney* (New York: Macmillan Co., 1935), chap. xvi. Van Buren also consulted with Taney on banking problems. *Ibid.*

89. *Ibid.,* pp. 498–502.

90. David Silver, *Lincoln's Supreme Court* (Urbana: University of Illinois Press, 1956), p. 63. Willard King, *Lincoln's Manager: David Davis* (Cambridge, Mass.: Harvard University Press, 1960), pp. 204, 207–8, 251; David Hughes, "Salmon P. Chase: Chief Justice," chap. iv.

91. David Hughes, *op. cit.,* pp. 300–302.

92. Elting E. Morrison (ed.), *The Letters of Theodore Roosevelt* (Cambridge, Mass.: Harvard University Press, 1952), V, 801–2, 804; VI, 1336, 1393, 1487.

93. Henry Pringle, *The Life and Times of William Howard Taft* (New York: Farrar & Rinehart, 1939), I, 242–43.

94. See, for example, the *New York Times,* Sept. 9, 1953, p. 26, col. 1: "The Chief Justice's friendship with President Truman was one of the most important facts of their lives. . . . Both the President and the Chief Justice had telephones by their beds, and regularly held long talks late at night, in which the President received Mr. Vinson's advice and counsel on many problems.

Throughout the Truman Administration Mr. Vinson was regarded as one of the real inner circle at the White House, one of the 'top ten.' "

95. Arthur Link, *Woodrow Wilson and the Progressive Era 1900–1917* (New York: Harper & Row, 1954), pp. 28, 48.

96. Josephus Daniels to Franklin D. Roosevelt, Sept. 26, 1934, PPF File, Franklin D. Roosevelt Papers, Hyde Park. In this letter Daniels was urging the President to consult with Brandeis on current political and economic problems and was explaining how—and with what profit—Wilson had sought Brandeis' advice.

97. Quoted in Alpheus T. Mason, *Brandeis: A Free Man's Life* (New York: Viking Press, 1946), p. 521.

98. Quoted *ibid.,* p. 523.

99. Quoted *ibid.,* p. 522.

100. See generally, Alpheus T. Mason, *Harlan Fiske Stone,* chap. xvii.

101. April 28, 1924, Taft Papers.

102. Taft to Robert A. Taft, March 10, 1923, *ibid.*

103. Taft to Horace Taft, Sept. 29, 1923, *ibid.*

104. Rexford Tugwell, *The Art of Politics as Practiced by Three Great Americans* (New York: Doubleday & Co., Inc., 1958), pp. 247–48; and *The Democratic Roosevelt* (New York: Doubleday & Co., Inc., 1957), *passim.*

105. Arthur M. Schlesinger, Jr., *The Age of Roosevelt: The Politics of Upheaval* (Boston: Houghton Mifflin Co., 1960), III, 220, 280, 387–88.

106. Taft to Attorney General Sargent, April 21, 1925; Taft to Horace Taft, March 22, 1925; Taft to Judge Arthur Denison, March 22, 1925, Taft Papers.

107. Taft to Robert A. Taft, Jan. 10, 1925, *ibid.*

108. David Hughes, *op. cit.,* chap. vi.

109. Swisher, *Stephen J. Field,* p. 315; see also Fairman, *Mr. Justice Miller,* p. 298.

110. Dec. 2, 1928, Taft Papers.

111. Dec. 4, 1928, *ibid.*

112. Dec. 17, 1928, *ibid.*

113. Dec. 22, 1928, *ibid.*

114. Jan. 1, 1929, *ibid.*

115. Dec. 29, 1928, *ibid.*

116. Taft to Helen Taft Manning, Jan. 13, 1929, *ibid.*

117. Jan. 14, 1929, *ibid.*

118. Feb. 24, 1929, *ibid.*

119. Stone to Frankfurter, April 14, 1933; Frankfurter to Stone, April 17, 1933; Stone to Frankfurter, April 19, 1933; Frankfurter to Stone, April 22, 1933; Stone to Frankfurter, May 15, 1933, Harlan Fiske Stone Papers, Library of Congress.

6. THE POLITICAL CHECKS: PREVENTING OR MINIMIZING HOSTILE ACTION

1. Kent v. Dulles (1958), Dayton v. Dulles (1958); cf. the Court's handling of contempt of Congress convictions in Watkins v. United States (1957), Deutch v. United States (1961), and Yellin v. United States (1963). Regretfully to civil libertarians, the Court has not been consistent in its policy in this latter field, but the Justices in Aptheker v. Rusk (1964) carried out the threat implicit in the Passport cases by declaring unconstitutional the major passport provisions of the Internal Security Act of 1950.

2. See especially Cinn., N. O. & Tex. Pac. Ry. v. ICC (1896); ICC v. Cinn., N. O. & Tex. Pac. Ry. (1897); ICC v. Alabama Midland Ry. (1897).

3. For example: FTC v. Gratz (1920) and FTC v. Curtis Publishing Co. (1923). In the latter case Brandeis warned the Chief Justice that it was "not good statesmanship to tie down safety valves," and the two joined in a separate opinion, something Taft rarely agreed to do. Brandeis to Taft, Dec. 23, 1922; William Howard Taft Papers, Library of Congress. For a full discussion of FTC and Clayton Act cases, see Carl McFarland, *Judicial Control of the Federal Trade Commission and the Interstate Commerce Commission 1920–1930* (Cambridge, Mass.: Harvard University Press, 1933).

4. Peters v. Hobby (1955), Cole v. Young (1956), Service v. Dulles (1957), Vitarelli v. Seaton (1959), Greene v. McElroy (1959).

5. Cf. Robert A. Dahl, "Decision-Making in a Democracy: The Supreme Court as a National Policy-Maker," 6 *J. of Pub. L.* 279, 286–91 (1957).

6. For instance: Ex parte Milligan (1866), Carter v. Carter Coal Co. (1936), and Greene v. McElroy (1959).

7. Taft to Henry Taft, March 27, 1925, Taft Papers.

8. Taft, for instance, told his son Robert that even if some of the Progressives' Court-curbing bills were enacted into law, the Progressives would still have "great difficulty" when these statutes were subjected to judicial review. April 16, 1923, *ibid.*

9. The letter is reprinted in U.S. Senate, Committee on the Judiciary, *Hearings on Reorganization of the Federal Judiciary,* 75/1, Part III, pp. 488–92.

10. See especially West Coast Hotel v. Parrish (1937), NLRB v. Jones and Laughlin (1937), NLRB v. Fruehauf Trailer Co. (1937), NLRB v. Friedman, Harry Marks Clothing Co. (1937).

11. Joseph Alsop and Turner Catledge, *The 168 Days* (New York: Doubleday & Co., Inc., 1938), p. 206.

12. Sen. Rept. 711, 75/1.

13. Taft to Henry Taft, May 18, 1926, Taft Papers.

14. Taft to Thomas Shelton, April 6, 1924, *ibid.*

15. Taft to Elihu Root, Jan. 4, 1926, *ibid.*

16. Taft to Robert A. Taft, April 5, 1924, *ibid.*

17. Dec. 2, 1924, *ibid.*

18. Henry Taft to Taft, May 29, 1925, *ibid.*

19. 48 *A.B.A. Repts.* 406, 410–14, 415–16 (1925); the ABA had also disapproved of earlier versions of the Caraway bill in 1916, 1918, 1920, and 1923.

20. Taft to Henry Taft, May 18, 1926, Taft Papers.

21. Reed to Taft, March 21, 1928, *ibid.*

22. Taft to Reed, March 22, 1928, *ibid.*

23. Taft to Nicholas Longworth, March 28, 1928, *ibid.*

24. Longworth to Taft, March 28, 1928, *ibid.*

25. *New York Times,* April 23, 1922, VI, p. 5, col. 1; May 7, 1922, VII, p. 8, col. 4; see also Norris' comments at 62 *Cong. Rec.* 5107 ff.

26. S. 3151, 70/1.

27. George Norris to Taft, April 14, 1927, Taft Papers.

28. Memorandum of April 18, 1927, *ibid.* This memorandum is not addressed to anyone and is not signed or initialed. It was written on the typewriter of Taft's secretary and bears the marks of the Chief Justice's happily inimitable prose style.

29. 69 *Cong. Rec.* 2885.

30. *Ibid.,* p. 6378.

31. Sen. Rept. 626; 69 *Cong. Rec.* 5414.

32. March 29, 1928, Taft Papers.

33. April 5, 1928, *ibid.*

34. Taft to George Wickersham, March 29, 1928, *ibid.*

35. Taft to Newton Baker, April 5, 1928, *ibid.*

36. April 7, 1928, *ibid.*

37. Henry Taft to Taft, April 18, 1928, *ibid.*

38. 69 *Cong. Rec.* 8078–80.

39. 53 *A.B.A. Rept.* 425 (1928).

40. 69 *Cong. Rec.* 8077, 8080.

41. Ex. O. 10865; 25 Fed. Reg. 1583 (1960).

42. David Silver, *Lincoln's Supreme Court* (Urbana: University of Illinois Press, 1956), p. 63.

43. Willard King, *Lincoln's Manager: David Davis* (Cambridge, Mass.: Harvard University Press, 1960), pp. 207–8.

44. Chase to J. W. Schuckers, Sept. 24, 1866, reprinted in J. W. Schuckers, *The Life and Public Services of Salmon Portland Chase* (New York: D. Appleton & Co., 1874), p. 541.

45. David F. Hughes, "Salmon P. Chase: Chief Justice" (Ph.D. diss., Princeton University, 1963), pp. 300 ff.

46. Rexford Tugwell, *The Art of Politics as Practiced by Three Great Americans* (New York: Doubleday & Co., Inc., 1958), pp. 247–48.

47. For a brief account of these maneuverings and countermaneuverings, see my *Congress and the Court* (Chicago: University of Chicago Press, 1962).

48. Compare my conclusions in *Congress and the Court,* chap. xi, with the remarks of Robert McCloskey, "Deeds without Doctrines: Civil Rights in the 1960 Term of the Supreme Court," 56 *Am. Pol. Sci. Rev.* 71, 87 (1962).

7. ETHICS AND STRATEGY

1. Harry R. Davis and Robert C. Good (eds.), *Reinhold Niebuhr on Politics* (New York: Charles Scribner's Sons, 1960), p. xi.

2. Carl B. Swisher, *Roger B. Taney* (New York: Macmillan Co., 1935), p. 501.

3. May 1, 1924, William Howard Taft Papers, Library of Congress.

4. Cf. Justice Field's comments. Carl B. Swisher, *Stephen J. Field: Craftsman of the Law* (Washington, D.C.: Brookings Institution, 1930), p. 315.

5. Hugo L. Black to Franklin D. Roosevelt, July 25, 1940, PPF File, Franklin D. Roosevelt Papers, Hyde Park.

6. "The Bill of Rights," 35 *N.Y.U.L. Rev.* 865 (1960).

7. "The Supreme Court in the Mirror of the Justices," 105 *U. Pa. L. Rev.* 781 (1957).

8. Alan Westin (ed.), *An Autobiography of the Supreme Court* (New York: Macmillan Co., 1963), p. 35.

9. Thomas Aquinas, *Summa Theologica,* I–II, Q. 101, a. 3.

10. Jefferson to Ritchie, Dec. 25, 1820, Andrew A. Lipscomb (ed.), *The Writings of Thomas Jefferson* (Washington, D.C.: Thomas Jefferson Memorial Association, 1903), XV, 298.

11. Jefferson to Livingston, March 25, 1825, *ibid.,* XVI, 114.

12. Marshall, of course, did not originate the practice, but he established it as the rule of the Court. Karl M. ZoBell, "Division of Opinion in the Supreme Court: A History of Judicial Disintegration," 44 *Corn. L. Q.* 186 (1959).

13. Harlan B. Phillips (ed.), *Felix Frankfurter Reminisces* (New York: Doubleday & Co., Inc., 1960), p. 346.

14. Quoted in Westin, *op. cit.,* p. 26.

15. Chambers v. Florida (1940). Cf. the comments of Benjamin F. Wright: "The history of judicial review does not furnish the evidence to indicate that the Supreme Court will, in periods of intense feeling or of hysteria, afford a sanctuary to those whose views run counter to the popular will." *The Growth of American Constitutional Law* (Boston: Houghton Mifflin Co., 1942), p. 254.

16. Box 6, Bridges v. Wixon file, Frank Murphy Papers, Michigan Historical Collections, Ann Arbor, Mich.

17. I must confess that I have contributed to this misunderstanding. See my "Mr. Justice Jackson, Free Speech, and the Judicial Function," 12 *Vand. L. Rev.* 1019, 1044 (1959).

18. Frankfurter wrote Stone that Black had said this about the decision in Hirabayashi v. United States (1943). Frankfurter to Stone, June 4, 1943, Harlan Fiske Stone Papers, Library of Congress.

19. Jackson v. Alabama (1954).

20. David Hughes, "Salmon P. Chase: Chief Justice" (Ph.D. diss., Princeton University, 1963), pp. 251–52.

21. Gideon Welles, *Diary of Gideon Welles* (Boston: Houghton Mifflin Co., 1911), III, 320.

22. James Ford Rhodes, *History of the United States 1850–1877* (New York: Macmillan Co., 1906), VI, 74.

23. Aquinas, *op. cit.*, I–II, Q. 13, a. 5.

24. Cf. Alexander M. Bickel, *The Least Dangerous Branch: The Supreme Court at the Bar of Politics* (Indianapolis: Bobbs-Merrill Co., Inc., 1962), chap. iv; cf. John P. Roche, "Judicial Self-Restraint," 49 *Am. Pol. Sci. Rev.* 762 (1955).

25. George Graham, *Morality in American Politics* (New York: Random House, 1952), p. 200.

8. JUDICIAL DECISION-MAKING AND JUDICIAL STRATEGY

1. For an important exception, see Joel Grossman, "Role Playing and the Analysis of Judicial Behavior: The Case of Mr. Justice Frankfurter," 11 *J. of Pub. L.* 285 (1962).

2. For example, Connecticut General Life Ins. Co. v. Johnson (1938).

3. Undated memorandum by Herbert Wechsler, Law Clerk file, Harlan Fiske Stone Papers, Library of Congress.

4. See Alpheus T. Mason, *Harlan Fiske Stone: Pillar of the Law* (New York: Viking Press, 1956), pp. 472–76.

5. Robert McCloskey, *The American Supreme Court* (Chicago: University of Chicago Press, 1960), pp. 229–30.

6. William O. Douglas, *We the Judges* (New York: Doubleday & Co., Inc., 1956), p. 445.

7. Taft to Sutherland, Sept. 10, 1922, William Howard Taft Papers, Library of Congress.

8. Taft to Helen Taft Manning, Nov. 26, 1922, *ibid.* Taft made similar comments in a letter to Charles P. Taft, II, Sept. 10, 1922, *ibid.* Cf. the observations on the Progressives by Arthur M. Schlesinger, Jr., *The Age of Roosevelt: The Politics of Upheaval* (Boston: Houghton Mifflin Co., 1960), III, 413.

9. Schlesinger, *op. cit.*, p. 221.

10. "The Presidential Campaign," in Paul T. David (ed.), *The Presidential Election and Transition 1960–61* (Washington, D.C.: Brookings Institution, 1961), p. 57.

11. Pendleton Herring, *Public Administration and the Public Interest* (New York: McGraw-Hill Book Co., 1936), p. 138.

12. "Politics as a Vocation," in H. H. Gerth and C. Wright Mills (trans. and eds.), *From Max Weber: Essays in Sociology* (New York: Oxford University Press, 1946), pp. 121, 123.

13. Foreword to Sir Henry Slesser, *The Art of Judgment* (London: Stevens & Sons, Ltd., 1962), p. vii.

＊

Case Index

Subject Index